O9-ABH-109

Advance praise for *Who Killed Jesus?*

"For centuries, the Good Friday liturgy of the church has said that 'the Jews' killed Jesus. With clarity and passion, Crossan persuasively argues that the gospel stories of Jesus' passion are not primarily history remembered, but a creative (and ultimately destructive) combination of prophecy historicized and early Christian propaganda. Written at a popular and engaging level, important for both Christians and scholars, this book by today's premier Jesus scholar is the primary alternative to Raymond Brown's reading of the history behind these narratives of suffering that have caused so much suffering."

—Marcus J. Borg, Hundere Distinguished Professor of Religion, Oregon
State University; author of *Jesus: A New Vision, Meeting Jesus Again for the
First Time,* and *Jesus in Contemporary Scholarship*

"An important and intriguing book. Crossan demonstrates in a compelling fashion that the Gospel's version of the death of Jesus was a theological tool used to point the finger of blame at the Jewish people. This book should be read by those who struggle with the question of the role of New Testament in the history of anti-Semitism. More importantly, it should be read by those who do not struggle with this question: they will no longer be able to remain oblivious to this issue."

—Deborah E. Lipstadt, Emory University; author of
Denying the Holocaust: The Growing Assault on Truth & Memory

"John Dominic Crossan has shown how bold historical scholarship vindicates Christianity of charges of being necessarily anti-Semitic. He shows with passion and lucidity that the anti-Jewish moments of the Gospels are not essential to Christian faith but the product of the bitter struggles between some of the earliest Christians and other Jews. These became anti-Semitic in their force only with Christianity's political domination that began in the fourth century."

—Daniel Boyarin, Taubman Professor of
Talmudic Culture, University of California, Berkeley; author of
A Radical Jew: Paul and the Politics of Identity

"Since Raymond Brown's *The Death of the Messiah* will surely become the classic in the field for decades, Crossan's codicil of principled dissent is welcome and important. Here is a clash between two scholarly temperaments and of two understandings of the scholar's responsibility in the public arena. Both are needed. What to Brown is 'not totally lacking in verisimilitude' is to Crossan just plain impossible, and to him it is a moral duty to say so. Which he does with flair."

—Krister Stendahl, Andrew W. Mellon Professor Emeritus,
Harvard Divinity School

Who Killed Jesus?

Who Killed Jesus?

Exposing the Roots of Anti-Semitism
in the Gospel Story of the Death of Jesus

John Dominic Crossan

HarperSanFrancisco
A Division of HarperCollins*Publishers*

HarperSanFrancisco and the author, in association with the
Basic Foundation, a not-for-profit organization whose primary
mission is reforestation, will facilitate the planting of two trees
for every one tree used in the manufacture of this book.
A TREE CLAUSE BOOK

Library of Congress Cataloging-in-Publication Data

Crossan, John Dominic.
    Who killed Jesus? : exposing the roots of anti-Semitism in
the Gospel story of the death of Jesus / John Dominic Crossan.
— 1st ed.
        p.   cm.
    Includes bibliographical references and index.
    ISBN 0–06–061479–X (cloth : alk. paper)
    ISBN 0–06–061480–3 (pbk. : alk. paper)
    1. Jesus Christ—Passion—Role of Jews—History of doctrines.
2. Jesus Christ—Resurrection—History of doctrines.   3. Passion narratives (Gospels).   4. Bible. N.T. Gospels—Criticism, interpretation, etc.   5. Gospel of Peter—Criticism, interpretation,
etc.   6. Christianity and anti-Semitism—History.   I. Title.
BT431.5.C76   1995   94-40200
232.96—dc20   CIP

95 96 97 98 99 ❖ RRD(H) 10 9 8 7 6 5 4 3 2 1

For Sarah

CONTENTS

Anti-Semitism means six million Jews on Hitler's list but only twelve
hundred Jews on Schindler's list. This book is about anti-Semitism, not,
however, in its latest European obscenity, but in its earliest Christian la-
tency. It is about the historicity of the passion narratives, those terribly
well-known stories about Jesus' arrest and trial, abuse and crucifixion,
burial and resurrection. It is about the accuracy and honesty of Christian
scholarship in its best reconstruction of those ancient yet ever-present
events. Biblical exegesis and historical analysis may often seem but distant
murmurs from an ivory tower. Why should ordinary people care about
discussions and debates among scholars? Two examples, one very small
and one very large, indicate why the historicity of the passion narratives is
not a question just for scholars and experts but for anyone with a heart
and a conscience.

In the gospel of Mark, Jesus is tried by both a Jewish and a Roman
tribunal, and each juridical process concludes with physical abuse and
mockery. After the Jewish trial in Mark 14:65, "some began to spit on
him," mocking him as a pseudo-prophet. After the Roman trial in Mark
15:19, "the soldiers . . . spat upon him," mocking him as a pseudo-king. If
you are being scourged and crucified, being spat upon or even slapped
may seem a very minor indignity and hardly worth consideration then or
now. But, as Father Raymond E. Brown, S.S., notes in his recently published *The Death of the Messiah: From Gethsemane to the Grave—A Commentary on the Passion Narratives in the Four Gospels,* those mockeries were
recalled by "the Passiontide ceremony in the 9th–11th cents. in which a
Jew was brought into the cathedral of Toulouse to be given a symbolic
blow by the count—an honor!" (575 note 7). No Roman, one notices,
was accorded a like honor.

Brown insists that his "commentary will not ignore the ways in
which guilt and punishment for the crucifixion of Jesus have been inflicted on Jews by Christians, not the least in our own times" (7). Yet, despite that statement and a long section on anti-Judaism (383–97), the best

he can say about the historicity of those twin spittings is this: At the Jewish trial, "Such abuse is not at all implausible historically" (586). At the Roman trial, "There is no way of knowing whether this happened historically; at most one can discuss the issue of verisimilitude. . . . The content of what is described in the Gospels about the Roman mockery is not implausible, whether historical or not" (874, 877). Is that really the best that historical scholarship can offer?

It is not a question of certitude, a word that Brown uses regularly to avoid final decision: "there are severe limitations imposed by method and matter in our ability to acquire certitude about that history. . . . Certitude about the historicity of details is understandably infrequent" (22). Or again: "Absolute negative statements (e.g., the account has no historical basis) most often go beyond the kind of evidence available to biblical scholars" (1312). But historical scholarship is not called to absolutes or to certitudes but only to its own best reconstructions given accurately, honestly, and publicly. Even in our courts, with life and death in the balance, our best judgments are given "beyond a reasonable doubt." We seldom get to beyond *any* doubt. But, in the end, judgments must be made, and most historical reconstructions are based on "this is more plausible than that" rather than "this is absolutely certain" or "that is absolutely wrong." None of this allows us to hedge or to fudge or to hide behind double negatives like "not implausible" or "not impossible." *Who Killed Jesus?* shows how we can get beyond that impasse by beginning, for example, with a biblical text like this:

> I gave my back to those who struck me, and my cheeks to those who pulled out the beard; I did not hide my face from insult and spitting.
> (Isaiah 50:6)

Does the abuse of Jesus come from history remembered, or from prophecy historicized? Does it come from Christians investigating their sources to know what happened as historical event, or does it come from Christians searching their Scriptures to create what happened as prophetic fulfillment?

Consider that small spitting or slapping scene from Mark, and widen it into the following far more terrible scene:

> When Pilate saw that he could do nothing, but rather that a riot was beginning, he took some water and washed his hands before the crowd, saying, "I am innocent of this man's blood; see to it yourselves." Then the people as a whole answered, "His blood be on us and on our children!"
> (Matthew 27:24–25)

Brown is, once again, very aware of the latent anti-Semitism in that passage. "In commenting on this passage, one cannot ignore its tragic history in inflaming Christian hatred for Jews" (831), and he agrees (I presume) with a quotation that describes it as "'one of those phrases which have been responsible for oceans of human blood and a ceaseless stream of misery and desolation'" (831 note 22). Yet he can go on to describe it as "the most effective theater among the Synoptics, outclassed in that respect only by the Johannine masterpiece" (832), and his best historical judgment is that it is "a Matthean composition on the basis of a popular tradition reflecting on the theme of Jesus' innocent blood and the responsibility it created. . . . There may have been a small historical nucleus; but the detection of that nucleus with accuracy is beyond our grasp" (833). I ask, once again, is that the best we can do? *Who Killed Jesus?* proposes a flat alternative to Brown's *The Death of the Messiah* and argues that we can and must do much better. If, in my smaller example, we must assess the role of prophecy in creating history, we must, in this larger one, assess equally the role of apologetics and polemics in continuing and expanding that creation.

Here is the question at the heart of my book. Jesus stands before a Roman governor who declares him innocent and wants him released while a Jewish crowd declares him guilty and wants him crucified. The crowd wins. Is that scene Roman history, or Christian propaganda? When I am speaking of those first centuries, by the way, I use terms like *Christians* or *Christianity* exactly as I would use terms such as *Essenes, Pharisees, Sadducees,* or *Zealots.* These are groups with different and differing Jewish options about the best vision, program, and leadership for the Jewish future in a very dangerous age. History or propaganda, then, that is the question. It will take my entire book to answer it adequately, but, here to conclude the preface, I present two passages that appear later in the book to emphasize their importance:

> For Christians the New Testament texts and the gospel accounts are inspired by God. But divine inspiration necessarily comes through a human heart and a mortal mind, through personal prejudice and communal interpretation, through fear, dislike, and hate as well as through faith, hope, and charity. It can also come as inspired propaganda, and inspiration does not make it any the less propaganda. In its origins and first moments, that Christian propaganda was fairly innocent. Those first Christians were relatively powerless Jews, and compared with them the Jewish authorities represented serious and threatening power. As long as Christians were the marginalized and disenfranchised ones, such passion fiction about Jewish

responsibility and Roman innocence did nobody much harm. But, once the Roman Empire became Christian, that fiction turned lethal. In the light of later Christian anti-Judaism and eventually of genocidal anti-Semitism, it is no longer possible in retrospect to think of that passion fiction as relatively benign propaganda. However explicable its origins, defensible its invectives, and understandable its motives among Christians fighting for survival, its repetition has now become the longest lie, and, for our own integrity, we Christians must at last name it as such.

Externally, records of pagan contempt and records of pagan respect for Judaism started as soon as Greek culture and Roman power integrated the eastern Mediterranean into a somewhat unified whole. Internally, divergent groups within Judaism opposed one another in those same centuries with everything from armed opposition through rhetorical attack to nasty name calling. Read, for example, Josephus on any other Jews he dislikes, or read the Qumran Essenes of Dead Sea Scrolls fame on those other Jews they opposed. Christianity began as a sect within Judaism and, here slowly, there swiftly, separated itself to become eventually a distinct religion. If all this had stayed on the religious level, each side could have accused and denigrated the other quite safely forever. But, by the fourth century, Christianity was the official religion of the Roman Empire, and with the dawn of Christian Europe, anti-Judaism moved from theological debate to lethal possibility. Think, now, of those passion-resurrection stories as heard in a predominantly Christian world. Did those stories of ours send certain people out to kill?

History and Prophecy

History Remembered and Prophecy Historicized

Recently Peter Steinfels was preparing a news report for the Sunday edition of the *New York Times* on the monumental two-volume study *The Death of the Messiah: From Gethsemane to the Grave,* by Father Raymond E. Brown, S.S., which had just been published by Doubleday. He knew that my own book *The Cross That Spoke: The Origins of the Passion Narrative,* published by Harper & Row in 1988, represented a very different scholarly interpretation and called me for a dissenting opinion:

> "Basically the issue is whether the passion accounts are prophecy historicized or history remembered," said John Dominic Crossan, a professor of religious studies at DePaul University in Chicago. "Ray Brown is 80 percent in the direction of history remembered. I'm 80 percent in the opposite direction." (*New York Times,* March 27, 1994, National section)

That quotation accurately cites how I summed up the difference between our viewpoints. But reading it in cold print, I wondered how many readers had the faintest idea what it meant. What is "history remembered," and what is "prophecy historicized"? What is 80 percent one way or the other? And why should a wider population care about debates between scholars?

Darkness at High Noon

An example may clarify what I meant by those comments to Peter Steinfels. There are five different accounts of the crucifixion of Jesus, in the gospels of Matthew, Mark, Luke, John, and Peter, and hereafter I use those names to designate not authors but texts. The first four are in the Christian New Testament, the last one is not, and I hold further comments on all five sources until the next section (see the appendix at the end of this book for the Gospel of Peter). But for now, four of those gospels mention a darkness at high noon during the execution of Jesus. Here are the texts, with key words italicized for later explanation:

(1) Mark 15:33: When it was noon, *darkness* came over the whole land until three in the afternoon.

(2) Matthew 27:45: From noon on, *darkness* came over the whole land until three in the afternoon.

(3) Luke 23:44: It was now about noon, and *darkness* came over the whole land until three in the afternoon, the *sun* having been eclipsed.

(4) Peter 5:15 and 6:22: Now it was *midday* and a *darkness* covered all Judaea. And they became anxious and uneasy lest the *sun* had already set. . . . Then the *sun* shone (again), and it was found to be the ninth hour.

A note on the time designations in the original Greek of those versions: The first three have, literally, the sixth and the ninth hours. The last one has, as translated, midday and the ninth hour. The day is divided according to the four watches of Roman military discipline:

First day-watch: morning to third hour, 6:00 A.M. to 9:00 A.M.

Second day-watch: third to sixth hour, 9:00 A.M. to 12 noon

Third day-watch: sixth to ninth hour, 12 noon to 3:00 P.M.

Fourth day-watch: ninth hour to evening, 3:00 P.M. to 6:00 P.M.

Leaving aside differences for the moment, all four sources agree that there was darkness from high noon until 3:00 P.M. during the execution of Jesus.

To explain those accounts as "history remembered" means that Jesus' companions observed the darkness, recorded it in memory, passed it on in tradition, and recalled it when writing their accounts of the crucifixion. It happened in history, and that is why it is mentioned in gospel. In one sense that is the obvious explanation, and my alternative reading can be justified only if it is what *they* intended rather than what *we* expected.

To explain those accounts as "prophecy historicized" requires more detailed commentary. The first Christians were all Jews, and, in trying to understand what had happened to Jesus and themselves, they turned to their sacred writings, the Hebrew Scriptures, which they studied in Greek and would eventually call their Old Testament, as distinct from the New Testament they themselves had created. In that Old Testament they

read the book of the prophet Amos, for example. Sometime in the 750s
B.C.E. this peasant prophet denounced the prosperous state of the Jewish
homeland's northern half during the forty-year reign of its king Jeroboam II. The reason for his denunciation was the aristocracy's preference for commerce over compassion and for liturgical worship over
social justice. In 8:4–6 Amos addresses them accusingly:

> Hear this, you that trample on the needy,
> and bring to ruin the poor of the land,
> saying, "When will the new moon be over
> so that we may sell grain;
> and the sabbath,
> so that we may offer wheat for sale?
> We will make the ephah [a weight] small and the shekel [a coin] great,
> and practice deceit with false balances,
> buying the poor for silver and the needy for a pair of sandals,
> and selling the sweepings of the wheat"

After those accusations against the long and prosperous rule of Jeroboam
II, Amos warns that a terrible day is coming when God's avenging wrath
will be unleashed in punishment, according to Amos 8:9–10, with words
corresponding to key words in gospel texts italicized:

> On that day, says the Lord God,
> I will make the *sun* go down at noon [Greek: midday],
> and *darken* the earth in broad daylight.
> I will turn your feasts into mourning,
> and all your songs into lamentation;
> I will bring sackcloth on all loins,
> and baldness on every head;
> I will make it like the mourning for an only son,
> and the end of it like a bitter day.

Darkness at high noon meant, of course, a cosmic cataclysm, a world
turned upside down and inside out, a terrible and presumably imminent
catastrophe. And before the generation that heard Amos's threats were all
gone, the northern kingdom of Israel was devastated by the brutal mili-
tarism of the Assyrian Empire. But, in any case, midnight at noon,
whether as alleged actuality or symbolic possibility, is an obvious indication of disaster. It was even said by first-century authors such as Josephus,
Plutarch, and Pliny the Elder to have accompanied the assassination of
Julius Caesar on March 15 of 44 B.C.E.

By "prophecy historicized" I mean that no such *historical* three-hour-long midnight at noon accompanied the death of Jesus, but that learned Christians searching their Scriptures found this ancient description of future divine punishment, maybe facilitated by its mention of "an only son" in the second-to-last line, and so created that *fictional* story about darkness at noon to assert that Jesus died in fulfillment of prophecy. That is, of course, only a single example, but it is the working hypothesis of this book that specific units such as that one, general sequences such as the abuse or mockery, and even the overall framework of passion and vindication were dictated and controlled by exactly similar processes. Hence the first thesis of this book: *the units, sequences, and frames of the passion narrative were derived not from history remembered but from prophecy historicized.* The question is not, I emphasize now once and for all, whether you or I think that way, whether you or I find such exegetical discoveries persuasive or delusive, whether you or I prefer historical details to prophetic fulfillments. The question is whether that is what interested those first Christians and whether that is, therefore, what they did. And, as emphasized in the Preface, whether we are today reading history or prophecy in the passion story is a question of conscience after what began and developed from accepting it all as fact for so long.

Unbroken Love or Spreading Contagion

That explains what I meant by the terms *history remembered* and *prophecy historicized,* but what does that 80 percent mean? Imagine a spectrum with 100 percent history remembered and 100 percent prophecy historicized as the extreme ends of its range. To describe the passion story as 100 percent history remembered means that everything happened exactly as narrated so that it is, as it were, a court transcript of the proceedings against Jesus combined with a journalist's factual description of the surrounding events. To describe the passion story as 100 percent prophecy historicized means either that Jesus did not exist or, if he did, that he was never executed and that the first Christians made him and/or it up to fulfill the Scriptures. Raymond Brown does not claim 100 percent history, nor do I claim 100 percent prophecy, so I chose 80 percent as an emblematic rather than a mathematical indication of our divergent conclusions. But what do I include in my 20 percent history, what from Gethsemane to the grave or from Crime, through Arrest, Trial, and Abuse, to Execution and Burial is most likely historical in my best judgment and reconstruction?

Jesus' death by execution under Pontius Pilate is as sure as anything historical can ever be. For, if no follower of Jesus had written anything for one hundred years after his crucifixion, we would still know about him from two authors not among his supporters. Their names are Flavius Josephus and Cornelius Tacitus, and, once again, I hold for the next section any fuller details about those sources. We have, in other words, not just Christian witnesses but one major Jewish and one major pagan historian who both agree on three points concerning Jesus: there was a *movement,* there was an *execution* because of that movement, but, despite that execution, there was a *continuation* of the movement.

In describing civil disturbances during Pontius Pilate's rule over the Jewish homeland's southern half between 26 and 36 C.E., Josephus mentions Jesus and followers called Christians. His text was later preserved under Christian control, and I give their delicate but deliberate improvements italicized within brackets so that you can ignore them:

> About this time there lived Jesus, a wise man, [*if indeed one ought to call him a man*]. For he was one who wrought surprising feats and was a teacher of such people as accept the truth gladly. He won over many Jews and many of the Greeks. [*He was the Messiah.*] When Pilate, upon hearing him accused by men of the highest standing amongst us, had condemned him to be crucified, those who had in the first place come to love him did not give up their affection for him. [*On the third day he appeared to them restored to life, for the prophets of God had prophesied these and countless other marvellous things about him.*] And the tribe of the Christians, so called after him, has still to this day not disappeared. (*Jewish Antiquities* 18.63)

In describing the nine-day Roman fire of late July in 64 C.E., Tacitus mentions the Christians and, in explaining their name, tells us about the one called Christ:

> Christus, the founder of the name, had undergone the death penalty in the reign of Tiberius, by sentence of the procurator Pontius Pilatus, and the pernicious superstition was checked for the moment, only to break out once more, not merely in Judaea, the home of the disease, but in the capital itself, where all things horrible or shameful in the world collect and find a vogue. (*Annals* 15.44)

Despite the studied impartiality of Josephus and the sneering partiality of Tacitus, they both agree on those three points: movement, execution, continuation. They also agree that the term *Christian* derives from the name Christ. Tacitus mentions it without Jesus, but Josephus knows both names because later, in *Jewish Antiquities* 20.200, he speaks of "James, the brother of Jesus who was called the Christ." Josephus but not Tacitus mentions the role of both Jewish and Roman authority in Jesus' execution.

The basic historical facts that I presume concerning Jesus are those three linked items: movement, execution, and continuation. But all those details that fill out the passion-resurrection must be reviewed to see what also goes into that 20 percent that is history remembered and what must be placed in that 80 percent that is prophecy historicized.

A Basic Conflict of Interpretation

The purpose of this book is to ensure that a wider population, and not just scholarly experts, knows as clearly as possible that there already existed a radically different interpretation of the passion stories from that given in Raymond Brown's *The Death of the Messiah*. That different interpretation is based on six fundamental disagreements between Brown and myself. But before getting into those six disagreements, I emphasize six agreements.

First, we agree on the importance of Mark among the synoptic gospels (Matthew, Mark, and Luke). Although Brown separates "Comment" (on the evangelists' messages) from "Analysis" (on the evangelists' sources), he always places Mark in first place both in the unit translations at the start of each section and in the total translations at the end of the two volumes. That is actually a historical rather than a canonical priority (Matthew is first in the canon of the New Testament), a case of "Analysis" preceding "Comment," an indication of the difficulty in maintaining his artificial separation of those two categories. But, in any case, we agree on Mark as the source for Matthew and Luke in their passion narratives.

Second, we agree that the gospel of Peter must be taken seriously and not simply dismissed or ignored. Even though Brown is writing "A Commentary on the Passion Narratives in the Four Gospels," he gives a new translation of the gospel of Peter, comments on it at all appropriate places, and has a full appendix on it (1317–49). The gospel of Peter, about which more later, is not among those four New Testament or canonical texts and is termed apocryphal or extracanonical. Third, we agree that, however one explains the relationship between the canonical accounts and Peter, direct literary or scribal copying cannot explain the process: there is "the difficulty of hypotheses of careful literary dependence in either direction" (1325). I emphasize, however, that direct, literary, or scribal dependence (such as the dependence of Matthew and Luke on Mark, about which, again, more later) is not the only form or mode of dependence; it is simply the easiest to document and prove. Fourth, the specific vocabulary does not help very much in either direction. If you could find the peculiar or individual vocabulary, syntax, or style of a canonical gospel in Peter, for example, then Peter would have to be dependent. That does not work, in either direction. Fourth, there is one striking agreement between Brown and myself. Brown admits that there is a "consecutive" or textually continuous source independent of the canonical passion narratives that contains the story of the guarded tomb and the visible resurrection (1305–7; see also 1301). But there could never have been such an independent story without some preceding account of condemnation and crucifixion. No story could ever have begun with the entombment. Therefore, there must have been an independent and "consecutive" account involving at least three major parts: (1) Condemnation and Crucifixion, (2) Burial and Guards, (3) Resurrection and Report. That is, as you will see, exactly what I have postulated as existing and have termed the Cross Gospel (see the appendix at the end of this book). Brown has now accepted the existence at least of two-thirds of what I call the Cross Gospel, and he will logically have to postulate a preceding third section. Sixth, after giving his explanation of Peter as derived from hearing or reading the canonical versions but as writing from distant memory, Brown appends a footnote of special pleading: "How can I possibly hope to detect the exact composition of a section of the *Gospel of Peter?*" (1334 note 29). It would be easy and tempting to mock that special pleading, especially when it is accompanied by a dismissal of my own alternative hypothesis. (I must admit, sorry for this, that I love the critical overkill my name elicits from Brown, from "inconceivable" and "absurd" at the start of his two volumes [14–15] to "incomprehensible" and "utter implausibility" at the end [1333, 1342]). But, with that out of the way, I agree with Brown that, whether in his or in my hypothesis, the exact and precise processes of dependency are no longer discernible. Whether one moves from the canonical gospels to Peter (Brown) or Peter to the canonicals (myself), we cannot reconstruct the procedures of transmission as easily as we can, for instance, from Mark to Matthew or Luke.

Those are the six fundamental agreements. Of the six fundamental disagreements, I discuss the first four in the present chapter, the fifth much later under "Herod and the People" in chapter 3 on the Trial, and the sixth later still under "Responsibility for Innocent Blood" in chapter 5 on Execution.

What follows is the first and most important of the six fundamental disagreements between Brown and myself on the passion narratives. It concerns whether they are basically prophecy historicized or history re-membered. But a warning before proceeding. The various sections in Brown's massive study are regularly divided into Comment and Analysis, in that order both of sequence and importance:

> The COMMENT seeks to discover and explain what the evangelist wanted to convey by the passage; it is by far the most important part of my treatment and receives primary attention. . . . The much shorter ANALY-SIS . . . studies possible dependence of one Gospel on another, proposed preGospel traditions, and factors pertinent to historicity—unavoidable questions, answered of necessity by theorizing, but scarcely the heart of a commentary. (ix–x)

That is quite clear, open, and honest. What is of foremost concern for Brown is commentary, and that is described quite positively:

> the primary aim of this book [is] *to explain in detail what the evangelists intended and conveyed to their audiences by their narratives of the passion and death of Jesus.* (4)

> my primary goal is to offer solid understanding of the meaning intended and conveyed by the evangelists themselves in the 1st cent. and thus to sup-ply material for reflective interpretation of the passion by the readers themselves. (7)

History gets a somewhat more negative description, for example, "specu-lating" or "speculate" (5) or "obsession with the historical" and "obsessive history-hunting" (24). My debate with Brown does not concern *commen-tary* but *history.* His commentary is massive, monumental, and magisterial and will be used as an encyclopedia of basic reference well into the next millennium. But on questions of historicity, he is fighting, in my judg-ment, a rear guard action against the inevitable implications of his own pronounced principles. I emphasize that by debating *history* rather than *commentary* in this counterbook, I am deliberately reversing Brown's de-clared order of concern because I think it should be reversed in this par-ticular case.

His book is subtitled *A Commentary on the Passion Narratives of the Four Gospels.* One can legitimately write all sorts of commentaries: for example, historical or geographical, literary or structural, philological or theological, or all of the above together. Brown is interested in writing a theological commentary, something that is absolutely legitimate and can often be done without ever raising questions of historicity. But *can* it, and more important as I ask in the last section below, *should* it be done with regard to the passion narratives?

There are four versions, and they have been amalgamated into one harmonized whole in Christian art and imagination, liturgy and sermon, devotion and theology. And that whole has been seen as basically historical. The more brilliantly Brown dissects the different accounts, the more acutely the historical question presses. Yet it is immediately dismissed as "speculation" and "obsession" (5, 8, 24). He does, however, have a quite clear opinion on the subject, and it is given at the very start of his two-volume work:

> It is inconceivable that they [the Twelve] showed no *concern* about what happened to Jesus after the arrest. True, there is no Christian claim that they were present during the legal proceedings against him, Jewish or Roman; but it is absurd to think that some information was not available to them about why Jesus was hanged on a cross. . . . Thus from the earliest days available historical raw material *could* have been developed into a PN [passion narrative] extending from the arrest to the burial, no matter what form it might receive in the course of evangelistic use and how it might have been embellished and added to by Christian imagination. (14, my italics)

I have italicized *concern* because that term falsifies the issue, which is not concern but knowledge: what did Jesus' companions *know* about the passion events? It also falsifies the issue to combine knowledge and concern when, later, Brown speaks of not "descending into the nihilism of assuming that no writer *knew or cared* about anything that happened in Jesus' passion" (1361 note 20, my italics). The debate is over *knowledge,* not *concern.* I have also italicized *could* because the debate is not over *could* but over *did,* not over what could have happened but what, in one's best historical reconstruction, did. Despite those two details, however, Brown's position seems so obvious and reasonable that you may well wonder why anyone might contradict it. But on the very next page he mentions two modern contradictors:

> The issue of scriptural background becomes more debatable in views like those of Koester and J. D. Crossan, who . . . dismiss any rooting of the passion in Christian memory. Koester states with assurance that in the beginning there was only belief that Jesus' passion and resurrection happened according to the Scriptures so that "the very first narratives of Jesus' suffering and death would not have made any attempt to remember what actually happened" [Koester, 1980:127; see also 1990:216–240]. Crossan . . . goes

even further: "It seems to me most likely that those closest to Jesus *knew* almost nothing about the details of the event. They knew only that Jesus had been crucified, outside Jerusalem, at the time of Passover, and probably through some conjunction of imperial and sacerdotal authority" [Crossan, 1988:405]. He does not explain why he thinks this "most likely," granted the well-founded tradition that those closest to Jesus had followed him for a long time, day and night. Did they suddenly lose all interest, not even taking the trouble to inquire about what must have been the most traumatic moment of their lives? (15–16, my italics)

There you have, at the very start of Brown's massive study, the two basic positions in contemporary critical scholarship on the passion-resurrection narratives, but you never again hear about that alternative viewpoint. By the way, but in the interest of fair debate, Brown's own position is argued deductively by holding the opposite opinion as "inconceivable" and "absurd" on the *opening* pages of his book. He cites my own opposition in *The Cross That Spoke* from its *closing* pages where I was summing up what I had inductively discovered. The entire preceding book explains why I found that conclusion "most likely." But, in any case, what do Helmut Koester and I hold, and why?

There are three main points in our position. We agree on the first two, which are by far the more important ones. We disagree on the third, which is the least important of the three:

1. The passion narratives are not history remembered but prophecy historicized

2. There is only one independent source for our present passion narratives

3. That single independent source is

   a. a source now lost but used by Mark, John, and Peter, which are all independent of one another (Koester)

   b. a source, the Cross Gospel, still discernible within Peter, and used by Mark, Matthew, Luke, and John, with the last three also dependent on Mark (myself)

The reason for my disagreement on that third point is that I think John's passion-resurrection narratives are dependent on those in Matthew, Mark, and Luke. I discuss the major reason for that conclusion in detail in chapter 3 on the Trial. If I left that aside, the difference between a source common to Mark and Peter but now lost (Koester) and a source common to Mark and Peter but still discernible within Peter (myself) is of almost no substantive importance.

Why do we agree on those first two points and (apart from the problem of John) come very, very close on that third one? I emphasize that question because our position seems to affront common sense. The passion story is the most word-for-word and hour-by-hour sequence in all the four gospels. Its succession of Crime, Arrest, Trial, Abuse, Execution, Burial is exactly what one expects in such a case. And there are, within the New Testament itself, four separate versions all remarkably similar in general sequence and specific content. Of course, one argues, this must be history remembered, and very well remembered indeed. Why, then, that strange alternative proposal that it is, apart from barest skeletal information, all composed from prophecy historicized? These are our general reasons:

- Nobody outside the gospels knows this linked passion-resurrection narrative: if it was there as history remembered from the very beginning, why is it not found all over the various strands of tradition?

- All four gospels are in remarkable general agreement until Mark ends at the empty tomb in 16:8, but when Mark stops they all go their very separate ways: what happened to history remembered when Mark stopped and left the others on their own?

- It is extremely difficult to find independent versions of this earliest history-remembered passion story. Even in Brown there are only two, Mark and John, although he also talks of popular passion traditions. If it was so important and so early recorded, why are there not more independent versions of it?

- Individual units, general sequences, and overall frames of the passion-resurrection stories are so linked to prophetic fulfillment that its removal leaves nothing but the barest facts, almost as in Josephus or Tacitus.

The final argument, of course, is the detailed study of the narratives themselves. I did that in *The Cross That Spoke,* but most scholars focused on whether I had or had not proved where that single passion-resurrection source could be located (point 3b above). In this popularization of that earlier book, I intend to emphasize much more the first two points, especially that first and crucial one. Indeed, if one accepts the first point, the second one is almost a necessary corollary. Here is what I think actually happened.

Jesus' Kingdom movement among the *illiterate* peasant class could have died out within one or two generations as a local or regional phenomenon had not *literate* leadership from at least the lower echelons of the scribal or retainer class been also early at work. Understand the importance of that distinction between the illiterate peasant and the literate retainer class. Peasants know quite well the basic stories of their tradition and could easily tell the story of David and Goliath with knowing innuendo about the Roman Goliath and the Jewish David today. But they could not know, could not find, and could not read that actual story in 1 Samuel 17. They knew how to tell the *story* but not how to read the *source*.

Recall my earlier example about the darkness at noon from Amos 8:9. The ability to recall or find *that* text and to cite it properly demands literate, scribal, and exegetical skill. We are dealing here with learned and scholarly activity, which is not and need not be for everyone. That activity is what I imagine in the immediate days, months, and years after Jesus' execution, among circles of his learned followers. They are not searching their Scriptures for apologetical or polemical arguments with which to defend their own positions or refute those of opponents—that will all come much later. Their questions are these: Was Jesus' death a divine judgment against his program? Did God destroy Jesus? How does it now stand between God and Jesus? And the question above all was this: Do *we* have a future? Like any people asking if they have a future, they went back into their past to see what it might indicate. Searching the Scriptures was internally constitutive for their faith and their identity, not just externally useful for their debates and arguments. They knew, of course, what they were looking for in those texts. Could God's Holy One (by whatever title) be killed, and what sort of vindication would God obtain for him? But, I repeat, all this was the delicate and difficult work of learned Christian exegetes and did not do much for the *popular* Christian imagination.

Somewhere, sometime, somebody did something rather extraordinary with those dozens of Old Testament texts "foretelling" the passion-vindication of Jesus. *This author combined them into a coherent story with those prophetic texts as a now hidden substratum.* That was an act of religious genius, for once the popular or illiterate memory knew the story, teachers and preachers could much more easily move from "fulfillment" in the story back to "prophecy" in the Scriptures. Thereafter, two streams of tradition continued in some creative interaction with each other. First, that original single narrative with prophecy once and for all historicized was the basis for all the passion narratives we have. Second, that learned process of searching the Scriptures also continued, and we shall see its results throughout this book. In the beginning was passion prophecy; thence came passion narrative; thereafter, both continued as interactive streams of tradition. If dozens of discrete passion *prophecies* gave rise but once to a single coherent passion *narrative,* that explains why we cannot find earlier evidence of a passion narrative or more than one independent version for the one we have.

Dependent and Independent Passion Stories

In the last section I mentioned the major sources used in this book: the histories of Josephus and Tacitus as well as the gospels of Matthew, Mark, Luke, John, and Peter. Here is what you should know about those works (and two other gospels) not just their dates, times, and places but much more their presumptions, presuppositions, and prejudices. I tell you about my own in the epilogue (which you may want to read now to see if you can trust me). Also, even when I speak more simply of passion stories, I always have in mind passion-resurrection stories, because this book, un-like Brown's *The Death of the Messiah,* adamantly refuses to separate pas-sion and resurrection stories in critical discussion. No gospel story warrants separating execution from vindication, and neither Josephus's unbroken love nor Tacitus's spreading contagion do so either.

Josephus

In his self-defensive autobiography the Jewish historian Josephus claims descent from the royal priesthood of the Hasmoneans and records his birth into the Jerusalem Temple's aristocracy in 37 C.E. He also notes, in *Life* 9, that

> while still a mere boy, about fourteen years old, I won universal applause
> for my love of letters; insomuch that the chief priests and the leading men
> of the city used constantly to come to me for precise information on some
> particular in our ordinances.

I cite that story to invite critical intelligence in using *all* our sources and to admit immediately that I do not take such youthful brilliance too liter-ally, neither for fourteen-year-old boys called Josephus in *Life* 9 nor for twelve-year-old boys called Jesus in Luke 2:42–47. Later, in the First Roman War, Josephus was more or less in charge of the Jewish revolt in Galilee and eventually surrendered to the attacking general Vespasian in 67 C.E. Having foretold that his captor would become emperor, he was released when that prophecy was accomplished in 69 C.E. He observed the siege, fall, and destruction of Jerusalem and its Temple as interpreter for Vespasian's son Titus and returned to Rome under patronage of the new Flavian dynasty of Vespasian, Titus, and Domitian, from 69 to 96 C.E. He wrote his first historical work, the *Jewish War,* between the mid-70s and early 80s, and then a second and much larger work, the *Jewish Antiquities,* in the early 90s. Because the former study described Jewish history from about 175 B.C.E. to 74 C.E. and the latter from the creation of the world to 66 C.E., we have two overlapping Josephan accounts for first-century events in the Jewish homeland. We therefore must read those twin versions in critical comparison with each other. The point is not that Josephus changed from being pro-Roman to anti-Roman or from anti-Jewish to pro-Jewish. He was, in his own way, always both pro-Roman and pro-Jewish, and those attitudes never changed. But he began as apologist for Romans to Jews, and he ended as apologist for Jews to Romans.

Indeed, to be fair to Josephus, he is extremely open and honest about his own prejudices, as in his appeal to his fellow countrymen from outside the walls of besieged Jerusalem:

> Fortune, indeed, had from all quarters passed over to them [the Romans], and God who went the round of the nations, bringing to each in turn the rod of empire, now rested over Italy. . . .
>   You are warring not against the Romans only, but also against God. . . . the Deity has fled from the holy places and taken His stand on the side of those with whom you are now at war. (*Jewish War* 5.367, 378, 412)

Josephus's religiopolitical and socioeconomic biases agree that, because it is God's will that the Jewish homeland be ruled by a priestly aristocracy under Roman control, any revolt of Jews against Romans or of Jewish lower classes against Jewish upper classes is opposing God and inviting disaster. Always remember those presuppositions in reading his histories.

Tacitus

Both Josephus and Tacitus were aristocratic historians, the former from the Jewish priestly elite, the latter from the Roman consular nobility. Both lived to their early sixties, but Cornelius Tacitus, born around 55, was a younger contemporary of Flavius Josephus. Both remained profoundly faithful to their origins, Tacitus to the senatorial ideals of the Roman republic, Josephus to the priestly ideals of the Jewish theocracy. But both could have been accused of collaboration with imperial tyranny, and both would have replied that such was preferable to suicide.

Tacitus: "We should also have lost our memory along with our voice, had it been as easy to forget as to keep silence" (*Agricola* 2). Josephus: "Never may I live to become so abject a captive as to abjure my race or to forget the traditions of my forefathers" (*Jewish War* 6.107). They could even have met at Rome because there, between the 70s and 90s under the new Flavian dynasty, Tacitus's career was just beginning and Josephus's was coming to a climax.

Tacitus's interest was in dynastic degeneration, imperial corruption, and how "the souls of tyrants . . . show bruises and wounds . . . [from] cruelty, lust, and malice" (*Annals* 6.6). He saw the open and more superficial evil in persons and individuals but not the hidden and more profound evil in structures and systems. And because of that he sought the roots of Roman decline not in its empire but in its emperors, never recognizing the latter as but the former's personification. In his *Histories,* written in the first decade of the second century, he chronicled the decline and fall of the Flavians, Rome's second imperial dynasty, from Vespasian to Domitian between 69 and 96. In his *Annals,* written in the following decade, he repeated that process for the Julio-Claudians, Rome's first imperial dynasty, from Augustus to Nero between 14 and 68. Twice it had begun with such high hopes, with an Augustus or a Vespasian, and twice it had degenerated, first in a hundred years and then in only twenty-five, to a Nero and a Domitian. The somber mood that suffuses Tacitus's brilliant prose is not just nostalgia for Rome's republican past but the fear or certainty that, although he now writes under a new dynasty's high hopes, that too must pass.

Read Tacitus for history as aristocratic politics, dynastic intrigues, and imperial wars. Do not read him for anything about socioeconomic realities, about the lower classes, or about anything that Tacitus and a few thousand aristocratic equals did not find of interest. And he lived in a Rome of somewhere under a million people and a Roman Empire of about 50 to 60 million. He was equally contemptuous of eastern religions, maybe of anything east of Suez. If he had met Josephus, for example, they would probably not have liked each other, even if the demands of aristocratic honor and the dictates of imperial patronage made polite respect much wiser than open contempt. Tacitus, with both general ethnocentrism and specific anti-Judaism, claimed that "toward every other people they [the Jews] feel only hate and enmity" (*Histories* 5.5.1). His dislike for Judaism was matched, of course, by that for Christianity. He called it "a class of men, loathed for their vices" (*Annals* 15.44). Had he really seen the Roman future, his comments would have been even more biting and his tone even more dismal and disconsolate.

Matthew

Like Josephus and Tacitus, Matthew, Mark, Luke, John, and Peter were real people, but, unlike Josephus and Tacitus, the writings that bear their names were attributed to them rather than written by them. Originally Matthew, and all the other gospels, circulated anonymously and were probably sponsored by the communities for whom they were written rather than by the individuals through whom they were composed. Eventually, in the second century, each was fictionally tied directly or indirectly to important apostolic authorities as claims of unbroken tradition became increasingly important. When I use the terms *Matthew, Mark, Peter,* and so on, I mean the books, not the authors, for we have their contents even if we can only guess at their authors. For all the gospels we have to decide when, where, why, and with what biases they were written from *internal* data alone (which is probably a good general principle even when we know the actual author of a work). We have no *external* data to assist us. Those titles, in other words, refer to the books themselves and not to their fictional authors.

The gospel attributed to Matthew was probably written around 85 to 90 C.E. and possibly in Antioch, capital of the Roman province of Syria and third largest city in the empire. But arguments about date and place pale to insignificance before one conclusion for which there is now massive scholarly consensus: *Matthew used Mark as one of the two major sources in composing his gospel.* I should write that sentence not in italics but in neon because, almost all by itself, it forms the basis for the scholarly study of the gospels. Please think about its implications for a moment. If you read Matthew and Mark in parallel columns as scholars do, you can easily see how Matthew omits, changes, and adds to his Markan source. That is a heady introduction to authorial creativity, to the freedom one gospel writer takes in using another. It is a creative freedom we would scarcely dare suggest until the evidence in front of us demanded it.

During the First Roman War the Temple of Jerusalem was burned to the ground as it fell to Titus's troops in the year 70 C.E. The Jewish aristocratic class of priests, or Sadducees, was destroyed forever, and it was the scribal class of legal experts, or Pharisees, who inherited that vacuum in Jewish leadership. They met at Yavneh, west of Jerusalem near the Mediterranean coast, to save Judaism. They not only advocated religious fidelity and moral integrity, but also extended the lost Temple's ritual purity into every Jewish home. The home and its regular meals would be observed as once was the Temple and its sacrificial meals. This program was opposed by Jewish Christians such as those in Matthew's community, for whom Jesus' words and deeds and not rabbinical decisions and decrees were the proper interpretations of God's law. You can see that clash in this text:

> You are not to be called rabbi, for you have one teacher, and you are all students. And call no one your father on earth, for you have one Father—the one in heaven. Nor are you to be called instructors, for you have one instructor, the Messiah. (Matthew 23:8–10)

But that is a very mild example, and the terrible bitterness against Pharisaic rabbis throughout Matthew's gospel shows that the rabbis are winning, that more and more of the Jewish people are accepting the rabbinical rather than the Matthean vision for the future, and that Matthew's community is slowly but surely being pushed out of Judaism forever. Watch, then, for two features of Matthew's gospel, especially in the passion narrative. Watch where he is adding to or changing his Markan source, and watch, most particularly, when those changes or additions indicate bitter animosity against a Judaism that has refused his leadership.

Mark

The author is again unknown despite the later attribution to Mark but Mark's gospel was composed soon after the First Roman War of 66 to 73–74 C.E. Mark 13:14 refers to "the desolating sacrilege set up where it ought not to be (let the reader understand)." That "desolating sacrilege" is the presence of Titus's victorious army and "where it ought not to be" is within Jerusalem's Temple, which it has just destroyed in 70 C.E. Understand, dear reader? Locations for the gospel's composition have ranged from urban Rome to rural Syria, but that former suggestion seems unlikely because no early Christian Roman writings show any knowledge of Mark.

In any case, apart from external questions of time and place, two of Mark's special concerns are internally very clear. First of all, he writes for and to a community that has suffered severely from lethal persecution and not just social discrimination or political opposition. He has Jesus foretell as distant future what he knows full well as immediate past,

> As for yourselves, beware; for they will hand you over to councils; and you will be beaten in synagogues; and you will stand before governors and kings because of me, as a testimony to them. . . . When they bring you to trial and hand you over, do not worry beforehand about what you are to say. . . . Brother will betray brother to death, and a father his child, and

children will rise against parents and have them put to death; and you will
be hated by all because of my name. (Mark 13:9–13)

If it was terrible to be Jewish in the Jewish homeland during that First
Roman War, it may have been even more terrible to be Jewish Christian
or even Gentile Christian. At a time when identity lines were being
drawn in blood, where exactly did they fit?

A second concern is even more unusual and striking. Throughout his
gospel, and with increasing rather than diminishing emphasis, Mark criti-
cizes the Twelve Apostles, then the special Three who are named first
among them and given special privileges, and, finally or especially, Peter,
who is clearly their leader. The point of this criticism seems to be their
lack of understanding and acceptance of Jesus' suffering destiny, on the
one hand, and of the admission of pagans to Christianity, on the other.
Two examples will suffice. Jesus multiplies loaves and fishes twice, first on
the Jewish shore of the Sea of Galilee in Mark 6:32–44 and then on the
Gentile shore in 8:1–10, to show that one bread is common to all and suf-
ficient for all. But then, in a boat between those twin shores in 8:14–21,
he upbraids the disciples for their stubborn refusal to accept his vision
("hardness of heart") and warns them not to become his opponents, like
the Pharisees and the Herodians. The inner Three are allowed to witness
the Transfiguration of Jesus in 9:2–10 and are all in favor of such triumphant glorification ("it is good for us to be here") but dislike intensely
Jesus' talk of his impending death and either rebuke it in 8:32 (Peter) or
ignore it in 10:37 (James and John). One interpretation is that Mark has
those closest to Jesus fail him dismally *back then* in order to reassure those
who have themselves failed him under persecution *just now.* Another one,
probably more likely, is that he is opposing certain viewpoints advocated
in the name of Peter, the Three, and the Twelve within Christian communities he wishes to criticize or oppose. Watch for both those concerns
throughout his gospel but especially in the passion story.

Luke-Acts

The author of what we now call the gospel of Luke is, once again,
anonymous. Only later attribution gave us that identification. It probably
dates to the same period as did Matthew, say 85–90 C.E., and its composition can be placed in any Greek city of the Roman Empire, possibly
even in Greece itself. But, as with Matthew, arguments about date and
place pale to insignificance before one conclusion for which there is

now massive scholarly consensus. *Luke also used Mark as one of the two major sources in composing his gospel.* As before, read those italics in neon. Scholarly study of the gospels is based on a detailed comparison of how Matthew *and* Luke, independently of one another and with quite divergent processes and emphases, omitted, changed, and added to Mark. That is what forces us to acknowledge the tremendous creative freedom of one gospel writer in using another and even or especially in dealing with the words and deeds of Jesus himself. Keep Luke's Markan source constantly in mind when reading the passion narrative he adopted and adapted from it.

There is, however, an even more important point in understanding this gospel. Its anonymous author would be vastly surprised to see our present New Testament with what we now call "The Gospel of Luke" and "The Acts of the Apostles" separated by "The Gospel of John." Originally what was planned and written was a single linked, two-volume work so divided because each part filled a standard scroll. The end of the former volume (our Gospel of Luke) leaves the readers hanging for the start of the latter one (our Acts). These linkages are placed between the end of Luke and the start of Acts:

(1) I am sending upon you what *my Father promised;* so stay here in the city until you have been clothed with *power from on high.* (Luke 24:49, my italics)

(2) While staying with them, he ordered them not to leave Jerusalem, but to wait there for the *promise of the Father.* "This," he said, "is what you have heard from me; for John baptized with water, but you will be baptized with the *Holy Spirit* not many days from now. . . . You will *receive power* when the *Holy Spirit* has come upon you; and you will be my witnesses in Jerusalem, in all Judea and Samaria, and to the ends of the earth." (Acts 1:4–5, 8, my italics)

The former volume ends with its readers waiting, as it were, to find out who or what is the *promise of the Father* and *power from on high,* which is only explained at the start of the latter volume as meaning the *Holy Spirit.* And the disciples are left waiting at the end of one book for Pentecost at the start of the other. The gospel or good news is *all* of that two-volume work, and it records how the Holy Spirit took Jesus from Galilee to Jerusalem and then the church from Jerusalem to Rome. Good news: the Holy Spirit has moved headquarters from Jerusalem to Rome.

Compare, as another example, the final sentences of the twin volumes, one in Luke and the other in Acts:

(1) They . . . returned to Jerusalem with great joy; and they were continually in the temple blessing God. (Luke 24:52–53)

(2) He [Paul] lived there [under house arrest in Rome] two whole years at his own expense and welcomed all who came to him, proclaiming the kingdom of God and teaching about the Lord Jesus Christ with all boldness and without hindrance. (Acts 28:30–31)

The climax of Luke's gospel is not the disciples and the church in Jerusalem but Paul and the church in Rome, and to emphasize that point its author ignores what happened to Paul, whom we have watched making his way to imperial trial since Acts 21. We never hear that Paul was executed under Nero, because it is not his death at Rome but his presence in Rome that counts. The final image is of the Kingdom of God proclaimed freely and boldly in the very heart of the Roman Empire. And that, for this two-volume work, is good news indeed. Luke's passion story, therefore, must always be seen in that wider two-volume context and not just within what we now call the Gospel of Luke.

John

The earliest piece of the New Testament so far discovered is a torn papyrus page containing fragmented remnants of John 18:31–33 on one side and 18:37–38 on the other. It is dated from writing style to about 125 C.E. Those verses contain the trial of Jesus before Pilate and the latter's famous if fictional question, What is truth? Almost everything else about this gospel is also a question demanding final answer or even massive consensus. Matthew, Mark, and Luke are often called the Synoptic gospels because it is easy to place them in parallel columns and see them at a single glance. Not so John. It is often called the Fourth Gospel, and, because the others are seldom called the First, Second, and Third ones, that special title underlines its distinctiveness. It is attributed to John rather than written by him, dated to around 90 C.E., and written anywhere from Asia Minor to Syria. But, in comparison with Matthew, its community has been much more clearly forced outside the synagogues of the ascendant Pharisaic rabbis.

Two major features of John's theology must be kept in mind, especially in reading his passion-resurrection narratives. The major one is that, for John, Jesus is in complete control of what is happening to him. If Jesus is painfully human for Mark, he is serenely transcendental for John. In that latter version God may be the producer of the drama, but Jesus is more the controlling director than the controlled protagonist. The minor element is a constant exaltation of somebody called the Beloved Disciple over Simon Peter. The Beloved Disciple or the Disciple Whom Jesus Loved is the ideal model or leader in the Johannine tradition, and there is strong tension between that figure and Simon Peter, who is the ideal model or leader in the general Synoptic tradition, at least once Mark has been copied into Matthew and Luke. Watch for both those features, especially if, as I think, John uses the Synoptic tradition in his passion-resurrection stories. His extremely creative adaptations revolve massively around those twin points.

Major problem: is John independent of or dependent on the Synoptic gospels? This is a crucial question because, since Matthew and Luke are dependent on Mark, we have *so far* only a single independent source for the passion story. Which is John: a third dependent or the second independent version? I mentioned earlier a scholarly consensus on the Matthean and Lukan use of Mark; there is no such *present* consensus one way or another about John's relationship to the Synoptics. In sweeping outline: there was a consensus on dependence in the first third of this century; in the next third there was a consensus on independence; and in this final part of the century there is no consensus one way or the other!

What follows is the second of those six fundamental disagreements between Brown and myself on the passion narratives. It concerns the relationship between John and the three synoptic gospels. Brown judges that John is independent of the Synoptics: "I shall work with the thesis that John wrote his PN [passion narrative] independently of Mark's" (82). That completely possible thesis is seriously weakened, however, on the very next page where he notes the implausibility "of the Johannine evangelist working directly on the written Marcan PN, making dozens of inexplicable changes of order and words, and thus producing the very different PN that appears in John" (83). The problem is that the Synoptic dependence model in which Matthew and Luke worked directly and editorially with Mark's written work before them and in which you can show usually word for word and unit for unit how Matthew did that and Luke did this, is only one possible dependence model. I too find that model implausible for John, whose dependence is filtered through the teaching and preaching, cult and liturgy of a brilliantly independent creativity. My own judgment on John's relationship to the Synoptics is (sorry!) more complicated than simple dependence or independence.

At a first stage John had traditions about miracles and sayings of Jesus that were quite independent of the Synoptics and could get on very well without any of them. These were combined in an extremely creative and original way so that physical miracles performed by Jesus (on bread or wine, on sight or life) become *signs* of spiritual realities offered by Christ ("I am the bread of life" or "I am the true vine"; "I am the light of the world" or "I am the resurrection and the life"). This first stage minimizes the deeds and maximizes the words of Jesus, and three features stand out in this process. Many of the units can be moved around with no change in the overall design, almost any one of them contains the entire Johannine gospel in miniature, and again and again Jesus is opposed in Jerusalem. But does that last mean that Jesus went historically several times to that city, or that each unit, as gospel in miniature, must always contain the lethal possibility of what happened but once in that city?

At a second stage the Johannine community comes under increasing pressure from both the tradition of the Synoptic gospels and the authority of Peter in their environs. The Johannine style of physical/spiritual symbolism developed through powerful monologue and dramatic dialogue was forced to adjust to the Synoptic autobiographical narrative by adding John the Baptist traditions at its start and the Easter story of Jesus' passion-resurrection at its end. It did that with superb resistance by restating all the Synoptic data in its own special understanding. As mentioned earlier, my major argument for the dependence of the Johannine Easter story on the Synoptic and Markan model will be given in detail in chapter 3 on the Trial.

That general understanding of John's composition means that, for me, he is independent of the Synoptics for the miracles and sayings of Jesus but not for the passion and resurrection stories. That is, I know, more complicated than a simple decision for total dependence or independence, but it is the only way I can read the evidence. The result is that I find only a single independent source, Mark, behind all four of the New Testament passion stories. I remind you that journalistic ethics and historical reconstruction must tread very carefully when they have but a single independent source. In looking at anything from John's passion (and resurrection) story, I emphasize with equal force both Synoptic dependence and Johannine creativity.

Peter

Now the complications multiply and my discussion lengthens. The gospel of Peter is not found in the New Testament, and we hear of it for the first time in western Syria at the end of the second century. But within the last hundred years came two fascinating discoveries.

Ancient Panopolis, modern Akhmîm, on the east bank of the Nile about two hundred fifty miles south of Cairo, contained several Christian monasteries founded by Pachomius in the fourth century. During the winter season of 1886–87 the French Archaeological Mission in Cairo found in the cemetery of Panopolis a small papyrus book buried in a monk's grave. It is inventoried as Papyrus Cairensis 10759 and was officially published in 1892. This precious pocketbook for eternity contained several fragmentary texts, including one beginning in midsentence during what is clearly the trial of Jesus and ending in midsentence during what is presumably an apparition of the risen Jesus at the sea of Galilee (see appendix). The text records in 7:26 that "I mourned" and in 14:60 that "I, Simon Peter . . . went to the sea," so scholars have presumed that this is a fragment of that long-lost Gospel of Peter. The handwriting in this Panopolis fragment is from the seventh to the ninth centuries. That is, of course, very, very late, but a second discovery vastly improves the evidence.

Ancient Oxyrhynchus, modern El Bahnasa, on the west bank of the Nile about halfway between Akhmîm and Cairo, was one of the chief Christian centers in ancient Egypt. Among the thousands of papyri that have been recovered from its rubbish dumps since 1897 by London's Egypt Exploration Fund were two tiny fragments containing Peter 2:3–5a but with considerable variations from the Panopolis version. It is inventoried as Papyrus Oxyrhynchus 2949 and was officially published in 1972. What is most significant, however, is the dating of its handwriting to the late second or early third century.

Major problem (just as before with John): is Peter dependent on or independent of the four New Testament gospels? We just saw, in the case of John, that scholarship moved from a consensus on dependence to one on independence to the present split consensus. In the case of Peter, split consensus was there at the very beginning and probably still is. Some interpreters find Peter no more than a direct or indirect *Reader's Digest*–type condensed version of the other four gospels. Others find at least certain parts of it to be quite independent of them. Read straight through the text for yourself (in the appendix), and ask yourself the big questions: If it is *dependent,* why is it so changed; for example, Herod and the people, not Pilate and the soldiers, are in charge of the crucifixion (anti-Judaism?)? If it is *dependent,* why does it have sections not in the other gospel texts, for example, that resurrection scene with Jewish and Roman authorities looking on? If it is *independent,* why does that burial scene seem such an adaptation to the other gospels; for example, Joseph of Arimathea asks Herod and Herod asks Pilate for the body? If it is *independent,* why do the women at the tomb seem such a rewrite of Mark 16:1–8? No simple either-or solution seems possible, and it is very easy, when somebody opts one way or the other, to bring up the contrary objections; but, at the end, the text is still there and still needs explanation.

What follows is the third of those six fundamental disagreements between Brown and myself on the passion narratives. It concerns the relationship of Peter's gospel to the four canonical gospels. Brown holds that Peter's gospel had *heard or read* the canonical gospels (at least Matthew, Luke, and John) in the *distant* past and wrote its own account based on those *memories* as well as some *popular* elements independent of them (for example, the guards at the tomb and the resurrection account). Peter, in other words, is dependent on the canonical versions. I maintain the opposite, that the canonical versions are dependent on a section of Peter.

Recall how, in my opinion, the Johannine tradition and community came under pressure to conform to Synoptic orthodoxy and the apostle Peter's authority and so gave us the hybrid gospel of John, *independent* for miracle and saying sources, *dependent* for passion and resurrection stories. Something similar happened to produce this hybrid gospel of Peter (see appendix for details). An original and independent core, which I term the Cross Gospel, involving crucifixion by *enemies,* burial by *enemies,* and apparition to *enemies,* was later expanded into burial by *friends,* tomb found empty by *friends,* and, presumably, apparition to *friends,* as the text breaks off. The Cross Gospel itself, that independent passion-resurrection story, could have been composed as early as the middle of the first century, but it had to adapt itself to the gathering orthodoxy of the fourfold gospel and Peter's importance by the second half of the second century. Brown, as noted before, also finds an independent source in Peter for two of those segments, the guards at the tomb and the resurrection of Jesus, that is, for two-thirds of my hypothetical Cross Gospel (1307). But how could those two-thirds have ever existed and come down to Peter without some equally independent trial and crucifixion preceding them?

Another major problem: if the Cross Gospel, now embedded in the gospel of Peter, is not dependent on the four New Testament gospels, are they dependent on it? In effect, does Mark use it, do Matthew and Luke use it and Mark, and does John use it and the Synoptic triad? I think they do, and my general reason, to be seen in more detail as we move through the following chapters, is that every unit that it and they have in common *seems to be original or primitive in it and more developed or adapted in them.*

That seems to me the most economical working hypothesis. It poses fewer problems than its alternatives and solves more problems than it creates. I have no idea if the text of the Cross Gospel that we now have in Peter is exactly what those others knew long ago, and I have no idea what steps may have intervened between its composition and their usage of it. For example, most of Brown's arguments against my position presume the Synoptic method of direct literary copying, but one could reply (although I would not) by turning his own explanation against him: maybe they had all heard or read Peter in the distant past and worked from just those memories. In other words, and more seriously, whether Peter is dependent on the canonicals (Brown) or the canonicals on Peter (Crossan), that process was certainly not on the Synoptic model of text-in-front-of-me copying, and its own precise model is terribly hard to imagine. I return to this debate under "The Two Thieves as a Test Case" in chapter 5 on the Execution. In any case, my working hypothesis of canonical dependency on the Cross Gospel within Peter leaves me with a second major thesis for this work: *there is only a single independent source for the passion narrative, so that prophecy historicized moved from the Cross Gospel through Mark, Matthew, and Luke into John.* I note, by the way, that if we omitted Peter completely, I would still have only a single linked source, Mark.

Q Gospel

A massive scholarly consensus agreed, as stated earlier, that Matthew and Luke used Mark as a major source in composing their own gospels. After drawing that conclusion, scholars noticed that there were other sections common to Matthew and Luke but *not present in Mark.* Where did they come from? The general sequence and specific content of those non-Markan passages common to Matthew and Luke led scholars to postulate a second written Greek source used along with Mark by those other two Synoptic writers. That other major source is called Q, because it was German exegetes who discovered it and *Quelle* is the German word for source. I term it, to give it full honor, the Q Gospel because I do not think of it as just somebody else's source. Those conclusions are usually called the two-source theory, meaning that Matthew and Luke each used two main sources, Mark and Q, as the basis for their own writings. The Q Gospel was completed, most likely in two major steps, by the middle of the first century and was probably composed in Galilee and its immediate environs.

In the Q Gospel's vision, divine Wisdom came down to earth and spoke through the prophets of old, spoke through John the Baptist and Jesus recently, and continues to do so today through the Q community. But here is Wisdom's accusation, now in Luke 11:49–51:

> The Wisdom of God said, "I will send them prophets and apostles, some of whom they will kill and persecute," so that this generation may be charged with the blood of all the prophets shed since the foundation of the world, from the blood of Abel to the blood of Zechariah, who perished between the altar and the sanctuary. Yes, I tell you, it will be charged against this generation.

The Q community knows not only about rhetorical opposition but also about lethal persecution, yet there is not a hint about any passion-resurrection story *from* Q in Matthew or Luke. This absence must always be remembered even in focusing on those five gospels, Matthew, Mark, Luke, John, and Peter, that do have a passion-resurrection account. If the passion narrative is history remembered, why is there not a trace of it in the extant text of the Q Gospel?

Thomas

We return once more to ancient Oxyrhynchus and the fragmentary manuscripts discovered in its rubbish dumps by the Egypt Exploration Fund. Papyri Oxyrhynchus 1, 654, and 655 were found between 1897 and 1904 and contained sayings of Jesus on pages dated to the year 200 for the earliest and 250 for the latest ones. It was not then known that those three fragments were from three different Greek versions of the Gospel of Thomas. That became clear only when a fourth complete, but somewhat different, version of that text was discovered in 1945 (recall the differences seen earlier between the two versions of Peter). This full version was not in the original Greek but in Coptic, the language of ancient Egypt written more or less with the Greek alphabet. It was discovered as part of a small library buried in a sealed jar beneath the Nile-side cliffs near Nag Hammadi, a modern town about three hundred seventy miles south of Cairo.

Judas Didymus Thomas is simply Judas bilingually nicknamed the Twin (Didymus in Greek and Thomas in Syriac). He is best known from the polemic against him as Doubting Thomas in John 20:24–28. Traditions about him center at Edessa in eastern Syria beyond the Euphrates, and that is the best location for this gospel's original composition. Its date is more problematic. It, like the Q Gospel, may have been composed in two major steps. The first stage has a lot of sayings common to it and the Q Gospel, dates to the 50s and 60s of the first century, and emphasized the authority of James, the brother of Jesus martyred in 62 C.E.:

> The followers said to Jesus: "We know that you are going to leave us. Who will be our leader?"
>
> Jesus said to them: "No matter where you are, you are to go to James the Just, for whose sake heaven and earth came in to being." (Thomas 12)

The second stage has many sayings special to itself, dates to the 70s and 80s of that first century, and now emphasizes the authority of Thomas, especially against Peter and Matthew:

> Jesus said to his followers: "Compare me to something and tell me what I am like."
>
> Simon Peter said to him, "You are like a just messenger."
>
> Matthew said to him, "You are like a wise philosopher."
>
> Thomas said, "Teacher, my mouth is utterly unable to say what you are like." (Thomas 13a)

For that confession, Thomas is rewarded with secret revelations that he refuses to tell the others lest they stone him.

The Gospel of Thomas consists exclusively of sayings, parables, and dialogues of Jesus—of words, that is, rather than deeds. There are no birth stories, miracles, passion or resurrection narratives. Neither is there any overall compositional design in the arrangement of Jesus' sayings. It is like the Q Gospel in depicting divine Wisdom as challenging the world and being rejected:

> Jesus said: "I took my stand in the midst of the world, And in flesh I appeared to them. I found them all drunk, and I did not find any of them thirsty. My soul ached for the children of humanity, because they are blind in their hearts and do not see, for they came into the world empty, and they also seek to depart from the world empty. But now they are drunk. When they shake off their wine, then they will repent." (Thomas 28)

But, unlike the Q Gospel, it is profoundly antiapocalyptic, looking to the perfect past rather than the ideal future for the solution to the evil present, finding the Kingdom of God here and now through ascetic celibacy, and thereby reestablishing Eden before the Androgynous One was split into Adam and Eve, into male and female.

My point in mentioning Thomas is that this relatively early text shows, like the Q Gospel, not the faintest knowledge of any passion-resurrection narrative. If the passion narrative was, as alleged, the earliest and best case of history remembered, it was not so remembered in Thomas.

Sources and Theories

How does that discussion of sources and theories connect with the preceding one on prophecy historicized versus history remembered?

The Synoptic gospels. Brown and I are in complete agreement here: the passion narratives of Matthew and Luke are directly dependent on that in Mark. This is much clearer for Matthew, who follows Mark closely, almost woodenly, and whose changes on his Markan source are quite obvious. It is not nearly so clear for Luke, whose use of Mark is much more creative in both general sequence and specific content. It is precisely because Matthew and Luke use Mark in a quite direct and literary manner, with his text open before them, as it were, that there has developed such a massive consensus on the independent priority of Mark. You can actually see and eventually almost predict their minds at work on him.

It is, however, a theory, an operationally most successful one, to be sure, but not an absolute certitude, because such is *never* available in these matters. There is, for example, one very strong objection to it: what about those cases where Matthew and Luke are copying from Mark but both contain an element not present in Mark? Scholars call these *the minor agreements of Matthew and Luke against Mark.* Here are two examples from the account of Jesus' trial before the Jewish authorities.

The first one records what happened to Jesus after he was declared guilty as he was abused by those around him:

(1) Mark 14:65: Some began to spit on him, to blindfold him, and to strike him, saying to him, "Prophesy!" The guards also took him over and beat him.

(2) Matthew 26:67: Then they spat in his face and struck him; and some slapped him, saying, "Prophesy to us, you Messiah! *Who is it that struck you?*"

(3) Luke 22:63: Now the men who were holding Jesus began to mock him and beat him; they also blindfolded him and kept asking him, "Prophesy! *Who is it that struck you?*" They kept heaping many other insults on him.

Matthew and Luke each make their own separate changes on their Markan source, and that represents no theoretical problem. But how does one explain those words I italicized found in both of them but not in Mark?

The second example records what happened to Peter after his triple denial of Jesus as he recalled the prophecy of Jesus:

(1) Mark 14:72: Then Peter remembered that Jesus had said to him, "Before the cock crows twice, you will deny me three times." And he broke down and *wept.*

(2) Matthew 26:75: Then Peter remembered what Jesus had said: "Before the cock crows, you will deny me three times." *And he went out and wept bitterly.*

(3) Luke 22:61: Then Peter remembered the word of the Lord, how he had said to him, "Before the cock crows today, you will deny me three times." *And he went out and wept bitterly.*

Once again you can see the problem. If Matthew and Luke are copying from Mark, their changes over Mark are explicable, but how do you explain their agreement in those words I italicized not found in Mark? Brown postulates oral tradition and argues that there would have been other accounts of those stories in circulation and that those influenced the Matthean and Lukan agreements against Mark. But no theory of oral tradition and human memory that I know of works that way, so I do not think that Matthew and Luke follow *written* Mark completely except for a few *minor* words that break in from an *oral* alternative. An easier postulate is that their text of Mark and ours differed on those verses. Is that just special pleading? Recall the differences between the copies of Peter and Thomas noted earlier, and recall that, while Matthew and Luke were reading Mark's text in the 80s of the first century, *we* do not have a manuscript of Mark's gospel dated earlier than around 250. It would be special pleading to presume that their Markan text of the 80s and ours of the 250s were exactly the same on minor details and free from any copyist errors or changes.

What is the point of all that? However one explains those minor agreements, scholars do not judge them an objection adequate to destroy the basic two-source theory. Hence a very important lesson: A theory does not have to be perfect or even able to answer absolutely all objections against it. *A theory must simply be better than its alternatives; it must solve quantitatively and qualitatively more problems than it raises.*

The Johannine gospel. Brown and I agree on John's independence from the Synoptic gospels for the sayings and miracles of Jesus but disagree on his independence from them for the passion and resurrection narratives. Imagine yourself on a jury deciding a charge of plagiarism. The closer the defendant sticks to the order and content of the plaintiff's book, the easier your decision will be. In the passion narratives, for example, your jury might well agree unanimously that Matthew copied Mark, could possibly become a hung jury on Luke, and would probably find John innocent. The reason is that John's alleged use of Mark is so profoundly creative that we are dealing with a total transformation in the theological depths, hence a thorough adaptation on the narrative surface.

But, when that theological change from the painfully human Jesus of Mark to the serenely transcendental Jesus of John is constantly kept in mind, I do not find anything in John that requires independent passion tradition. But here the meaning of dependence has probably changed. With Matthew's and Luke's use of Mark, you can imagine direct and literary copying. You can imagine them working with a copy before them. It is much more difficult to imagine John working with the Synoptics in similar fashion. There the Synoptic passion-resurrection traditions were filtered and changed in the teaching and preaching, liturgy and meditation of a community whose own tradition was already as original and creative as anything else in the entire New Testament. Dependence and even dependent creativity come in many ways, shapes, and forms. Nevertheless, my principal reason for accepting Johannine dependence on the Synoptics for his passion-resurrection stories must wait for fuller explanation in chapter 3 on the Trial.

The Petrine Gospel. If you are still on that jury, you will have the hardest time of all with Peter. Maybe that is why most scholars have simply ignored it or presumed its dependence on the New Testament gospels in general rather than argued that position in detail. I recall to your mind two basic possibilities:

1. Peter is dependent on the passion-resurrection narratives of the four New Testament gospels (Brown, in general).

2. The passion-resurrection narratives of the four New Testament gospels are dependent on Peter (myself, in general).

Both those positions find serious difficulties in explaining how *exactly* the author of Peter operated in using the New Testament foursome or the New Testament foursome operated in using Peter. It was clearly a more complicated process than the Synoptic model of direct and literary copying as at a scholar's desk. Brown's appendix 1 in *The Death of the Messiah* (1317–49) is a detailed analysis of that problem. Here are two expressions of his basic conclusion:

> [The Gospel of Peter] draws on the canonical Gospels (not necessarily from their written texts but often from memories preserved through their having been *heard* and recounted orally). (1001, my italics)

> [The Gospel of Peter] as I have contended throughout the commentary, was not produced at a desk by someone with written sources propped up before him but by someone with a memory of what he had *read and heard* (canonical and noncanonical) to which he contributed imagination and a sense of drama. (1336, my italics)

It is clearly not easy to explain how Peter got from the four New Testament gospels to his own rather special version. It presumes memories of things heard or maybe read (long?) before. Close your eyes and review, if you can, your own general memory of the Christian passion story from film, novel, or Bible. Now read the version from Peter in my appendix to this book. We now know that memory, unless deliberately programmed from a written text drilled into memory verbatim, is plausible reconstruction of a general structure rather than precise remembrance of a specific sequence. Does that theory of memory explain Peter's text? If not, what theory of memory does?

I have no intention of appealing to memory about gospels heard or read to explain Peter. But my point is not that Brown's explanation has problems and mine has none. The major objection against my position is this: if all four New Testament gospels knew Peter, why is it that no two of them ever use the same item from it; for example, only Matthew uses the guards at Jesus' tomb; only Luke uses the good thief crucified with Jesus; only John uses the leg breaking during crucifixion. I have no particularly good answer to that objection. I insist, however, as noted earlier, that a theory need not be perfect but simply better than its alternatives. You will have to judge for yourself whether Peter is best explained as a medley of canonical and noncanonical gospels filtered through memory or as the original passion-resurrection narrative used by the New Testament gospels. In any case, my position will have to be shown in case after case throughout this book.

Finally, please remember that, however one decides about Peter, it is the first two of those three theses mentioned in the last section that are crucial: first, the passion-narratives are prophecy historicized rather than history remembered; second, there may well be only a single independent version of that linked narrative (whether the Cross Gospel in Peter; the common source behind Mark, John, and Peter; or Mark himself).

Anti-Judaism and Anti-Semitism

At the start of the chapter I asked this question, and I now repeat it: what is at stake in all of this? Why should the interested reader, as distinct from a scholarly specialist, care about how many sources we have for the passion-resurrection stories, whether they derive from prophecy or history, and how Brown and myself disagree on this, that, or the other? The answer, which was already given in my preface earlier, involves the passion-resurrection stories as the matrix for Christian anti-Judaism and eventually for European anti-Semitism. I distinguish those two terms because anti-Semitism only arrives in history when anti-Judaism is combined with racism. Anti-Judaism is religious prejudice: a Jew can convert to avoid it. Anti-Semitism is racial prejudice: a Jew can do nothing to avoid it. They are equally despicable but differently so.

Stories That Send People Out to Kill

Josephus's final work, written at the very end of the first century, is a defense against "malicious calumnies. . . . malignity and deliberate falsehood. . . . scurrilous and mendacious statements about us" (*Against Apion* 2–4; Thackeray et al., 1.162–65). Externally, records of pagan contempt and records of pagan respect for Judaism started as soon as Greek culture and then Roman power integrated the eastern Mediterranean into a somewhat unified whole. Internally, divergent groups within Judaism opposed one another in those same centuries with everything from armed opposition through rhetorical attack to nasty name calling. Read, for example, Josephus on any other Jews he dislikes or the Qumran Essenes of Dead Sea Scrolls fame on those other Jews they opposed. Christianity began as a sect within Judaism and, here slowly, there swiftly, separated itself to become eventually a distinct religion. If all this had stayed on the religious level, each side could have accused and denigrated the other quite safely forever. But, by the fourth century, Christianity was the official religion of the Roman Empire, and with the dawn of Christian Europe, anti-Judaism moved from theological debate to lethal possibility. Think, now, of those passion-resurrection stories as heard in a predominantly Christian world. Did those stories of ours send certain people out to kill?

Go back, for a moment, to that darkness at high noon from Amos 8:9 at the start of this chapter and recall how its prophetic threat was "fulfilled" at the execution of Jesus. I now add quotations from two very famous Christian scholars on either side of the Mediterranean around the end of the second century. The first one is from Irenaeus of Lyons in Gaul:

> Those, moreover, who said [in Amos 8:9–10ab],
>
> > "On that day, says the Lord God,
> >   I will make the sun go down at noon
> >   and darken the earth in broad daylight.
> > I will turn your feasts into mourning,
> >   and all your songs into lamentation,"

plainly announced that obscuration of the sun which at the time of His crucifixion took place from the sixth hour onwards, and that after this event,
those days which were their festivals according to the law, and their songs,
should be changed into grief and lamentation when they were handed over
to the Gentiles [=Romans]. (*Against Heresies* 4.33.12; Roberts et al., 1.510)

Not only is the "darkness" fulfilled at the death of Jesus, but the "mourning" is fulfilled at the destruction of Jerusalem by the Romans.

The second example is from Tertullian of Carthage in Roman Af-
rica, and it has that same double fulfillment, but now Amos's darkness at
noon is intertwined with the darkness at Passover from Exodus:

For that which happened at His passion, that mid-day grew dark, the
prophet Amos announces saying [in Amos 9:9–10abc],

On that day, says the Lord God,
　　I will make the sun go down at noon,
　　and darken the earth in broad daylight.
I will turn your feasts into mourning,
　　and all your songs into lamentation;
I will bring sackcloth on all loins,
　　and baldness on every head;
I will make it like the mourning for an only son,
　　and the end of it like a bitter day.

For that you would do thus at the beginning of the first month of your
new (years) even Moses prophesied, when he was foretelling that all the
community of the sons of Israel were to immolate at eventide a lamb, and
were to eat this solemn sacrifice of this day (that is, of the passover of unleavened bread) "with bitterness"; and added that "it is the *passover of the
Lord*" [in Exodus 12:1–11: "The Lord said to Moses and Aaron in the land
of Egypt: This month shall mark for you the beginning of months; it shall
be the first month of the year for you. Tell the whole congregation of Israel
that . . . they are to take a lamb for each family . . . [and] slaughter it at
twilight. . . . They shall eat the lamb that same night . . . with unleavened
bread and bitter herbs. . . . It is the passover of the Lord"], that is, the *passion of Christ*. Which prediction was thus also fulfilled, that "on the first day
of unleavened bread" you slew Christ; and (that the prophecies might be
fulfilled) the day hastened to make an eventide, that is, to cause darkness,
which was made at mid-day; and thus [in Amos 8:10a]

your feasts God turned into mourning,
and your songs into lamentation.

For after the passion of Christ there overtook you even captivity and dis-
persion, predicted before through the Holy Spirit. (*An Answer to the Jews*
10; Roberts et al. 3.167; my italics)

Does your head spin a little and your eyes glaze over in following that last argument? It is very difficult to read such scholarly exegesis, but that is what passion *prophecy* looked like before and continued to look like after it had been turned into passion *narrative* for a more popular audience. Exegesis is for experts, story is for everyone.

My point in quoting those texts is to force the ethical issue of historicity, the moral necessity of making a judgment on what actually happened. Was there or was there not an actual darkness at noon when Jesus was crucified? Did it historically happen, or was it created to declare, in Christian faith, that Jesus died according to the Scriptures, that is, within the will of God? No more and no less?

Those twin texts were taken from a time when the Roman Empire was still pagan and when Christians could do no more against Jews than argue and accuse. Here is one final text from a Lenten sermon of Cyril, bishop of Jerusalem between 349 and 387:

> Do you seek at what hour exactly the sun failed? Was it the fifth or the eighth or the tenth? Give the exact hour, O prophet, to the unheeding Jews; when did the sun set? The prophet says [in Amos 8:9]:
>
>> "On that day, says the Lord God,
>> I will make the sun go down at noon
>
> (for there was darkness from the sixth hour),
>
>> and darken the earth in broad daylight."
>
> What season is this, O prophet, and what sort of day [in Amos 8:10a]?
>
>> "I will turn your feasts into mourning,
>> and all your songs into lamentation"
>
> (for it was in the Azymes that this event took place, and at the feast of the Pasch); then he says [in Amos 8:10c]:
>
>> "I will make it like the mourning for an only son,
>> and the end of it like a bitter day."
>
> For the day of Azymes and at the time of the feast the women mourned and wept, and the Apostles who had hidden themselves were overwhelmed with anguish. How wonderful the prophecy! (*Catechetical Lectures* 13.25; McCauley and Stephenson 2.21)

There is no new content here over Irenaeus and Tertullian, but the *date* makes all the difference. That sermon was delivered, in Jerusalem, in the middle of the fourth century when Christianity was assuming imperial power over those "unheeding Jews."

That is what is at issue in this book, and that is why it is written for a general audience. There may well be some stories in the New Testament that one can leave as "maybe historical" and avoid asserting one's best historical judgment or reconstruction about them. But the passion-resurrection stories are different because they have been the seedbed for Christian anti-Judaism. And without that Christian anti-Judaism, lethal and genocidal European anti-Semitism would have been either impossible or at least not widely successful. What was at stake in those passion stories, in the long haul of history, was the Jewish Holocaust.

The Ethics of Verisimilitude

What follows is the fourth of those six fundamental disagreements between Brown and myself on the passion narratives. It concerns the ethics of historical reconstruction. His book *The Death of the Messiah* is acutely aware of the problem of anti-Judaism, and he has a special section entitled "Responsibility and/or Guilt for the Death of Jesus" (383–97). No one could read that chapter and accuse Brown of either anti-Judaism or anti-Semitism. He insists quite rightly,

> *One must understand that religious people could have disliked Jesus.* (391)

> If one takes the Gospels at face value (and even if one examines them through the microscope of historical criticism), there emerges a Jesus capable of generating intense dislike. (392)

> The Gospel portrait implies that Jesus would be found guilty by the self-conscious religious majority of any age and background. (393)

> *In Jesus' time religious opposition often led to violence.* (393)

> At any time and in any place those who contribute to the execution of an accused are responsible for that death; they are guilty only if they know that the accused is undeserving of such punishment or have been negligible in discerning innocence. (395–96)

> *The religious dispute with Jesus was an inner Jewish dispute.* (396)

I do not find any unfair, illegitimate, or invalid criticism of Judaism's religious tenets anywhere in Brown's book, and I emphasize that most strongly to offset any misunderstanding. *What is lacking, however, is a fair, legitimate, and valid criticism of Christianity's passion stories.* And that lack touches on the ethics of public discourse.

I emphatically do not ask about the ethics of persons or individuals (such as Brown or myself), but I emphatically do ask about the ethics of processes and procedures. The passion narratives are a section of the

Christian New Testament where sectarian intra-Jewish polemics ("the Jews" as all those *other* Jewish groups besides *our* Jewish group) prepared the ground for theological anti-Judaism, which prepared the ground, in the terrible fullness of time, for genocidal anti-Semitism. Brown knows that all too well and confronts it explicitly and directly:

> . . . this commentary will not ignore the way in which guilt and punishment for the crucifixion of Jesus have been inflicted on Jews by Christians, not the least in our own times. (7)

> . . . a Christian commentator is aware of and concerned about the harmful way in which the PNs [passion narratives] have been misused against Jews; and Christian readers need to be forcefully reminded of hostile elements in their own readings of the PNs. (386)

But it is not just a question of how the passion narratives were misused or misread but of what they were in the first place. What is actual history, and what is creative polemics in those stories? When a Roman governor insists on Jesus' innocence and a Jerusalem crowd insists on Jesus' crucifixion, is that factual history, or Christian propaganda? It is quite possible to understand and sympathize with a small and powerless Jewish sect writing fiction to defend itself. But once that Jewish sect became the Christian Roman Empire, a defensive strategy would become the longest lie. The passion narratives challenge both the honesty of Christian history and the integrity of Christian conscience.

Here are some exemplary points about the way Brown handles questions of historicity throughout the passion narratives. He speaks of "verisimilitude," which means that something is possible or could have happened but "it is not the same as historical likelihood" (18 note 24). Of course, but why use such an expression at all except to hint at historicity without having to affirm it. Or again, he uses double negatives such as "not implausible" or "not impossible." Of course, but since most historical reconstructions deal with comparative rather than absolute implausibility, those judgments are of little help. Here are the main cases:

> Attendants slap or beat Jesus after his Jewish interrogation: "Such abuse is not at all implausible historically" (586).

> Pilate asks Jesus if he is the King of the Jews: "There is nothing implausible in the initial question" (719).

> Pilate asks Jesus why he will not respond: "In itself that is not an implausible judicial reaction" (719).

> The crowd demands Jesus' crucifixion: "As for whether historically such an outcry of crowds occurred during the trial of Jesus by Pilate, we can speak only of verisimilitude" (721).

The soldiers mock Jesus as king: "There is no way of knowing whether this happened historically; at most one can discuss the issue of verisimilitude" (874); "The content of what is described in the Gospels about the Roman mockery is not implausible, whether historical or not" (877).

Simon carries Jesus' cross: "there is no inherent implausibility that there could have been a Cyrenian Jew named Simon in Jerusalem at the time of Jesus' death and that he could have become a Christian" (915).

Wine is offered to Jesus: "What Mark describes is not totally lacking in verisimilitude" (940).

Soldiers guard the crucified Jesus: "There is verisimilitude here" (962).

Soldiers mock Jesus on the cross: "it is not unlikely" (1027).

Passersby mock Jesus on the cross: "it is not implausible. . . . [but] it is impossible to decide whether a specific memory from Golgotha was at the root of the Mark/Matt scene" (1027).

Members of the Sanhedrin are present at the cross: "is not at all implausible" (1027).

Reactions to Jesus' death: "With rare exceptions there is little implausibility in what is described, so that one may speak of general verisimilitude" (1192).

Finally, there are two statements that articulate clearly what I sensed everywhere as guiding principles in Brown's analysis. The first one states that "what is logically surmised to have happened more often than not actually did happen" (1274). In other words: just because you made it up, does not mean it did not happen. My disagreement with that principle is ethical, not epistemological. It is surely correct on an absolute level, but it destroys any discipline for historical reconstruction and any protection for legal accusation. The second statement is, "historicity should be determined not by what we think possible or likely, but by the antiquity and reliability of the evidence" (1469). In *public* discourse, however, possibility and likelihood are also factors. If not, how could we distinguish history from fiction in accounts of an execution in Jerusalem in the first century or an assassination in Dallas in the twentieth?

Think for a moment about the ethics of judging events as having "verisimilitude" or the morality of judging happenings with double negatives such as "not implausible." Think of ourselves in court and judged by those standards; we all go straight to jail. Historians should be ready and willing to say, This, in my best professional reconstruction, is what happened; that did not. And if with other subjects we can hedge on historicity decisions, Christian exegetes, theologians, and historians cannot do so on the passion narratives—not just because of what happened then, but because of what has happened since.

By now, it is clear that there are two great partings of the ways, two sets of massively divergent forking paths as Christians read the Bible, which they agree is the inspired word of God. The first and most obvious divergence is between fundamental and contextual interpretation. *Fundamental* interpretation holds, in general, that anything that can be taken literally and historically must be so taken. *Contextual* interpretation disagrees and maintains that biblical texts must be understood in their full contextual situation. That includes not only authorial intentions and generic expectations as narrowest context but also a tensile dialectic between reason and revelation as widest context. But now comes a second great division within contextual interpretation itself. *Selective contextualism* takes that basic principle but applies it, as Brown does, in a highly selective manner. For example, it may simply pronounce the principle and hardly ever apply it; or it may apply it to the Christian Old Testament but not to the Christian New Testament; or it may apply it to the start of Jesus' life by taking symbolically the physicality of the virginal conception but not to the end of Jesus' life by taking symbolically the physicality of the risen body. *Consistent contextualism* is the alternative. The physical sciences, for example, help us understand that Genesis 1 should be taken symbolically not because they are infallible but because, in that dialectic of reason and revelation, they discipline our reason with the theory of evolution. That also makes clear what is of revelation in Genesis 1. God observed the Sabbath in creating the world so that it is bigger than creation and almost, as it were, bigger than God. Genesis 1 is not rational information about how the world began but revelatory challenge about the importance of the Sabbath. I not only accept that application of contextualism but try to follow it consistently with regard to the physical, social, and human sciences throughout the entire Bible from one end to the other with no selectively protected areas anywhere. The Bible, for me, does not furnish information about the physicality of the world's beginning or the world's ending. Nor does it furnish information about the physicality of Jesus' beginning or Jesus' ending. Brown and I both operate theoretically within contextual interpretation, but we part decisively thereafter. I consider that the historicity of the passion narratives is handled with selective contextualism in *The Death of the Messiah* and consider *Who Killed Jesus?* to exemplify the alternative, consistent contextualism.

CHAPTER ONE

Crime

In the Territory of Antipas

Herod the Great ruled the entire Jewish homeland for over thirty years with the title King of the Jews. After his death, the Roman emperor Augustus divided his territories, placing Galilee and Perea, areas northwest and east of the Jordan, under his son Herod Antipas with the title of tetrarch, and placing Samaria, Judea, and Idumea, areas west and southwest of the Jordan, under a Roman governor with the title of prefect.

Why did two peasant movements, that of John and that of Jesus, arise in Perea and Galilee rather than in Samaria, Judea, or Idumea? Why did they arise under the Herodian kingling Antipas rather than under his father, Herod the Great, who ruled the entire country from 37 to 4 B.C.E., or under his half-nephew Agrippa I, who ruled the entire country from 41 to 44 C.E.? And, because Antipas ruled between 4 B.C.E. and 39 C.E., why did they arise in the late 20s rather than in any other period of that long reign? Why did two movements, the Baptism movement of John and the Kingdom movement of Jesus, arise in the late 20s of that first common-era century in the two separated regions of Antipas's territory, John in Perea east of the Jordan and Jesus in Galilee to its northwest? Why precisely there, why exactly then?

This Land Belongs to God

The Roman world was an aristocratic society, a preindustrial empire in which the peasantry produced a very large agricultural surplus. But, as in any agrarian empire, a tiny minority of political and religious elites, along with their supporters and retainers, held the peasantry at subsistence level and thereby obtained levels of luxury those exploited and oppressed peasants could hardly even imagine. The Roman Empire, however, was no longer a *traditional* but rather a *commercialized* agrarian empire, and the Jewish peasantry was being pushed into debt and displaced from its holdings at higher than normal rates as land became, under the commercializing Roman economy, less an ancestral inheritance never to be abandoned and more an entrepreneurial commodity rapidly to be exploited. In a traditional or uncommercialized agrarian empire, business or investment intrudes minimally if at all *between* aristocrats and peasants. There exists almost a steady state situation in which peasants produce and aristocrats take, and it almost looks like an inevitable if not natural process. Peasants resist exploitation, of course, but in the same fatalistic way that they resist other unfortunate but implacable phenomena such as storm, flood, or disease. But with commercialization even the guarantee of owning one's own familial plot of well-taxed land is gone, and the peasantry, having learned that things can change for the worse, begin to ponder how they might also change for the better, even for the ideal or utopian better. As ancient commercialization, let alone modern industrialization, intrudes into an agrarian and aristocratic empire, the barometer of possible political rebellion and/or social revolution rises accordingly among the peasantry. That was precisely the situation in the Mediterranean world of the first century. The Roman civil wars, from Julius Caesar against Pompey to Octavius against Antony, had ended with Octavius emerging as the victorious Augustus, and this Augustan Peace opened the Roman Empire to an economic boom. But booms do not boom alike for everyone.

The Jewish peasantry was prone, over and above the resistance expected from any colonial peasantry, to refuse quiet compliance with heavy taxation, subsistence farming, debt impoverishment, and land expropriation. Their traditional ideology of *land* was enshrined in the ancient scriptural laws. Just as God's people were to rest on the seventh or Sabbath Day, so God's land was to rest on the seventh or Sabbath Year:

> For six years you shall sow your land and gather in its yield; but the seventh year you shall let it rest and lie fallow, so that the poor of your people may eat; and what they leave the wild animals may eat. You shall do the same with your vineyard, and with your olive orchard. (Exodus 23:10–11)

> When you enter the land that I am giving you, the land shall observe a sabbath for the Lord. Six years you shall sow your field, and six years you shall prune your vineyard, and gather in their yield; but in the seventh year there shall be a sabbath of complete rest for the land, a sabbath for the Lord: you shall not sow your field or prune your vineyard. (Leviticus 25:2–4)

On that seventh or Sabbath Year, moreover, Jewish debts were to be re-
mitted and Jewish slaves were to be released.

> Every seventh year you shall grant a remission of debts. And this is the
> manner of the remission: every creditor shall remit the claim that is held
> against a neighbor, not exacting it of a neighbor who is a member of the
> community, because the Lord's remission has been proclaimed. Of a for-
> eigner you may exact it, but you must remit your claim on whatever any
> member of your community owes you. . . .
>
> If a member of your community, whether a Hebrew man or a He-
> brew woman, is sold to you and works for you six years, in the seventh year
> you shall set that person free. And when you send a male slave out from
> you a free person, you shall not send him out empty-handed. Provide lib-
> erally out of your flock, your threshing floor, and your wine press, thus giv-
> ing to him some of the bounty with which the Lord your God has blessed
> you. (Deuteronomy 15:1–3, 12–14)

Finally, there was even a Jubilee Year, the year after seven sets of Sabbath
Years. In that fiftieth year all expropriated lands and even village houses,
but not city ones, were to revert to their original or traditional owners:

> You shall hallow the fiftieth year and you shall proclaim liberty throughout
> the land to all its inhabitants. It shall be a jubilee for you: you shall return,
> every one of you, to your property and every one of you to your
> family. . . .
>
> But if there is not sufficient means to recover it [a piece of property],
> what was sold shall remain with the purchaser until the year of jubilee; in
> the jubilee it shall be released, and the property shall be returned. (Leviti-
> cus 25:10, 28)

It is hard to know now what is ideal and what is real, what is ideological
and what is actual in those decrees. Most likely the Jubilee Year was not im-
plemented at all by the first century, but the Sabbath Year was probably still
more or less enforced. My point, however, is that those ancient laws precisely as ideal vision or ideological promise refuse to see debt, slavery, or
land expropriation simply as standard business transactions and normal economic activities. The land is a divine possession, not a negotiable commodity, or, as Leviticus 25:23 put it, "The land shall not be sold in perpetuity, for
the land is mine; with me you are but aliens and tenants." The Jewish peasantry, therefore, had a long tradition in flat contradiction with a first-century boom economy that saw land accumulation as sensible business
practice and debt foreclosure as the best and swiftest way to accomplish it.

Lower Galilee's 470 square miles are divided by four alternating hills and valleys running in a generally west–east direction. It is rich in cereals on the valley floors and in vines and olives on the hillside slopes. But the Galilean peasantry had their own very particular pressures at the time of John and of Jesus, and this gives an answer to that opening question: Why did those two movements arise under Antipas in the late 20s? Sepphoris, about four miles northwest of Nazareth, and Tiberias, about twenty miles northeast of Nazareth, alternated as capitals of Galilee in the first century. Sepphoris was burned and its population enslaved as the Romans reestablished control over those several sections of the Jewish homeland that had broken into open rebellion at the death of Herod the Great in 4 B.C.E. Herod Antipas rebuilt the city almost immediately. But then, around 19 C.E., he finished another city on the western shore of the Sea of Galilee, named it after the Roman emperor Tiberius, and transferred his capital there from Sepphoris. But two new cities of about twenty-four thousand population apiece, in close proximity and also in administrative competition, must have increased demands and exactions on their local peasantry for both food production and investment opportunity. New cities, as mentioned earlier, are not good news for the local peasantry, at least not as a whole—especially where, in ancient law, the land belongs to God.

Crossing over Jordan

What do we know about John's vision and program? For what crime was he executed by Herod Antipas? Our sources are the New Testament gospels and Josephus, but both must be read critically and combined carefully. Josephus does not admit that John was an apocalyptic visionary announcing the imminent and avenging advent of God. And the New Testament gospels do not admit that it was God rather than Jesus whose advent John was announcing.

Antipas abandoned his first wife, a daughter of King Aretas of the desert Nabateans east of the Jordan, to marry Herodias, his half-brother's wife. And John was executed, according to one account, for reprimanding that action:

> For Herod himself had sent men who arrested John, bound him, and put him in prison on account of Herodias, his brother Philip's wife, because Herod had married her. For John had been telling Herod, "It is not lawful for you to have your brother's wife." (Mark 6:17–18)

But another account puts that story in a wider context, which shows that there was much more than a moral reprimand involved in John's crime. Here is Josephus's description of John the Baptist:

> Herod had put him [John, surnamed the Baptist] to death, though he was a good man and had exhorted the Jews to lead righteous lives, to practice justice towards their fellows and piety towards God, and so doing to join in baptism. In his view this was a necessary preliminary if baptism was to be acceptable to God. They must not employ it to gain pardon for whatever sins they committed, but as a consecration of the body implying that the soul was already thoroughly cleansed by right behaviour.
>
> When others too joined the crowds about him, because they were aroused to the highest degree by his sermons, Herod became alarmed. Eloquence that had so great an effect on mankind might lead to some form of sedition, for it looked as if they would be guided by John in everything that they did. Herod decided therefore that it would be much better to strike first and be rid of him before his work led to an uprising, than to await for an upheaval, get involved in a difficult situation and see his mistake. . . . John, because of Herod's suspicions, was brought in chains to Machaerus . . . and there put to death. (*Jewish Antiquities* 18:116–119)

I divided that unit into two separate paragraphs to emphasize how strangely they go together and how difficult it is to see what exactly was John's crime. The reason is that Josephus does not want us, or maybe even himself, to see it too accurately. But, no matter how much Josephus obscures it, John was offering a radical alternative to the Temple cult as an apocalyptic visionary announcing the cataclysmic advent of God to restore an evil world to justice and holiness.

In that first paragraph John seems to preside over a convocation of otherworldly saints who, having already achieved *spiritual* perfection by themselves, come to John just for *physical* purification. But Josephus's apologetic insistence on what John was *not* doing lets us see exactly what he *was* doing: he was offering a free and populist alternative to the Temple's purification process for sin. That is the first point that Josephus, himself a Temple priest before its destruction, wishes to obscure about John's program.

In that second paragraph, the tone changes completely. We now hear about crowds aroused to the highest degree by John's sermons and about eloquence potentially leading to some form of sedition, uprising, or upheaval. How did we get from select saints to dangerous crowds? What is Josephus hiding now? Before proceeding, recall that the Roman Empire had God's approval as far as Josephus was concerned. Furthermore, he had no sympathy with Jewish messianic or apocalyptic hopes and expectations. Those prophecies were fulfilled in Vespasian and his Flavian dynasty:

> What more than all else incited them [the Jews] to the [First Roman] war was an ambiguous oracle . . . found in their sacred scriptures, to the effect that at that time one from their country would become ruler of the world. This they understood to mean someone of their own race, and many of their wise men went astray in their interpretation of it. The oracle, however, in reality signified the sovereignty of Vespasian who was proclaimed Emperor on Jewish soil. (*Jewish War* 6.312–13)

The second feature Josephus deliberately obscures about John's program is that those sermons were dangerous apocalyptic promises announcing the imminent arrival of an avenging God. That, of course, is why they aroused his audience, and that, of course, is why Antipas struck.

This apocalyptic scenario is very clear in the New Testament accounts of John's message, although those texts now presume that he prepares for Jesus rather than God:

> You offspring of vipers! Who warned you to flee from the coming fury? Change your ways if you have changed your mind. Don't say, "We have Abraham as our father." I am telling you, God can raise up children for Abraham from these stones. Even now the ax is aimed at the root of the trees. Every tree that does not bear good fruit is cut down and thrown into the fire. . . . I am plunging you in water; but one who is stronger than I is coming, one whose sandals I am not worthy to touch. He will overwhelm you with holy spirit and fire. His winnowing fork is in his hand to clear his threshing floor and gather the wheat into his granary. The chaff he will burn with a fire that no one can put out. (Q Gospel in Matthew 3:7–12=Luke 3:7–9, 16b–17)

There are, finally, two features that Josephus does not mention but the New Testament accounts affirm. He has nothing about John baptizing in the *Jordan* and nothing about his location in the *desert* on its east bank. You might guess that last point because he is taken to the Machaerus fortress in southern Perea, east of the Jordan, but both those points are quite explicit in the New Testament accounts, as is the fact that baptism and forgiveness went together:

> John the baptizer appeared in the wilderness, proclaiming a baptism of repentance for the forgiveness of sins. And people from the whole Judean countryside and all the people of Jerusalem were going out to him, and were baptized by him in the river Jordan, confessing their sins. (Mark 1:4–5)

How does that all hang together: desert location, Jordan baptism, apocalyptic scenario? You can work it out by reading Josephus's account of another movement with which he has no sympathy and that he is willing to describe without any obscuration. This took place about thirty years later when the Roman governor Felix was in charge of the entire country between 52 and 60 C.E.

> A still worse blow was dealt at the Jews by the Egyptian false prophet. A charlatan, who had gained for himself the reputation of a prophet, this man appeared in the country, collected a following of about thirty thousand dupes, and led them by a circuitous route from the desert to the mount called the mount of Olives. From there he proposed to force an entrance into Jerusalem and, after overpowering the Roman garrison, to set himself up as tyrant of the people, employing those who poured in with him as his bodyguard. (*Jewish War* 2.261–62)

> At this time there came to Jerusalem from Egypt a man who declared that he was a prophet and advised the masses of the common people to go out with him to the mountain called the Mount of Olives, which lies opposite the city at a distance of five furlongs. For he asserted that he wished to demonstrate from there that at his command Jerusalem's walls would fall down, through which he promised to provide them an entrance into the city. (*Jewish Antiquities* 20.169–70)

Those twin accounts, even with nastier language in the first one (charlatan, dupes) than the second (prophet, masses), make it quite clear what is happening. The Egyptian and his peasant followers are reenacting the scenario of Exodus and Conquest when, under Moses and Joshua, the Israelites left Egypt (notice his title-name), came out of the eastern desert, and crossed the Jordan, and Jericho's walls had fallen at their feet by divine power. Surely, they believed and hoped, God would do the same now for them. If they but marched with faith and hope, God would do to Roman Jerusalem as once before and long ago to Canaanite Jericho. They were unarmed, not only because they had no weapons, but because they needed none. They expected an apocalyptic intervention by God to restore their Promised Land once again. We are dealing primarily with peasants rather than scholars, and while the latter write and live, the former march and die. The governor moved swiftly, and a massacre ensued, although the Egyptian himself escaped.

When John's movement is compared with that later one, similarities and differences become apparent, and what actually happened is clearer than in either Josephus or the New Testament. The reenactment of the

Exodus-Conquest scenario is also the logic behind John's apocalyptic vision. He too is drawing people into the desert east of the Jordan, but instead of gathering a large crowd there and bringing them into the Promised Land in one great march, he sends them through the Jordan individually, baptizing away their sins in its purifying waters and telling them to await in holiness the imminent advent of the avenging God. That is, in a way, even more dangerous than the Egyptian's program. John plants ticking time bombs of apocalyptic expectation all over the Jewish homeland. That left Antipas no crowd to strike at, so he struck at John himself.

The Kingdom of God

John was executed because his apocalyptic vision radically criticized and fundamentally subverted the religious, political, social, and economic bases for Herodian and Roman control of the Jewish homeland. He operated in and was executed in the territory of Antipas.

What about Jesus? He operated in that same territory but was not charged or executed by Herod Antipas. He was executed, instead, at Jerusalem in Judea, under the Roman prefect Pontius Pilate. What was Jesus' own vision and program? Did he pick up the fallen mantle of John, as Elisha did for Elijah in the Old Testament, and continue the same apocalyptic message? And why was he executed in Judea, not in Galilee?

Before attempting answers, a few words about terms and concepts. When a people is exploited by colonial occupation, one obvious response is armed revolt or military rebellion. But sometimes that situation of oppression is experienced as so fundamentally evil and so humanly hopeless that only transcendental intervention is deemed of any use. God, and God alone, must act to restore a ruined world to justice and holiness. This demands a vision and a program that is radical, countercultural, utopian, world-negating, or, as scholars say, *eschatological.* That term comes from the Greek word for "the last things" and means that God's solution will be so profound as to constitute an ending of things, a radical world-negation. But now comes a great parting of the ways as that world-negating radicalism is articulated and programmed in one of two ways.

The first way is called *apocalyptic eschatology,* and that is what we just saw as John's message. The word *apocalypsis* is Greek for "revelation," and apocalyptic eschatology announces that God has given *us alone* (some specific in-group) a special and secret revelation about an imminent and cataclysmic divine intervention to restore peace and justice to a disordered world. Whether thereafter there will be heaven on earth or earth in heaven is left rather vague, but the evil oppressors will be gone forever and the holy oppressed will be in charge under God. An example of apocalyptic eschatology's divine revelatory promise is, from the ancient world, John of Patmos, Greece, and from the modern world, David Koresh of Waco, Texas. This future but imminent apocalyptic radicalism is dependent on the overpowering action of God's moving to restore justice and peace to an earth ravished by injustice and oppression. Believers can, at the very most, prepare or persuade, implore or assist its arrival, but its accomplishment is consigned to divine power alone. And despite a serene vagueness about specifics and details, its consummation would be objectively visible and tangible to all, believers and unbelievers alike, but with appropriately different fates.

The second way is called *sapiential eschatology,* and this is what eventually became Jesus' own message. The word *sapientia* is Latin for "wisdom," and sapiential eschatology announces that God has given *all human beings* the wisdom to discern how, here and now in this world, one can so live that God's power, rule, and dominion are evidently present to all observers. It involves a way of life for now rather than a hope of life for the future. An example of sapiential eschatology's radical life-style challenge is, from the ancient world, Diogenes of Greece living in his barrel, and from the modern world, Gandhi of India living in nonviolence. Apocalyptic eschatology is world-negation stressing *future and imminent* divine intervention; sapiential eschatology is world-negation emphasizing *present and immanent* divine intervention. In apocalyptic eschatology, we are waiting for God to act. In sapiential eschatology, God is waiting for us to act.

Jesus certainly began as a follower of the Baptist, because, as surely as we know anything about him, we know that he was baptized by John: Mark 1:9–11 admits it, Matthew 3:14–15 explains it, Luke 3:21–22 obscures it, and John 1:29–34 ignores it. Their evident embarrassment certifies it as fact. But John was killed, and God did not intervene. John was executed, and there was no apocalyptic advent of an avenging God. When we finally hear Jesus' own voice, it is not to continue the Baptism movement but to proclaim the Kingdom movement. Jesus changed, possibly schooled by John's fate and God's nonintervention, from apocalyptic to sapiential eschatology:

> I tell you, among those born of women no one is greater than John;
>> yet the least in the kingdom of God is greater than he.
> (Q Gospel in Matthew 11:11 = Luke 7:28)

In two earlier books, *The Historical Jesus: The Life of a Mediterranean Jewish Peasant* and *Jesus: A Revolutionary Biography,* I reconstructed Jesus' religiopolitical vision and socioeconomic program; I will simply summarize it here.

Jesus' phrase *Kingdom of God* evokes an ideal vision of political and religious power, of how this world here below would be run if God, not Caesar, sat on an imperial throne. As such it always casts a caustically critical shadow on human rule. It includes especially an eschatological rejection of the world as it is currently run. But the solution is that we must act now to incarnate God's power on earth rather than that God must act soon to do it for us.

Thus the sayings and parables of the historical Jesus often describe a world of radical egalitarianism in which discrimination and hierarchy, exploitation and oppression should no longer exist. This is his utopian dream of the Kingdom of God in which both material and spiritual goods, political and religious resources, economic and transcendental favors are equally available to all without interference from brokers, mediators, or intermediaries. Think, for example, of his parable about the feast, in which the servant finally brings in anyone he can find so that female and male, married and unmarried, slave and free, pure and impure, rich and poor could all be gathered together around an open and indiscriminate table for the same meal. But there was also a program behind that vision, a political challenge behind the poetic rhetoric. The place where one can most clearly see that program in action is in these three independent sources, two of which date from the earliest stratum of the Jesus tradition. What is mandated by these texts is a reciprocity of free healing and open eating. The members of the Kingdom movement must eat with those they heal, and that conjunction enacts the Kingdom itself. They are not sent, above all, to bring others back to Jesus. It is not a matter of Jesus' power but of their empowerment. He himself has no monopoly on the Kingdom; it is there for anyone with the courage to embrace it.

> When you go into any land and walk about in the districts, if they receive you, eat what they will set before you, and heal the sick among them. (Gospel of Thomas 14:2)

> Carry no purse, no bag, no sandals; and salute no one on the road. Whatever house you enter, first say, "Peace be to this house!" And if a son of peace is there, your peace shall rest upon him; but if not, it shall return to you. And remain in the same house, eating and drinking what they provide, for the laborer deserves his wages; do not go from house to house.

Whenever you enter a town and they receive you, eat what is set before you; heal the sick in it and say to them, "The kingdom of God has come near to you." But whenever you enter a town and they do not receive you, go into its streets and say, "Even the dust of your town that clings to our feet, we wipe off against you; nevertheless know this, that the kingdom of God has come near." (Q Gospel in Matthew 10:8–14=Luke 10:4–11)

He charged them to take nothing for their journey except a staff; no bread, no bag, no money in their belts; but to wear sandals and not put on two tunics. And he said to them, "Where you enter a house, stay there until you leave the place. And if any place will not receive you and they refuse to hear you, when you leave, shake off the dust that is on your feet for a testimony against them." So they went out and preached that men should repent. And they cast out many demons, and anointed with oil many that were sick and healed them. (Mark 6:8–13=Matthew 10:8–10a, 11=Luke 9:2–6)

Jesus called his program the presence of the Kingdom of God, but that expression must be interpreted primarily in light of what he himself did and what he also challenged his companions to do. It did not mean for Jesus, as it could for others, the imminent apocalyptic intervention of God to set right a world taken over by evil and injustice. It meant the presence of God's Kingdom here and now in the reciprocity of open eating and open healing, in lives, that is, of radical egalitarianism on both the socioeconomic (eating) and the religiopolitical (healing) levels.

That combination of vision and program, of word and deed, of thought and action could just as easily have led to Jesus' as it had to John's execution by Antipas. We know, however, that there was popular resentment against Antipas because of John's death. Recall that unnamed wife whom Antipas abandoned in favor of Herodias. Her royal father came after Antipas with an army:

In the ensuing battle, the whole army of Herod was destroyed. . . . But to some of the Jews the destruction of Herod's army seemed to be divine vengeance, and certainly a just vengeance, for his treatment of John surnamed the Baptist. (*Jewish Antiquities* 18:114, 116)

Popular resentment for the death of John probably persuaded Antipas not to move against Jesus. It was not worth risking any further discontent, especially among the peasantry. That explains why Jesus could have been but was not executed by Antipas in Galilee. It does not explain why Jesus was executed by Pilate in Judea.

My answer to that question involves Jesus and the Temple in Jerusalem, but first some background is needed on the attitude of Jewish peasants to that sanctuary, on crowded festival days as a flash point for trouble, and on what concerning the Temple could and could not get you executed. In the next section, therefore, I give two first-century incidents to establish parameters for each of those three topics but always as preparation for Jesus and the Temple in the final section of this chapter. The question is still, What crime led to Jesus' execution under Pilate in Judea?

Peasants in the Temple

What did the Jewish peasantry think about the Temple (Theissen 1992:95–114)? Were they for it, or against it? Was it the place of prayers and sacrifices, or the place of tithes and taxes? Was it divine dwelling, or central bank? Was it the link between God and themselves, between heaven and earth, or the link between religion and politics, between Jewish collaboration and Roman occupation? It was clearly both, and peasant attitudes were correspondingly ambiguous.

Ambiguous Peasant Responses

My first preparatory point for Jesus and the Temple concerns peasant attitudes toward that sacred building. Compare two very divergent peasant reactions to the Temple, one at the start of the 40s and the other at the end of the 60s of the first century. I cite them as instances of a more permanent and abiding ambiguity whose presence must always be recognized.

Caligula's statue. Gaius, nicknamed Caligula, was Roman emperor from 39 to 41 C.E., and the infamous story of Caligula's statue is told twice by Josephus, the Jewish historian seen so often before, and also by Philo, a Jewish philosopher from Alexandria who lived between 20 B.C.E. and 45 C.E. All three texts agree that Caligula, deeming the Jews disrespectful of his divinity, decided to place in Jerusalem's Temple statues of himself as Zeus incarnate. He ordered Petronius, the new Syrian governor, to do so by taking two legions immediately into Judea. Those two legions, at full strength about twelve thousand elite soldiers, represented half the forces stationed at Antioch to guard the eastern approaches of the empire, so obviously Caligula was expecting serious Jewish resistance. Petronius moved southward and put his troops into quarters for the winter of 39 to 40 C.E. at Ptolemais on the Mediterranean seacoast due west of Galilee. Here is what happened next, in two versions:

> Many tens of thousands of Jews ["with their wives and children" in *Jewish War* 2.192] came to Petronius at Ptolemais with petitions not to use force to make them transgress and violate their ancestral code. . . . He gathered up his friends and attendants and hastened to Tiberias. . . . As before, many tens of thousands faced Petronius on his arrival at Tiberias. . . . "On no account would we fight," they said, "but we will die sooner than violate our laws." And falling on their faces and baring their throats, they declared that they were ready to be slain. They continued to make these supplications for forty days. Furthermore, they neglected their fields, and that, too, though it was time to sow the seed. For they showed stubborn determination to die rather than to see the image erected. (Josephus, *Jewish Antiquities* 18.263–72=*Jewish War* 2.192–97)

> He also sent for the magnates of the Jews, priests and magistrates. . . . For he thought that if he could start by appeasing them he could use them to instruct all the rest of the population to abstain from opposition. . . . Smitten by his first words . . . they stood riveted to the ground, incapable of speech, and then while a flood of tears poured from their eyes as from fountains they plucked the hair from their beards and heads. . . . While they were thus lamenting, the inhabitants of the holy city and the rest of the country hearing what was afoot marshalled themselves as if at a single signal . . . and issued forth in a body leaving cities, villages and houses empty and in one rush sped to Phoenicia where Petronius chanced to be. . . . They were divided into six companies, old men, young men, boys, and again in their turn old women, grown women, maidens. . . . [and they said] if we cannot persuade you, we give up ourselves for destruction that we may not live to see a calamity worse than death. . . . The wheat crop was just ripe and so were the other cereals, and he [Petronius] feared that the Jews in despair for their ancestral rites and in scorn of life might lay waste the arable land or set fire to the cornfields on the hills and the plain (Philo, *Embassy to Gaius* 222–49)

Both writers agree that the crowds were unarmed, that they had brought their wives and children with them, that they were loyal both to Rome and to Caligula, but that they were willing to die if his statue profaned their Temple at Jerusalem, and that it all happened at an important agricultural moment, either for sowing or harvesting. Petronius, faced with a massive agricultural strike or sabotage backed up by an equally massive readiness for unresisting martyrdom, postponed the operation. He withdrew to Antioch and reported to Caligula, and only the latter's timely assassination in early 41 C.E. saved Petronius from execution.

That is one side of the peasantry's attitude toward their Temple. When a pagan emperor threatened to defile it, they were ready to die rather than cooperate. That was a case dividing along *religious* lines of Jews against pagans. But that is only one side; here is the other, about thirty years later. And now it is a case of dividing along *class* lines of Jews against Jews.

Zealot elections. The incident took place during the First Roman War, which had begun in the late summer of 66 C.E. By the spring of 67, as we saw before, the Roman general Vespasian had reconquered Galilee and taken Josephus prisoner. During the winter of 67 and the spring of 68 he moved inexorably southward toward Jerusalem leaving scorched earth behind him. Groups of peasant insurgents under bandit leadership were swept steadily inside the protection of Jerusalem's walls by the Roman noose. These were known collectively as the Zealots, and what happened on their arrival was a reign of terror by those peasant rebels against the aristocratic and high-priestly leadership of the war against Rome. Temple worship took second place to class warfare. Josephus himself was from an aristocratic priestly family, and his anger is quite palpable in the heated rhetoric of his description:

> In the end to such abject prostration and terror were the people reduced and to such heights of madness rose these brigands, that they actually took upon themselves the election to the high priesthood. Abrogating the claims of those families from which in turn the high priests had always been drawn, they appointed to that office ignoble and low born individuals, in order to gain accomplices in their impious crimes; for persons who had undeservedly attained to the highest dignity were bound to obey those who had conferred it. Moreover, by various devices and libellous statements, they brought the official authorities into collision with each other, finding their own opportunity in the bickerings of those who should have kept them in check; until, glutted with the wrongs which they had done to men, they transferred their insolence to the Deity and with polluted feet invaded the sanctuary. . . .
>
> To these horrors was added a spice of mockery more galling than their actions. For, to test the abject submission of the populace and make trial of their own strength, they essayed to appoint the high priests by lot, although, as we have stated, the succession was hereditary. As pretext for this scheme they adduced ancient custom, asserting that in old days the high priesthood had been determined by lot; but in reality their action was the abrogation of established practice and a trick to make themselves supreme by getting these appointments into their own hands. They accordingly summoned one of the high-priestly clans, called Eniachin, and cast

lots for a high priest. By chance the lot fell to one who proved a signal illustration of their depravity; he was an individual named Phanni, son of Samuel, of the village of Aphthia, a man who not only was not descended from high priests, but was such a clown that he scarcely knew what the high priesthood meant. At any rate they dragged their reluctant victim out of the country and, dressing him up for his assumed part, as on the stage, put the sacred vestments upon him and instructed him how to act in keeping with the occasion. To them this monstrous impiety was a subject for jesting and sport, but the other priests, beholding from a distance this mockery of their law, could not restrain their tears and bemoaned the degradation of the sacred honours. (*Jewish War* 4.147–48, 153–57)

I gave that section in full so you could appreciate Josephus's fury in recounting it. There are all those nasty words which impugn motivation rather than offer explanation. He is furious, first, because it is a case of peasants against aristocrats and, second, because what they did was actually ancient and valid tradition.

Some background is necessary here. As there was only one God, so there was only one Temple, and one high priest. Those individuals had been chosen from one single family, that of Zadok, from at least the time of Solomon until the early decades of the second century B.C.E. But when the Jewish dynasty of the Hasmoneans restored national control over their homeland in the 160s, they themselves assumed the high priesthood, although they were not of Zadokite lineage. It was probably legitimate Zadokite priests who withdrew in protest to Qumran where, among the Dead Sea Scrolls, their Community Rule decrees that "the lot come shall forth . . . [on] all matters concerning the Law or property or justice" (5:3). Thereafter, under the Herodians and the Romans, high priests were chosen from four main families, not of legitimate Zadokite lineage, and were appointed and fired almost like servants. What the peasant Zealots are doing is quite logical, coherent, and traditional against that background. They are ousting the aristocratic government of their country and replacing it with a peasant leadership chosen from legitimate Zadokite stock by the ancient method of lottery. That action, of course, was intended to leave the ultimate decision up to God. Because all of that lineage are legitimate, let God choose. They would not choose the smartest, or the tallest, or the richest, or the most powerful. Lottery was their radical egalitarianism in action. They also killed their chief opponents, Ananus II and Jesus, former high priests of 62 to 63 and 63 to 64 C.E., respectively.

Those two events, the protest against Caligula's statue and the Zealot elections, took place about thirty years apart, but they represent two very different peasant reactions to their Temple and its high priesthood. They indicate the extremities of peasant ambiguity with regard to that single and central sanctuary: mass martyrdom to protect it from pagan Romans; mass slaughter to wrench it from aristocratic Jews.

Trouble at the Festival

My second preparatory point for Jesus and the Temple concerns festivals as dangerous focal points for insurrection. Each year three feasts concentrated large numbers of pilgrims in the confined space of Jerusalem's Temple. The feast of Booths was in September–October, that of Weeks in May–June, and the one day of Passover leading into the one week of Unleavened Bread was in March–April. That last festival combined the Jewish homeland's pastoral (lamb) and agricultural (bread) bases into a commemoration of the Exodus from Egypt. But the Exodus celebrated divine deliverance from imperial slavery and imminent extermination, and that annual remembrance must have been especially difficult when Egypt had been replaced by Rome and the Jewish homeland was no longer the place of freedom but of colonial occupation. Imagine a very large group of people gathered together in a very confined space to celebrate their ancient freedom from slavery with a Herodian kingling or a Roman prefect now in charge and pagan soldiers looking down into the Temple courts from the Antonia fortress at its northwest corner. The pilgrim feasts in general, but Passover in particular, were flash points for trouble, and the authorities, whether Herodian or Roman, were always appropriately prepared. Once again, two cases about fifty years apart will suffice to make the point.

Archelaus at Passover. The first incident at Passover took place in 4 B.C.E. just after Herod the Great's death but before his son Archelaus had gone to Rome to plead his case before the emperor Augustus. He eventually received control of Idumea, Judea, and Samaria, which he held only until 6 C.E., when he was exiled and Roman prefects took direct control of those territories. Herod the Great had executed some teachers, interpreters, or doctors of the Law (an incident to be seen in the next section), and here is what happened at the following Passover:

> And now the feast of unleavened bread, which the Jews call Passover, came
> round; it is an occasion for the contribution of a multitude of sacrifices,
> and a vast crowd streamed in from the country for the ceremony. The pro-
> moters of the mourning for the doctors [executed by Herod the Great]
> stood in a body in the temple, procuring recruits for their faction. This

alarmed Archelaus, who, wishing to prevent the contagion from spreading to the whole crowd, sent in a tribune in command of a cohort, with orders to restrain by force the ringleaders of the sedition. Indignant at the appearance of the troops, the whole crowd pelted them with stones; most of the cohort were killed, while their commander was wounded and escaped with difficulty. Then, as if nothing serious had happened, the rioters returned to their sacrifices. Archelaus, however, now felt that it would be impossible to restrain the mob without bloodshed, and let loose upon them his entire army, the infantry advancing in close order through the city, the cavalry by way of the plain. The soldiers falling unexpectedly upon the various parties busy with their sacrifices slew about three thousand of them and dispersed the remainder among the neighbouring hills. The heralds of Archelaus followed and ordered everyone to return home; so they all abandoned the festival and departed. (*Jewish War* 2:10–13=*Jewish Antiquities* 17.204–5)

There is no point in giving the full text of both versions, but that second one mentions that "Passover [is] a commemoration of their departure from Egypt." It also explains more clearly the danger of the rebellion spreading *from* the ringleaders ("if there were any who clearly stood out from the rest in their eagerness to rebel, they were to be brought to him") *through* the crowd within the Temple ("infuriated") *to* the crowds encamped outside in the plain ("the cavalry, in order that they might prevent the people encamped there from helping those in the Temple"). The festival situation made escalation a serious possibility.

Cumanus at Passover. The second incident at Passover took place after the Romans had assumed direct control of the entire Jewish homeland in 44 C.E. and Ventidius Cumanus was governor between 48 and 52 C.E.

The usual crowd had assembled at Jerusalem for the feast of unleavened bread, and the Roman cohort had taken up its position on the roof of the portico of the temple; for a body of men in arms invariably mounts guard at the feasts, to prevent disorders arising from such a concourse of people. Thereupon one of the soldiers, raising his robe, stooped in an indecent attitude, so as to turn his backside to the Jews, and made a noise in keeping with his posture. Enraged at this insult, the whole multitude with loud cries called upon Cumanus to punish the soldier; some of the more hotheaded young men and seditious persons in the crowd started a fight, and, picking up stones, hurled them at the troops. Cumanus, fearing a general attack upon himself, sent for reinforcements. These troops pouring into the porticoes, the Jews were seized with irresistible panic and turned to fly from the temple and make their escape into the town. But such violence was used as they pressed round the exits that they were trodden under foot and crushed to death by one another; upwards of thirty thousand perished, and the feast was turned into mourning for the whole nation and for every household into lamentation. (*Jewish War* 2.224–27=*Jewish Antiquities* 20.106–12)

Once again it is not necessary to give the second version in full. It calls the feast "Passover," mentions the Antonia fortress, describes the guards as a smaller "company" rather than a larger cohort, deems the insult a "blasphemy against God," and numbers the dead as "twenty thousand."

Those troops, by the way, were not the legions, four of which, at that time and as mentioned before, were stationed near Syrian Antioch under the command of its first-rank governor. The second-rank governor in the Jewish homeland commanded five cohorts of infantry and one squadron of cavalry. Those auxiliary troops, with six hundred men to a cohort, were composed not of Jews but of soldiers from the several predominantly pagan cities in the Jewish homeland, especially from Sebaste in Samaria and Caesarea, the Roman capital on the coast. The point, once again, is that feasts in general and Passover in particular were dangerous situations as large crowds of people celebrated ancient deliverance in an occupied country.

An Oracle and an Eagle

My final preparatory point for Jesus and the Temple concerns what could and could not get you killed in words or deeds against it.

Oracle of a madman. His name was Jesus, and he was a peasant. He spoke against the Temple, was arrested and beaten by the Jewish authorities, and was handed over to the Roman authorities, who scourged him but then released him. But this Jesus was the son of Ananias, and the year was 62 C.E., under Albinus, Roman governor between then and 64 C.E. It was once again a festival, but now Booths in the fall rather than Passover in the spring. Here is Josephus's account of this incident, the closest parallel to the gospels' passion story from that first century:

> Four years before the war, when the city was enjoying profound peace and prosperity, there came to the feast at which it is the custom of all Jews to erect tabernacles to God, one Jesus, son of Ananias, a rude peasant, who, standing in the temple, suddenly began to cry out,
>
> > "A voice from the east,
> > a voice from the west,
> > a voice from the four winds;
> > a voice against Jerusalem and the sanctuary,

a voice against the bridegroom and the bride,
a voice against all the people."

Day and night he went about all the alleys with this cry on his lips. Some
of the leading citizens, incensed at these ill-omened words, arrested the fellow and severely chastised him. But he, without a word on his own behalf
or for the private ear of those who smote him, only continued his cries as
before. Thereupon, the magistrates, supposing, as was indeed the case, that
the man was under some supernatural impulse, brought him before the
Roman governor; there, although flayed to the bone with scourges, he neither sued for mercy nor shed a tear, but, merely introducing the most
mournful of variations into his ejaculation, responded to each stroke with
"Woe to Jerusalem!" When Albinus, the governor, asked him who and
whence he was and why he uttered these cries, he answered him never a
word, but unceasingly reiterated his dirge over the city, until Albinus pronounced him a maniac and let him go. During the whole period up to the
outbreak of war he neither approached nor was seen talking to any of the
citizens, but daily, like a prayer that he had conned [practiced], repeated his
lament, "Woe to Jerusalem!" He neither cursed any of those who beat him
from day to day, nor blessed those who offered him food: to all men that
melancholy presage was his one reply. His cries were loudest at the festivals. So for seven years and five months he continued his wail, his voice
never flagging nor his strength exhausted, until in the siege, having seen his
presage verified, he found his rest. For, while going his round and shouting
in piercing tones from the wall, "Woe once more to the city and to the
people and to the temple," as he added a last word, "and woe to me also,"
a stone hurled from the *ballista* struck and killed him on the spot. So with
those ominous words still upon his lips he passed away. (*Jewish War*
6.300–309)

Once again we are dealing with a peasant and with something that
started at a festival. But this is only speech, not action, and although Jewish authority takes it seriously enough to want the man executed, Roman
authority finds it all politically irrelevant, judges the man mad, and lets
him go free. His message was, of course, quite terribly correct.

The eagle on the Temple. That preceding incident took place over
thirty years after the death of Jesus of Nazareth. This incident of the eagle
on the Temple took place over thirty years before. It led, as just seen, to
that massacre by Archelaus in the Temple at Passover. The moment is just
before the death of Herod the Great in 4 B.C.E., as Josephus tells the
story:

There were in the capital two doctors [teachers] with a reputation as profound experts in the laws of their country, who consequently enjoyed the

highest esteem of the whole nation; their names were Judas, son of Sep-
phoraeus, and Matthias, son of Margalus. Their lectures on the laws were
attended by a large youthful audience, and day after day they drew together
a large army of men in their prime. . . . It was, in fact, unlawful to place in
the temple either images or busts or any representation whatsoever of a living creature; notwithstanding this, the king had erected over the great gate
a golden eagle. This it was which these doctors now exhorted their disciples to cut down. . . . At mid-day, accordingly, when numbers of people
were perambulating in the temple, they let themselves down from the roof
by stout cords and began chopping off the golden eagle with hatchets.
The king's captain . . . with a considerable force, arrested about forty of
the young men and conducted them to the king. . . . Those who had let
themselves down from the roof together with the doctors he had burnt
alive; the remainder of those arrested he handed over to his executioners.
(*Jewish War* 1:648–55=*Jewish Antiquities* 17.149–67)

Apart from the question of images, the golden *eagle* represented Roman
power over the Jewish Temple, and to destroy it was clearly a symbolic action. It did not, of course, destroy Roman control, nor did it intend to
start a general revolt. But with Jesus, son of Ananias, there was only *speech*
against the Temple involved. With those teachers and their students, there
was *action* involved, even or especially if that action was primarily a symbolical one. So the teachers and their students were executed, but the
prophet was released to his own fate.

Overturning the Tables

John and Jesus, each in his own way, engaged in a program of social revolution and political subversion in the name of the Jewish God. Both operated primarily in the territory of Herod Antipas, but Jesus, unlike John,
was executed by Pontius Pilate in Judea. In one sense, all we know of
Jesus' activities in Galilee could have got him executed anywhere in an
occupied country under Roman control. But did anything more specific
happen in Jerusalem? As you can tell from the preceding section, my answer will have to do with Jesus and the Temple. In that preceding section
I chose three sets of incidents immediately before and after the time of
Jesus, and I emphasize my conclusion: the peasantry was both for and
against their Temple; the pilgrim feasts and especially Passover were always potentially explosive; rather than speech alone, actions, even symbolic actions, against the Temple could get you killed.

There are three independent sources attesting that Jesus did and/or said something against Jerusalem's Temple, and that is very important for any decision about its historicity. An equally significant factor is the sense of unease or embarrassment with which two of those sources discuss the matter.

I Will Destroy This House

The first independent source on Jesus and the Temple is a terse saying unaccompanied by any action, found in the Gospel of Thomas, which, as you will recall from the prologue section "Dependent and Independent Passion Stories," is not among the New Testament gospels:

> I shall destroy [this] house, and no one will be able to build it . . .
> (Thomas 71)

There is, obviously, no mention of the Temple there, but "house" also appears in the saying part of the two other independent sources, as we shall see at Mark 11:17 and John 2:16–17, so I take it here to refer to the Temple as well.

The Gospel of Thomas has a long series of sayings against various forms of standard Jewish piety because they were deemed inadequate compared to the ascetic celibacy demanded by that community:

> His followers asked him and said to him, "Do you want us to fast? How should we pray? Should we give to charity? . . .
> Jesus said to them, "If you fast, you will bring sin upon yourselves, and if you pray, you will be condemned, and if you give to charity, you will harm your spirits." (6a, 14a)
> "If you do not fast from the world, you will not find the kingdom. If you do not observe the sabbath as a sabbath, you will not see the father." (27)
> His followers said to him, "Twenty-four prophets have spoken in Israel, and they all spoke of you."
> He said to them, "You have disregarded the living one who is in your presence and have spoken of the dead." (52)
> His followers said to him, "Is circumcision useful or not?"
> He said to them, "If it were useful, children's fathers would produce them already circumcised from their mothers. Rather the true circumcision in spirit has become valuable in every respect." (53)
> Jesus said, "Why do you wash the outside of the cup? Do you not understand that the one who made the inside is also the one who made the outside?" (89)

Why fast this day or that, when you should fast all the time? Why give alms, when you should have nothing to begin with? Thomas Christianity demands a more radical and total abstention from the material world than is advocated in standard Jewish piety. Prayer, fasting, almsgiving, Sabbath, circumcision, prophecy, purification are all negated in sayings of Jesus, so a word against the Temple is not unexpected as well. In Thomas, as is customary for that gospel, Jesus talks rather than acts. In the next two sources, there will be a union of deed and word, of action and speech.

Take These Things Away

The second independent source is in John. Recall my conclusion, in the prologue section "Dependent and Independent Passion Stories," that John is independent of the Synoptic gospels apart from his initial Baptist traditions and his terminal passion-resurrection stories. His story about Jesus and the Temple is in 2:13–22 and is independent from the one to be seen next in Mark 11:15–17.

John's account contains two sections, deed and word, event and saying (separated as A and B below). Its importance is signaled by the double "his disciples remembered" after each of its two component parts. That gloss indicates, I presume, some trouble with those twin units, some initial lack of understanding or misunderstanding that had to be explained by later comprehension. Here is the text:

> (A) The Passover of the Jews was at hand, and Jesus went up to Jerusalem. In the temple he found those who were selling oxen and sheep and pigeons, and the money-changers at their business. And making a whip of cords, he drove them all, with the sheep and oxen, out of the temple; and he poured out the coins of the money-changers and overturned their tables.

> (B1) And he told those who sold the pigeons, "Take these things away; you shall not make my Father's house a house of trade." *His disciples remembered* that it was written, "Zeal for thy house will consume me [=Psalm 69:9]."

> (B2) The Jews then said to him, "What sign have you to show us for doing this?" Jesus answered them, "Destroy this temple, and in three days I will raise it up." The Jews then said, "It has taken forty-six years to build this temple, and will you raise it up in three days?" But he spoke of the temple of his body. When therefore he was raised from the dead, *his disciples remembered* that he had said this; and they believed the scripture and the word which Jesus had spoken. (John 2:13–22, my italics)

Focus first on the *saying* section and on how greatly developed it is over Thomas 71 (B1–2). There are four points to be emphasized. One is the use of "house" for Temple, twice from Jesus himself and once from Psalm 69:9. Recall that usage from Thomas 71, and retain it for future reference with Mark. Another point is the double division (B1/B2) within that saying section, underlined by the double note that "his disciples remembered." That duplication allows a strong muting of Jesus' saying against the Temple. Now, all he does is protest against business in the Temple (B1), and the destruction theme is not Jesus destroying the Temple but "the Jews'" destroying his Temple/body (B2). John's text is very careful to protect Jesus against saying, "I will destroy." But the final point is the most important of all. On the one hand, this incident takes place at the very start, not the very end, of Jesus' public life. But, on the other, it takes place at Passover, and it does involve a discussion of Jesus' death, of Jesus' body being destroyed and raised.

Two conclusions: John has used the *saying* section (B1–B2) to interpret the *action* section (A) according to his own theology. But John locates this event at the very start rather than the very end of Jesus' career, so how can it be the immediate cause of his execution? But if John knew of that connection between Temple event and Jesus' execution, are there reasons why he might have relocated it to its present position? I see two possible reasons. In its new location that first Passover can form an overarching preparation for the last Passover. But, even more important, that allows John to give the following explanation for why the high-priestly authorities in Jerusalem wanted Jesus dead and eventually had him executed:

> Many of the Jews therefore, who had [seen the raising of Lazarus], believed in him. But some of them went to the Pharisees and told them what he had done. So the chief priests and the Pharisees called a meeting of the council, and said, "What are we to do? This man is performing many signs. If we let him go on like this, everyone will believe in him, and the Romans will come and destroy both our holy place and our nation." But one of them, Caiaphas, who was high priest that year, said to them, "You know nothing at all! You do not understand that it is better for you to have one man die for the people than to have the whole nation destroyed." He did not say this on his own, but being high priest that year he prophesied that Jesus was about to die for the nation, and not for the nation only, but to gather into one the dispersed children of God. So from that day on they planned to put him to death. (John 11:45–53)

That is theology, not history. The crime for which the Jewish authorities wanted Jesus executed had to make sense not only to themselves but to Pilate as well. It could, of course, be phrased differently for each venue, but the above is a Johannine interpretation, not a historical indictment.

Learn from the Fig Tree

The *saying* of Jesus is quite clear in Thomas 71: he will destroy the Temple beyond any possibility of restoration. But John's version is much more muted: the *action* simply opposes business in the Temple's outer courts, and the *saying* first cites Psalm 69:9 and then mentions destruction not as a threat by Jesus against the Temple but as one by "the Jews" against Jesus' life. Mark's account, however, again with both action and saying, is not at all muted and very clear in its meaning.

We can see exactly how Mark understands Jesus' action, and it brings up a Markan literary technique or compositional device that will be of even greater importance in chapter 3 in discussing John's dependence on the Synoptics for his passion-resurrection stories. This device involves an *intercalation* of two events whereby Event 1 begins, is interrupted by a full account of Event 2, and then is completed. It is a stylistic device inviting the hearer or reader to interpret the frame event and the center event as mutually interactive, as casting important light on each other and as forming a linked pair for mutual interpretation. It has also been termed a sandwich technique, with the Event 1 as the twin slices of bread and Event 2 as the filler. I give several examples in chapter 3, but I concentrate here on the one that frames the Temple event with the start and finish of the fig tree event:

Event 1 begins (fig tree cursed):

On the following day, when they came from Bethany, he was hungry. Seeing in the distance a fig tree in leaf, he went to see whether perhaps he would find anything on it. When he came to it, he found nothing but leaves, for it was not the season for figs. He said to it, "May no one ever eat fruit from you again." And his disciples heard it. (Mark 11:12–14)

Event 2 starts and finishes (Temple symbolically destroyed):

Action: And they came to Jerusalem. And he entered the temple and began to drive out those who sold and those who bought in the temple, and he overturned the tables of the money-changers and the seats of those who sold pigeons; and he would not allow any one to carry anything through the temple.

Saying: And he taught, and said to them, "Is it not written, 'My house shall be called a house of prayer for all the nations' [=Isaiah 56:7]? But you have made it a den of robbers [=Jeremiah 7:11]."

And when the chief priests and the scribes heard it, they kept looking for a way to kill him; for they were afraid of him, because the whole crowd was spellbound by his teaching. And when evening came, Jesus and his disciples went out of the city. (Mark 11:15–19)

Event 1 finishes (fig tree withered):

In the morning as they passed by, they saw the fig tree withered away to its roots. Then Peter remembered and said to him, "Rabbi, look! The fig tree that you cursed has withered." (Mark 11:20–21)

In Mark's mind, therefore, those events interpret each other: Jesus is symbolically destroying the Temple just as he had destroyed the fig tree. (A fig tree in springtime is not a perfect example of culpable fruitlessness, but Mark is doing his best.) In any case it is interesting to see how Luke and Matthew handle that intercalation. Luke simply omits the entire fig tree incident, and Matthew puts cursing and withering together at the same moment:

In the morning, when he returned to the city, he was hungry. And seeing a fig tree by the side of the road, he went to it and found nothing at all on it but leaves. Then he said to it, "May no fruit ever come from you again!" And the fig tree withered at once. (Matthew 21:18–19)

But Mark's purpose is quite obvious. Jesus does not cleanse or purify the Temple. He symbolically destroys the Temple by attacking its fiscal, sacrificial, and cultic necessities. It is all symbolic, of course, but so was removing the golden eagle. That action did not actually destroy Roman rule any more than Jesus' action destroyed the Temple's giant edifice. But later, as Jesus dies, Mark records that God ratifies his action by abandoning the Temple's inner sanctuary through a symbolic act of departure:

And the curtain of the temple was torn in two, from top to bottom. (Mark 15:38)

Finally, there are two significant features of Mark's *saying* section. Once again the term "house" appears (twice) for Temple, as in John (twice) and Thomas (once). Also, the scriptural quotes are not from the Psalms, as in John, but from the prophets Isaiah and Jeremiah.

What Happened in the Temple?

A warning before summation. Forget any interpretation of Jesus' action as Christianity reforming Judaism. Forget any idea that what was being done in the Temple was invalid or illegitimate. That giant complex had a clearly structured architectural hierarchy: first, the innermost Holy of Holies entered only once a year by the high priest on the Day of Atonement, then, as if in concentric circles widening outward, the courts of the priests, of the male Jews, of the female Jews, and finally of the Gentiles, who, despite Mark's complaint, could still pray in Jerusalem's Temple if they so wished. Different sections of the Temple were for different operations. But the Temple required pure animals and birds for sacrifice, and such were most easily bought close to the place of sacrifice and guaranteed as appropriate by priestly authority. And the Temple could not have been maintained without the tax paid annually from all across the Jewish world, and it was the job of the money changers to turn all the many currencies offered into the single official coinage. There is not a single hint that anyone was doing anything financially or sacrificially inappropriate. Cleansing or purification are, therefore, very misleading terms for what Jesus was doing, namely, an attack on the Temple's very existence, a destruction—symbolic, to be sure, but none the less dangerous for that. His *action,* in John and Mark, is quite clear. It is like going into a draft office during the Vietnam War and overturning drawers of file cards. It is symbolic negation of all that office or Temple stands for. And the *saying* is equally clear in Thomas and goes very well with that *action.* But in Mark and John the *saying* has been glossed by different scriptural quotes, none of which is original, and has been, especially in John, muted considerably in its meaning. Still, Mark and John connect the event with Passover and John, implicitly, Mark, explicitly, with the death of Jesus.

Imagine Jesus' action against all we read above concerning peasants and the Temple, festival and especially Passover tensions, and the difference between mere talk and talk plus action, even symbolic action, against the Temple. Imagine the Temple for what it was, the religious, political, social, and economic center of the Jewish homeland, and think of those four aspects as absolutely interwoven together. Imagine that in the disturbances after Herod the Great's death in 4 B.C.E., the Romans managed to loot more than four hundred talents from the Temple treasury (*Jewish War* 2.50=*Jewish Antiquities* 17:264). As an example for comparative purposes, the total annual revenues of Herod Agrippa I, who ruled the entire Jewish homeland from 41 to 44 C.E., amounted to two thousand talents (*Jewish Antiquities* 19.352). The Temple was, in effect, a central bank. Imagine that eighteen thousand workers were still involved in its construction after eighty years of work in the early 60s C.E. It was, in effect, an important employment agency.

My best historical reconstruction concludes that what led immediately to Jesus' arrest and execution in Jerusalem at Passover was that act of symbolic destruction, in deed and word, against the Temple. That sacred edifice represented in one central place all that his vision and program had fought against among the peasantry of Lower Galilee. In Jerusalem, quite possibly for the first and only time, he acted according to that program.

CHAPTER TWO

Arrest

Prophecies Old and New

Jesus' symbolic destruction of the Temple was the historical action that led most immediately to his execution. But scriptural texts were used to interpret that text in Mark and John. That was not a case of prophecy historicized, that is, of a historical event created to fulfill an ancient prophecy, but of actual history interpreted by more-or-less appropriate ancient texts. That is a delicate and absolutely crucial distinction between scriptural prophecies as *confirmative* or *constitutive* of historical events. Prophecy as confirmative of historical events means that the event happened, and prophecy is used to understand it, defend it, or vindicate its necessity. Prophecy as constitutive means that the event did not happen, but prophecy has been used to imagine it, describe it, and create it. But how do you tell whether prophecy is creating history as its fulfillment, or history is selecting prophecy as its confirmation? There are two noteworthy features of the biblical texts used in that Temple instance. First, the texts were quite different in each case: from the Psalms in John, from Isaiah and Jeremiah in Mark. Second, none of them seemed exactly adequate to the deed itself. Absolute destruction, not relative purification, was the meaning of Jesus' symbolic action. Now comes a third feature to watch for in making that distinction. When *both* ancient biblical prophecy *and* Jesus' recent prophecy focus on an event, we are usually dealing with history seeking prophecy (going backward) rather than prophecy creating history (going forward).

Consider, for example, Jesus' prophecies concerning his own forthcoming passion and resurrection. Here is how Mark gives them, in climactic triplicate:

(1) He began to teach them that the Son of Man must undergo great suffering, and be rejected by the elders, the chief priests, and the scribes, and be killed, and after three days rise again. (8:31)

(2) He was teaching his disciples, saying to them, "The Son of Man is to be betrayed into human hands, and they will kill him, and three days after being killed, he will rise again." (9:31)

(3) He took the twelve aside again and began to tell them what was to happen to him, saying, "See, we are going up to Jerusalem, and the Son of Man will be handed over to the chief priests and the scribes, and they will condemn him to death; then they will hand him over to the Gentiles; they will mock him, and spit upon him, and flog him, and kill him; and after three days he will rise again." (10:32–34)

There is no reason, after John's execution, that Jesus might not have imagined some similar fate for himself, but those precise prophecies were created and placed on Jesus' lips by Mark himself. They are found only in Mark and were copied from Mark into Matthew and Luke. They appear as a linked set of three, and triplication is a characteristic of Markan style. They are climactically arranged from indirect to direct speech and from general statement to very specific detail. They emphasize passion over resurrection. And they are followed in each case by a dismal failure in understanding from Peter or James and John or the disciples in general. Those prophecies have, in other words, Markan literary fingerprints all over them.

My point is that, for something as terrible as the crucifixion, it was not enough to select ancient biblical prophecies announcing it would happen in the future. It was necessary to create more recent prophecies from Jesus himself proclaiming his knowledge and acceptance of that destiny. A very similar situation occurs with another very significant event, the reaction of the disciples when Jesus is arrested. That is foretold in both ancient scriptural prophecy and recent Jesus prophecy. That does not mean, for me, that the Scriptures were actually talking about Jesus' disciples or that Jesus ever foretold their actions. But it tells me that the event took place historically, and that it was so traumatic that later double prophecy, prophecy old and prophecy new, was demanded to come to terms with it.

On the night of his arrest, Jesus made, according to Mark, three separate prophecies concerning his closest followers, all of which were fulfilled before that very night was over. I focus primarily on Mark because I consider him to be the source for the other three canonical gospels, but I will always bring them in where necessary. As usual Matthew follows Mark least creatively, Luke more creatively, and John most creatively of all. The Gospel of Peter's fragmented opening starts in midtrial, so it does not help us until the next chapter. Table 1 gives the general outline of what we must discuss.

As you can see, the three prophecies and their three fulfillments are given in the sequence Judas, disciples, and Peter. Take a look, first, at those three prophecies, but in the order disciples, Judas, Peter, to see the differences and similarities.

Disciples Flee

In Mark's gospel after the Last Supper and on the way to the garden of Gethsemane, but in John's gospel during the meal itself, Jesus says to his disciples,

> "You will all become deserters; for it is written, 'I will strike the shepherd, and the sheep will be *scattered.*'" (Mark 14:27, my italics)

> "The hour is coming, indeed it has come, when you will be *scattered,* each one to his home, and you will leave me alone. Yet I am not alone because the Father is with me." (John 16:32; my italics)

There is, in Mark explicitly and in John implicitly, a citation of Zechariah 13:7. Thus, for the disciples' flight there is a biblical *prophecy* applied by *Jesus* to an event that will almost immediately fulfill it. In Mark's story of the passion Jesus appears as terribly, painfully human, but in John's he is serenely and magnificently transcendental. You catch a first taste of that difference in those two prophecies: Jesus now alone in Mark, Jesus never alone in John. Compare, as well, how they are fulfilled in each gospel:

> And they all forsook him, and fled. (Mark 14:50)

> [Earlier, Jesus to the Father at the Last Supper:] "While I was with them, I protected them in your name that you have given me. I guarded them, and

Table 1

	Jesus' Prophecy	*Prophecy's Fulfillment*
Judas (betrayal)	Mark 14:18-21	Mark 14:43-46
Disciples (flight)	Mark 14:27-28	Mark 14:50
Peter (denials)	Mark 14:29-31	Mark 14:54, 66-72

not one of them was lost except the one destined to be lost, so that the scripture might be fulfilled." (John 17:12)

[Later, Jesus to those arresting him:] Again he asked them, "Whom are you looking for?" And they said, "Jesus of Nazareth." Jesus answered, "I told you that I am he. So if you are looking for me, let these men go." This was to fulfill the word that he had spoken, "I did not lose a single one of those whom you gave me." (John 18:8–9)

In Mark they flee. But in John Jesus takes care that they are allowed to go free. In Mark the authorities are in charge, at least for now. In John they are not even in charge for now; Jesus is always in charge, even of his own execution.

Judas Betrays

In the story of the betrayal by Judas, once again I give you both Mark and John, and, once again, there are two separate texts from John. Both are given at the Last Supper. I begin with the key verse from the ancient biblical text (but, if you have a Bible, read all of that prayer, and see how appropriate it is to the entire passion-resurrection sequence):

Even my bosom friend in whom I trusted, *who ate of my bread, has lifted the heel against me.* (Psalm 41:9, my italics)

And when they had taken their places and were eating, Jesus said, "Truly I tell you, one of you will betray me, one who is eating with me." They began to be distressed and to say to him one after another, "Surely, not I?" He said to them, "It is one of the twelve, *one who is dipping bread into the bowl with me.* For the Son of Man goes as it is written of him, but woe to that one by whom the Son of Man is betrayed! It would have been better for that one not to have been born." (Mark 14:18–21, my italics)

[Jesus at the Last Supper:] "I am not speaking of all of you; I know whom I have chosen. But it is to fulfill the scripture, *'The one who ate my bread has lifted his heel against me.'*" . . .
    After saying this Jesus was troubled in spirit, and declared, "Very truly, I tell you, one of you will betray me." The disciples looked at one another, uncertain of whom he was speaking. One of his disciples—the one whom Jesus loved—was reclining next to him; Simon Peter therefore motioned to him to ask Jesus of whom he was speaking. So while reclining next to Jesus, he asked him, "Lord, who is it?" Jesus answered, "It is the one to whom I give this piece of bread when I have dipped it in the dish." So when he had dipped the piece of bread, he gave it to Judas son of Simon

Iscariot. After he received the piece of bread, Satan entered into him. Jesus said to him, "Do quickly what you are going to do." Now no one at the table knew why he said this to him. Some thought that, because Judas had the common purse, Jesus was telling him, "Buy what we need for the festival"; or, that he should give something to the poor. So, after receiving the piece of bread, he immediately went out. And it was night. (John 13:18, 21–30, my italics)

In this case there is the same conjunction of ancient *prophecy* applied by *Jesus* to an immediate event. But now, in reverse of the last case, the prophecy is implicit in Mark and explicit in John. That simply emphasizes that these applications are older than either Mark or John, are part of their common heritage, and that John did not need to learn of them from Mark. But that story in John is dependent on Mark, and you can easily see how and why John has so developed it. First, it allows him to exalt the Beloved Disciple over Simon Peter, and we shall see that as a Johannine theme throughout the passion-resurrection narrative. Second, as above with the arresting forces, it shows Jesus in complete control of events. He not only knows about Judas's treachery, but it is accomplished at *his* command. *He* sends Judas out to betray him.

Peter Denies

The third case, the denial by Peter, is quite different from the two preceding ones. They had both ancient prophecy and Jesus' application of it. Here Jesus foretells what will happen, but no ancient prophecy is cited explicitly or even implicitly. Once again I give you both Mark and John, but, in this case, John remains very close to Mark. The context, as with the prophecy of the Disciples' Flight, is after the Last Supper in Mark, during it in John:

Peter said to him, "Even though all become deserters, I will not." Jesus said to him, "Truly I tell you, this day, this very night, before the cock crows twice, you will deny me three times." But he said vehemently, "Even though I must die with you, I will not deny you." (Mark 14:29–31a)

Peter said to him, "Lord, why can I not follow you now? I will lay down my life for you." Jesus answered, "Will you lay down your life for me? Very truly, I tell you, before the cock crows, you will have denied me three times." (John 13:37b–38)

I discuss the fulfillment of that prophecy at the start of the next chapter, but I ask you to remember that, unlike Judas's Betrayal and the Disciples' Flight, Peter's Denials contains no application of ancient prophecy by Jesus.

A Kiss in Public

Two contradictory positions: Judas's existence and betrayal *are* historical because Christians would never have made up such a character as one of their own and especially as one of the inner circle of twelve apostles. He is too bad to be false. Judas's existence and betrayal *are not* historical, because the name "Judas" resonates in Hebrew with the name "Jew" and so Judas was created to accuse Judaism of betraying Jesus. Judas is Juda[i]s[m], and he simply incarnates the anti-Judaism of earliest Christianity. Was there, or was there not Judas the traitor? I ask that question at its most minimal: not was he one of the Twelve, not did he do it in the way and for the reason that Mark records, but simply did he exist and somehow betray Jesus? Remember, as we proceed, that I consider Jesus' Temple action to be historical, but no gospel ever claimed or even hinted that Jesus was immediately captured there and then. There is, in other words, a problem left hanging at the end of the last chapter. Jesus did something that could and would get him executed. But Jesus was apparently not taken in the act, was not arrested on the spot. Somehow, for whatever reason, by whatever means, he escaped immediate constraint. What happened next?

Mark ends his list of the Twelve Apostles in 3:19 with "and Judas Iscariot, who betrayed him." Matthew 10:4 and Luke 6:16 copy that same terminal position and description. And just about every time Judas's name appears in the three Synoptic gospels, he is designated as "one of the Twelve." When, for example, he appears with the group arresting Jesus, he is called "Judas, one of the Twelve" in Mark 14:43, and that phrase is copied by Matthew 26:47 and Luke 22:47. So all that insistence on Judas the traitor as one of the Twelve is derived from a single source, Mark. But, as mentioned in my prologue section "Dependent and Independent Passion Stories," Mark, first, is extremely critical of Peter himself, of Peter, James, and John as the first three among the Twelve, and of the Twelve in general by mentioning Judas the Traitor as their last member. You cannot argue that *no* Christian would ever make up such a person. Mark might.

Second, he lived and wrote for Christians to whom these terrible words made immediate sense because they had lately seen them at work during the First Roman War:

> Brother will *betray* brother to death, and a father his child, and children will rise against parents and have them put to death. (Mark 13:12, my italics)

Know, says Mark, that if you were betrayed by one closest to you, so was Jesus long ago. Mark *could* have made up Judas himself as he made up that terrible Judas kiss.

A public handshake, embrace, or kiss committed the participants to increasing levels of closeness in loyalty, friendship, and mutual assistance. One example from Jesus' world will suffice. In the spring of 14, Herod the Great went to Asia Minor (in modern western Turkey) to intensify his good relations with the emperor Augustus by courting Marcus Vipsanius Agrippa, his military second-in-command. At the end of their sojourn together, the following act of ritualized friendship took place in public:

> Herod went up to him [Agrippa] and embraced him in grateful acknowl-edgment of his friendly attitude towards himself. To this too Agrippa re-sponded in friendly fashion and behaved like an equal, putting his arms around Herod and embracing him in turn. (*Jewish Antiquities* 16.61)

This is what we might term "kissing up." But, in that world, it was met by "kissing down" fictionally portrayed as "kissing equal." Agrippa and Herod would never be equals, because Agrippa, having Augustus's ear, could probably make or break Herod at will. But their embrace, which had nothing whatsoever to do with internal feelings, had everything to do with external attitudes. Read, now, against that background, how Mark describes Judas's betrayal of Jesus:

> Judas, one of the twelve, arrived; and with him there was a crowd with swords and clubs, from the chief priests, the scribes, and the elders. Now the betrayer had given them a sign, saying, "The one I will kiss is the man; arrest him and lead him away under guard." So when he came, he went up to him at once and said, "Rabbi!" and kissed him. Then they laid hands on him and arrested him. (Mark 14:43–46)

I do not presume any historicity in that description. What it does is paint Judas in the most shameful colors possible. For if, in that ancient Mediterranean world, to betray *after* a kiss was shameful, to betray *with* a kiss was infamous. But if, after all that, the only source I had for Judas's treachery were Mark, I would strongly doubt the historicity of Judas's very existence. But there is very strong independent evidence for Judas's treachery even if it does not necessarily extend to his being one of the Twelve.

Mark was interested only in the terrible shame of Judas's betrayal, and that is all we get from his text. Other Christian traditions, clearly presuming some such act, were interested in the terrible punishment of Judas's death. But watch the trajectory of shame from kiss to death. One who started with such a monstrous act, they reasoned, must surely have ended with an appropriately monstrous death. There are three independent versions of that appropriate fate, and they all presume a death that was immediate, terrible, according to the Scriptures, linked to a specific location in Jerusalem, and reminiscent of the horrible deaths of other infamous characters.

One account of Judas's death is in Matthew. Judas returned the blood money gained for betraying Jesus, and the authorities bought a field named and visible "to this day" as the Field of Blood. That fulfilled a prophecy made by interweaving Jeremiah 32:9, which mentions *buying a field for silver,* and Zechariah 11:12–13, which mentions *throwing thirty pieces of silver into the Temple.* Judas then died a suicide by hanging himself. That recalls the death of the traitor Ahithophel from 2 Samuel 17:23, about which much more in the next section.

> When Judas, his betrayer, saw that Jesus was condemned, he repented and brought back the thirty pieces of silver to the chief priests and the elders. He said, "I have sinned by betraying innocent blood." But they said, "What is that to us? See to it yourself." Throwing down the pieces of silver in the temple, he departed; and he went and hanged himself. But the chief priests, taking the pieces of silver, said, "It is not lawful to put them into the treasury, since they are blood money." After conferring together, they used them to buy the potter's field as a place to bury foreigners. For this reason that field has been called the Field of Blood to this day. Then was fulfilled what had been spoken through the prophet Jeremiah, "And they took the thirty pieces of silver, the price of the one on whom a price had been set, on whom some of the people of Israel [literally, "the sons of Israel," a phrase not in Zechariah!] had set a price, and they gave them for the potter's field, as the Lord commanded me." (Matthew 27:3–10)

Matthew has created an anti-Judaism tone in that citation by citing Zechariah's "them" as "the sons of Israel," that is, "the Jews." I presume there must have been a real field in Jerusalem known as the Field of Blood and the Judas death legend grew up in connection with it. But, though that story is not historical, its creation presumes Judas existed and did something worthy of an awful death.

Another and independent account of Judas's death appears in Luke. The context is a speech by Peter proposing a replacement for Judas within the Twelve (now eleven). But in this account Judas buys a field himself, bursts open in it, hence its name Field of Blood, and that fulfills two Psalm texts:

> [Judas] acquired a field with the reward of his wickedness; and falling headlong [*or* swelling up; *or* laid prostrate], he burst open in the middle and all his bowels gushed out. This became known to all the residents of Jerusalem, so that the field was called in their language Hakeldama, that is, Field of Blood. For it is written in the book of Psalms, "Let his homestead become desolate, and let there be no one to live in it" [=Psalm 69:25]; and "Let another take his position of overseer" [=Psalm 109:8]. (Acts 1:18–20)

That second Psalm text connects with the immediate situation of replacing Judas among the Twelve. But the first one, from Psalm 69:25, applies to the death of Judas *as owner* of that field and would not work with Matthew's account, in which the authorities own the field. Some scriptural background and some connection with the Field of Blood were given by the tradition, but thereafter the details could diverge creatively. Similarly, the death of Judas who betrayed Jesus was modeled, in Matthew, on Ahithophel, who betrayed David but, in Acts, on Nadin who betrayed Ahiqar. We will have much more about Ahiqar and Nadin (or Nadan, Nathan, Nadab) later in chapter 7 on the Resurrection, but for now it is enough to record, respectively, the Syriac, Armenian, and Arabic versions of the traitor Nadin's fate:

> (1) Nadan *swelled* up like a bag and died.
>
> (2) Nathan *swelled* up and all his body *burst* asunder.
>
> (3) Nadan . . . *swelled* up immediately and became like a blown-out bladder. And his limbs *swelled* and his legs and his feet and his side, and he was torn and his belly *burst* asunder and his entrails were *scattered,* and he perished, and he died. ("The Story of Aḥiḳar," Harris et al. 776, my italics)

As my italics indicate, *swelled, burst,* and *scattered* give the full details of Nadin's death. Similarly, *swelled* (?), *burst,* and *gushed* give the full details of Judas's death in Acts. But, once again, an awful death presumes an awful life, and that points to the historicity of Judas.

The final description of the death of Judas is found outside the New Testament recorded in two texts by Papias of Hieropolis, a bishop writing before the middle of the second century. His descriptions are now lost but are preserved in much later collections of commentaries on Matthew 27 and Acts 1. I give one on each:

> Judas lived his career in this world as an enormous example of impiety. He was so swollen in the flesh that he could not pass where a wagon could easily pass. Having been crushed by a wagon, his entrails poured out. (*Fragments of Papias* 3; Roberts et al. 1.153)

> Judas was a dreadful, walking example of impiety in this world, with his flesh bloated to such an extent that he could not walk through a space where a wagon could easily pass. Not even the huge bulk of his head could go through! It is related that his eyelids were so swollen that it was absolutely impossible for him to see the light and his eyes could not be seen by a physician, even with the help of a magnifying glass, so far had they sunk from their outward projection. His private parts were shamefully huge and loathsome to behold and, transported through them from all parts of his body, pus and worms flooded out together as he shamefully relieved himself. He died after many tortures and punishments, in a secluded spot which has remained deserted and uninhabited up to our time. Not even to this day can anybody pass by the place without shielding his nostrils with his hands! Such is the afflux that goes through his flesh [and even pours] out on the ground. (*The Fragments of Papias* 3; based on Marique 380–81)

Those accounts seem independent of both Matthew and Luke, and they continue, need it be said, the process of turning Judas into a physical as well as a moral monster. There may be faint and very distant echoes of the Field of Blood and Psalm 69:25 behind the phrase "a secluded spot which has remained deserted and uninhabited up to our time," but the main point is to describe his awful death. That description vastly expands the general Nadin model, seen above for Acts. Several of those new items (worms, stench) also appear in the infamous deaths of evil rulers (Brown 1409 note 28), but that wagon seems to be a special touch.

I accept Judas as a historical follower of Jesus who betrayed him. I do not think he was a member of the Twelve, because that symbolic grouping of Twelve new Christian patriarchs to replace the Twelve ancient Jewish patriarchs did not take place until after Jesus' death. There are, for example, whole sections of early Christianity that never heard of that institution. But different and independent early Christian traditions knew about him and, without any historical information whatsoever about it, described his death as it surely *must* have taken place: immediate, terrible, according to the Scriptures, and, with the happy coincidence of a real field near Jerusalem called the Field of Blood, in some connection with that place, right over there.

Suppliants on the Mount of Olives

Judas betraying, the disciples fleeing, Peter denying are all incidents. But what the gospels offer is not just incidents but a linked and consecutive story, a narrative with its own logical plausibility. What about that framing narrative in which Jesus crosses to Gethsemane, prays while the disciples sleep, is approached by Judas the traitor, and, thus located and identified, is finally arrested? This is a crucial question: if there are *historical* incidents linked to ancient prophecy for their understanding and also *unhistorical* incidents linked to ancient prophecy for their creation, what about that overall frame? Where does it come from? From that same matrix of ancient biblical texts, themes, and types: specifically, from 2 Samuel 15–17 in the Christian Old Testament.

David was king of Israel, almost a thousand years before the time of Jesus. But afterwards, he was much more than one dead king among many others. He became, like Arthur, the once and future king. As waves of social injustice, foreign domination, colonial exploitation, and royal oppression swept over Jewish territory, people imagined a future Davidic leader who would bring back once again the peace, glory, and justice of a bygone age hallowed by long nostalgia and suffused with utopian idealism. For those who thought like that, it was easy to imagine and portray Jesus himself as that ideal Davidic leader. That is the process at work here in the framing narrative of Jesus' last night. In the ancient stories, Absalom started a rebellion and proclaimed himself king in place of his father, David. What happened to David in the Christian Old Testament becomes a model for what happened to Jesus in the Christian New Testament. There are seven major parallels, but sometimes, once the basic alignment is established, it is hard to say how far one should press it.

First, there is a traitor in each case, and this may well be the link that created the parallelism. Ahithophel is to David as Judas is to Jesus:

> While Absalom was offering the sacrifices, he sent for Ahithophel the Gilonite, David's counselor, from his city Gilo. . . . David was told that Ahithophel was among the conspirators with Absalom. And David said, "O Lord, I pray you, turn the counsel of Ahithophel into foolishness." (2 Samuel 15:12, 31)

> Then Judas Iscariot, who was one of the twelve, went to the chief priests in order to betray him to them. (Mark 14:10)

The details are, of course, utterly different, but, in each case, a close and trusted confidant turns traitor.

Second, when David hears that Absalom is coming against him with an army, he flees eastward across the Kedron valley (or Wadi Kidron, a gully that became a stream in the rainy season) and up the Mount of Olives:

> The whole country wept aloud as all the people passed by; the king crossed the Wadi Kidron, and all the people moved on toward the wilderness. . . . But David went up the ascent of the Mount of Olives. (2 Samuel 15:23, 30a)

> When they had sung the hymn, they went out to the Mount of Olives. . . . They went to a place called Gethsemane [=olive oil press]. (Mark 14:16, 32)

Third, both David and Jesus appear as suppliants before God on the Mount of Olives, each distraught by what is happening to him.

> [David] weeping as he went, with his head covered and walking barefoot; and all the people who were with him covered their heads and went up, weeping as they went. (2 Samuel 15:30b)

> [Jesus] began to be distressed and agitated. And said . . . "I am deeply grieved, even to death. . . ." And going a little farther, he threw himself on the ground and prayed. (Mark 14:33–35a)

David's posture and that of those with him is one of prayer and supplication. So also is that of Jesus, but those with Jesus end up sleeping rather than praying.

Fourth, there is a *possible* parallel between Peter's insistence that he is ready to die with Jesus and the statement made to David by the faithful Ittai the Gittite:

> Ittai answered the king, "As the Lord lives, and as my lord the king lives, wherever my lord the king may be, whether for death or for life, there also your servant will be." (2 Samuel 15:21)

Although the general comparison between David and Jesus is quite clear, that element and the next two may be left as just possibilities.

Fifth, there is another *possible* parallel between the prayer of David accepting God's will for him and that of Jesus, both on the Mount of Olives:

> Then the king said to Zadok, "Carry the ark of God back into the city. If I find favor in the eyes of the Lord, he will bring me back and let me see both it and the place where it stays. But if he says, 'I take no pleasure in you,' here I am, let him do to me what seems good to him." (2 Samuel 15:25–25)

[Jesus] said, "Abba, Father, for you all things are possible; remove this cup from me; yet, not what I want, but what you want." (Mark 14:36)

Sixth, there is a final *possible* parallel in Ahithophel's request to be given soldiers so that he can go with them to capture David:

> Moreover Ahithophel said to Absalom, "Let me choose twelve thousand men, and I will set out and pursue David tonight. I will come upon him while he is weary and discouraged, and throw him into a panic; and all the people who are with him will flee. I will strike down only the king, and I will bring all the people back to you as a bride comes home to her husband. You seek the life of only one man, and all the people will be at peace." (2 Samuel 17:1–3)

> Immediately, while he was still speaking, Judas, one of the twelve, arrived; and with him there was a crowd with swords and clubs, from the chief priests, the scribes, and the elders. (Mark 14:43)

That parallel is, as in the preceding case, just a possibility. Ahithophel and his soldiers are a model for Judas and his arresting band.

Seventh, the last parallel is very secure because it lies behind Matthew's description of Judas's death as suicide by hanging:

> When Ahithophel saw that his counsel was not followed, he saddled his donkey and went off home to his own city. He set his house in order, and hanged himself; he died and was buried in the tomb of his father. (2 Samuel 17:23)

> Throwing down the pieces of silver in the temple, he [Judas] departed; and he went and hanged himself. (Matthew 27:5)

Not only, in other words, is there a linkage between *specific events* in Jesus' arrest and ancient biblical texts, there is also a linkage between their *framing sequences* and ancient biblical sequences. Although Mark's scenario for that last night is quite detailed, sequential, and logical, it comes from searching the Scriptures, not from remembering the history. I may judge isolated events to be historical, for example, the betrayal or the flight, but I do not presume that the framing narrative is historical. That parallelism of Ahithophel/Judas as traitors and of the betrayed David/Jesus as weeping and praying on the Mount of Olives is older than Mark, Matthew, and John, who, as well as knowing Mark's own narrative, know independently of the existence of the parallels. But remember above all from that parallelism that, despite an awful night on the Mount of Olives, David prevailed and so did Jesus.

Agony as Victory

Christians knew, of course, that Jesus must have prayed and, believing that he knew what was his destiny, they could easily imagine something like this:

> In the days of his flesh, Jesus offered up prayers and supplications, with loud cries and tears, to the one who was able to save him from death, and he was heard because of his reverent submission. Although he was a Son, he learned obedience through what he suffered; and having been made perfect, he became the source of eternal salvation for all who obey him. (Hebrews 5:7–9)

But Jesus' agony in the garden is much more detailed in Mark's account, and the signs of Markan creativity are all over it. Recall the characteristics of Markan theology mentioned in the prologue section "Dependent and Independent Passion Stories." Here Mark is severely critical of those privileged three disciples Peter, James, and John who sleep while Jesus is in agony. He is especially critical of Simon Peter, who is, as it were, temporarily unnamed. His real name is Simon, and he has a bilingual nickname, Peter in Greek or Latin and Cephas in Hebrew or Aramaic (Rocky, in English). After Simon was renamed Peter in Mark 3:16 ("Simon whom he surnamed Peter"), he is always called Peter until 14:37 (see below), where Jesus addresses Peter as "Simon." Furthermore, triplication is, as we saw with Jesus' prophecies of his passion-resurrection, a typical Markan literary device. If you are creating a unit, one way of expanding its content is to triple it. I admit, by the way, that this is not one of Mark's most creative triplications. Everything is given in the first unit, so that the second and third are not climactic but rather perfunctory. Here is the text from Mark 14:32–42:

> They went to a place called Gethsemane; and he said to his disciples, "Sit here while I pray." He took with him Peter and James and John, and began to be distressed and agitated. And said to them, "I am [literally, "my soul is"] deeply grieved, even to death; remain here, and keep awake."
>
> And going a little farther, he threw himself on the ground and prayed that, if it were possible, the hour might pass from him. He said, "Abba, Father, for you all things are possible; remove this cup from me; yet, not what I want, but what you want." He came and found them sleeping; and he said to Peter, "Simon, are you asleep? Could you not keep awake one hour? Keep awake and pray that you may not come into the time of trial; the spirit indeed is willing, but the flesh is weak."

And again he went away and prayed, saying the same words. And once more he came and found them sleeping, for their eyes were very heavy; and they did not know what to say to him.

He came a third time and said to them, "Are you still sleeping and taking your rest? Enough! The hour has come; the Son of Man is betrayed into the hands of sinners. Get up, let us be going. See, my betrayer is at hand."

There are some echoes of Psalm 42:6 ("My soul is cast down within me") and 42:11 ("Why are you cast down, O my soul, and why are you disquieted within me") behind Jesus' opening clause in the garden ("my soul is deeply grieved). That could reflect a pre-Markan application of ancient prophecy (actually, prayer) to Jesus' general situation. This is, as it were, how Jesus *must* have prayed before his death. But all the rest is a pure Markan creation.

It is fascinating to compare what Mark created to make his points with what John created, from Mark's account, to make very different points. But, in each case, they work within predictable theological purposes. For Mark, Jesus is in agony, and his disciples fail him by sleeping. For John, there is no agony at all, Jesus protects his disciples, and he is in control of the entire situation. I will not cite the full text of John 18:2–12 but draw attention to three points: Who falls to the *ground?* What does Jesus say about the *cup* of suffering? Who came to *arrest* him? Compare the twin accounts:

> And going a little farther, he threw himself on the *ground* and prayed that, if it were possible, the hour might pass from him. He said, "Abba, Father, for you all things are possible; remove this *cup* from me; yet, not what I want, but what you want." . . . Immediately, while he was still speaking, Judas, one of the twelve, arrived; and with him there was a *crowd* with swords and clubs, from the chief priests, the scribes, and the elders. (Mark 14:35–36, 43, my italics)

> So Judas brought a *detachment* of soldiers together with police from the chief priests and the Pharisees, and they came there with lanterns and torches and weapons. Then Jesus, knowing all that was to happen to him, came forward and asked them, "Whom are you looking for?" They answered, "Jesus of Nazareth." Jesus replied, "I am he." Judas, who betrayed him, was standing with them. When Jesus said to them, "I am he," they stepped back and fell to the *ground*. . . . Jesus said to Peter, ". . . Am I not to drink the *cup* that the Father has given me?" (John 18:3–6, 11b, my italics)

The arresting force in Mark is a "crowd" but in John it is a "detachment" led by a "captain" (18:12). That is the technical terminology for a cohort, for a unit of six hundred troops. It is, in other words, the complete body of Roman troops permanently garrisoned in Jerusalem. And it is those auxiliaries from the Roman authorities, says John, and not some motley crowd with swords and clubs from the Jewish authorities, that came out to arrest Jesus and found themselves thrown to the ground at his feet. That is a magnificent scenario, not historical at all for the time of Jesus but quite true, of course, by about three hundred years later. Mark imagines it as it might have been. John imagines it as it should have been. Neither is historical, but both are true.

My best historical conclusion ignores the Markan frame for the arrest of Jesus. The garden on the Mount of Olives, whether for agony with Mark or victory with John, is derived from 2 Samuel 15–17. I accept as historical the treachery of Judas, who was a follower of Jesus but not one of the Twelve, an institution that did not exist until after Jesus' death and was closely associated with Peter's mission to the Jews rather than Paul's to the pagans. Jesus' Temple event, Judas's treachery, and Jesus' arrest must somehow be linked, but our only linkage is a Markan creation: the authorities knew all about Jesus but needed Judas to arrest Jesus quietly at night. I cannot accept that linkage as historical but have no evidence for any replacement. My *guess* is that Judas may have been captured from among Jesus' companions during the Temple action and eventually told them *who* had done it and not just *where* he was. I also accept as historical the flight of Jesus' companions, but I do not presume that loss of nerve is the same as loss of faith. I hold for the next chapter any decision on the historicity of Peter's denials.

CHAPTER THREE

Trial

In the Beginning Was Psalm 2

In the book of Psalms from the Christian Old Testament Psalm 2 is a prayer for a royal coronation. God promises assistance to the newly anointed monarch who continues the Davidic dynasty with all the hopes and promises we mentioned in the last section as Jesus recapitulated David on the Mount of Olives. Nations or peoples, that is, any opposing *groups,* and kings or rulers, that is, any opposing *leaders,* may conspire against him, but God calls him Anointed, King, and Son, assuring him of final victory:

> *Why do the nations conspire,*
> *and the peoples plot in vain?*
> *The kings of the earth set themselves,*
> *and the rulers take counsel together,*
> *against the Lord and his <u>anointed</u>,* saying,
> "Let us burst their bonds asunder,
> and cast their cords from us."
>
> He who sits in the heavens laughs;
> the Lord has them in derision.
> Then he will speak to them in his wrath,
> and terrify them in his fury, saying,
> "I have set my <u>king</u>
> on Zion, my holy hill."
>
> I will tell of the decree of the Lord:
> He said to me, *"You are <u>my son</u>;*
> *today I have begotten you.*
> Ask of me, and I will make the nations your heritage,
> and the ends of the earth your possession.

You shall break them with a rod of iron,
  and dash them in pieces like a potter's vessel."
(Psalm 2:1–9, my italics and underlining)

Imagine, as you read those verses, that you were one of Jesus' companions searching the Scriptures after his execution in order to understand what had happened. You have found a perfect way to say that Jesus' death will be vindicated by God, that the end is not end but beginning. Psalm 2 is not just a prophecy about opposition but a prophecy about opposition and vindication for the one with three titles: the *Anointed One* [Messiah, in Hebrew; Christ, in Greek], the *King* on Zion, and the *Son of God*. It is precisely those titles that will appear in accusation against Jesus during his trials. Son of God would be a serious religiopolitical charge in a Jewish trial; Messiah could be a serious charge in either a Jewish or a Roman context, depending on its interpretation; but King on Zion, rephrased as King of Israel or King of the Jews would be a very serious politicoreligious charge in a Roman venue.

Luke gives two speeches in the Acts of the Apostles, one by the general Christian community and another by Paul, both of which apply Psalm 2 to the execution and resurrection of Jesus. As was customary in Greco-Roman rhetoric, those speeches themselves were Lukan compositions rather than historical transcripts. But at their heart is something that is historical, namely, early Christian interpretation of a vital Old Testament text for understanding God's will for Jesus and for themselves. Here are those twin speeches:

[Jesus' followers said] Sovereign Lord, who made the heaven and the earth, the sea, and everything in them, it is you who said by the Holy Spirit through our ancestor David, your servant: "Why did the Gentiles rage, and the peoples imagine vain things? The kings of the earth took their stand, and the rulers have gathered together against the Lord and against his Messiah" [=Psalm 2:1–2]. For in this city, in fact, both Herod and Pontius Pilate, with the Gentiles and the peoples of Israel, gathered together against your holy servant Jesus, whom you anointed, to do whatever your hand and your plan had predestined to take place. (Acts 4:24–28)

[Paul said] Because *the residents of Jerusalem and their leaders* [−hint of Psalm 2:1–2] did not recognize him or understand the words of the prophets that are read every sabbath, they fulfilled those words by condemning him. Even though they found no cause for a sentence of death, they asked Pilate to have him killed. When they had carried out everything that was written about him, they took him down from the tree and laid him in a tomb. But

God raised him from the dead; and for many days he appeared to those
who came up with him from Galilee to Jerusalem, and they are now his
witnesses to the people. And we bring you the good news that what God
promised to our ancestors he has fulfilled for us, their children, by raising
Jesus; as also it is written in the second psalm, *"You are my Son; today I have
begotten you"* [=Psalm 2:7]. (Acts 13:27–33, my italics)

In the original Psalm 2:1–2 there were only *two* categories of opposition
but doubled in standard Hebrew poetic parallelism: thus nations=peoples
and kings=rulers. Or, in other words, both *countries* and their *leaders* who
opposed the Lord's Anointed One would be destroyed. In Acts 4:24–28
these are now *four* categories: nations=Gentiles; peoples=Jews; kings=
Herod; rulers=Pilate. But no matter how many categories of opposition
are to be imagined in Psalm 2:1–2 they are all gathered together in one
single conspiracy against the God's newly anointed One, newly appointed King, newly begotten Son.

Think, now, of two options with regard to the application of that
Psalm to the trial of Jesus, one from Brown and the other from me, as in
Figure 1.

In general, for Brown, the trials in the canonical gospels give rise to
the trial in Peter, and the Psalm text was applied confirmatively or decora-
tively. In general, for me, the Psalm text was formative or constitutive for
the trial in Peter, and the trials in the canonical gospels were derived from
it. My hypothesis, in other words, is that the trial of Jesus was first created
by historicization of Psalm 2, and, *because that psalm imagines a composite or
corporate opposition, so does its first historicization in the gospel of Peter.* What it
did was take earlier Christian application of that Psalm 2 to Jesus' execution
and vindication and imagine a single trial scene involving Jewish religious,
Herodian civil, and Roman imperial authorities all coming together against
Jesus in one place. That hypothesis does not have to propose, as Brown
does, that Peter's strange memory collapsed the different trials in the
canonical gospels into one. But it will have to explain later why the canonical authors would have wanted to multiply the trials by separating in time

Figure 1

and place a double trial in Mark, with Jewish religious and Roman imperial authorities distinguished, or a triple trial in Luke, with Jewish religious, Herodian civil, and Roman imperial authorities distinguished.

Bad Memory or Popular Creativity?

From now on I will be dealing with five different versions of the passion story. As mentioned in the prologue section "Dependent and Independent Passion Stories," Mark is used with some change by Matthew, more change by Luke, and very great change by John. Peter is the fifth account, and there are two very striking features to be noted about it immediately. Its fragmented opening depicts a single composite trial involving all religious and civil authorities, that is, Jewish, Herodian, and Roman powers all together in one place. Then, as Pilate withdraws completely from the process, "the Jews . . . Herod the king . . . his judges" and "the [Jewish] people," rather than Pilate and his soldiers, proceed to execute Jesus. Roman power does not reappear except to furnish guards for the tomb. Rome has nothing whatsoever to do with condemning, abusing, crucifying, or burying Jesus.

As noted also in "Dependent and Independent Passion Stories," Brown and I disagree on the relationship between the canonical gospels and Peter. For Brown, Peter had a "distant memory of having heard them," that is, "the *GPet* author has heard or read Matt and knew traditions of Lucan and Johannine origin" (1306). But that author also knew "popular material" (1345), and their combination into a gospel "was not produced at a desk by someone with written sources propped up before him but by someone with a memory of what he had heard and read (canonical and noncanonical) to which he contributed imagination and a sense of drama" (1336). My theory is the exact opposite, and now is a first time to test those opposite explanations.

The opening of the gospel of Peter was already fragmented when somebody copied it into that papyrus pocketbook in which it was eventually found. Here is that opening situation:

> But of the Jews none washed their hands, neither Herod nor any one of his judges. And as they would not wash, Pilate arose. And then Herod the king commanded that the Lord should be marched off, saying to them, "What I have commanded you to do to him, do ye." . . . And he delivered him to the people on the day before the unleavened bread, their feast. (Peter 1:1–2, 5b)

Question: if Peter had distantly heard or read the canonical passion narratives, why did he get it so wrong? Why did he end up with one trial, instead of one and a half as in John, two as in Mark and Matthew, or three as in Luke? And why, above all, did he change from an execution by Pilate and soldiers to one by Herod and people? Admittedly, individuals have weird memories, but short of saying that Peter had inexplicable modes of remembrance, as Brown must presume, what about an alternative explanation, namely, that Peter's narrative does not stem from idiosyncratic memory but from popular creativity?

Herod and the People

Please reread that text from Peter 1:1–2, 5b at the beginning of this section. Pilate withdraws completely from the trial, Herod "the king" and his "judges" accept responsibility for Jesus' condemnation, and Herod hands him over to "the people." Thereafter, it is "they," that is, the people, who abuse Jesus, crucify Jesus, and take Jesus down from the cross (read Peter 3:6–6:22 in the appendix). Three problems present themselves. First, how could Herod Antipas, ruler of Galilee and Perea to the north, conduct a crucifixion in Judea to the south? Next, even if we imagine Pilate allowing that, how could "the people" execute a crucifixion? A stoning to death is something people can do, but crucifixion demands the trained brutality of a small squad of soldiers. Finally, and above all, how could Peter imagine such a historical situation? Restated in Brown's hypothesis, how could Peter have heard or read the canonical accounts and got it so wrong in memory? Restated in my hypothesis, how could Peter have heard or read the application of Psalm 2 to Jesus and come up with such a weird historicization? He knows full well about Pilate's authority and Pilate's soldiers, but he opts for Herod's authority and the people instead. Why?

Brown has a powerful answer to that question, and it demands careful scrutiny because there is a lot at stake in it. What follows is the fifth of those six fundamental disagreements between Brown and myself concerning the passion narratives. It concerns the anti-Judaism of the gospel of Peter. He reiterates constantly throughout *The Death of the Messiah* that Peter is more anti-Jewish than any of the canonical gospels, a feature which indicates that it is later than they are and also popular rather than official, heterodox rather than orthodox. In other words, Peter could have read the canonical gospels and deliberately made them more anti-Jewish. Here are all the passages in Brown I noted:

in the later *GPet* [*Gospel of Peter*], where one finds a popularization
freer from the controls of the standardized preaching and teaching
discernible in much of Matt[hew], the antiJewish feeling is even more
unnuanced (63)

sharply more antiJewish than the canonical Gospels (834)

this work is quite hostile to the Jews (868)

overtly antiJewish spirit (912)

antiJewish thrust (929)

antiJewish implication of hypocrisy (1037)

the antiJewish sentiment that is much more prominent in *GPet* than
in the canonical Gospels (1065)

strong antiJewish prejudice of *GPet* (1235)

I would hope that today Christians would recognize another heterodox
tendency in *GPet*: its intensified antiJewish depictions (1347 note 62)

My first point is that those comments are flatly wrong, not just interpre-
tively wrong from my viewpoint, but factually wrong from anyone's
viewpoint. Here is what *actually* happens in Peter:

It is "the Jews" and not the Romans who condemn Jesus, and it is
"the people" who abuse and execute him. So far Brown is absolutely correct. This is more anti-Jewish than anything in the canonical gospels. And
if the story stopped with that, Peter would be certainly the most anti-
Jewish of the five passion accounts. But then something very strange happens, and that must be read within the unfolding narrative development.
Those marvelous signs at the death of Jesus bring this reaction:

> Then the Jews and the elders and the priests, perceiving what great evil
> they had done to themselves, began to lament and to say, "Woe on our sins,
> the judgment and the end of Jerusalem is drawn nigh." (Peter 7:25)

At this point the Jewish *authorities* know they have done wrong, know
that they will be punished, but, far from being repentant, seek guards
from Pilate for Jesus' tomb lest the *people* harm them:

> But the scribes and Pharisees and elders, being assembled together and
> hearing that all the people were murmuring and beating their breasts, say-
> ing, "If at his death these exceeding great signs have come to pass, behold
> how righteous he was!" The elders were afraid and came to Pilate, entreat-
> ing him and saying, "Give us soldiers that we may watch his sepulchre for
> three days, lest his disciples come and steal him away and the people sup-
> pose that he is risen from the dead, and do us harm." (Peter 8:28–30)

A crucial distinction is now established between Jewish *authorities* and Jewish *people,* and this distinction reaches a climax in what follows. In Peter, both Roman and Jewish authorities are actually at the tomb and witness the resurrection of Jesus. The Roman authorities confess Jesus, but the Jewish *authorities* conspire with Pilate to deceive their own *people:*

> Then all came to him, beseeching him [Pilate] and urgently calling upon him to command the centurion and the soldiers to tell no one what they had seen. "For it is better for us," they said, "to make ourselves guilty of the greatest sin before God than to fall into the hands of the people of the Jews and be stoned." Pilate therefore commanded the centurion and the soldiers to say nothing. (Peter 11:47–49)

That is a strange phrase, "the people of the Jews." For this author there are two Jewish groups: first, the *authorities,* including several groups, and also called simply "the Jews," and, second, "the people" or "the people of the Jews."

My reading of Peter is that it is more anti-Jewish with regard to the *authorities* than any of the canonical gospels but also more pro-Jewish with regard to the *people* than any of them. If only, says this gospel, those awful Jewish authorities had not lied to their own people, they too would have known all about the resurrection of Jesus and would have confessed him just as the Romans did. However false that accusation, fictional that story, and unrealistic that hope, Peter bespeaks a time and place where its enemies were the Jewish authorities but not yet, or not completely, the Jewish people. For them, an "if only . . . " was still possible.

There is, furthermore, a disconcerting element in Brown's reiteration of the "anti-Jewish" context of Peter. He knows everything from my last paragraphs just as well as I do, and he spells it all out clearly and accurately in one single place:

> GPet 7:25–8:29 offers an interesting insight into the author's attitude towards the Jews, whom (having left the Romans completely out of the execution) he has described as responsible for the crucifixion and death of Jesus. One gets the impression that overall *GPet* envisions two Jewish groups, one unrepentant and one repentant. . . . As for *repentant* Jews, one gets the impression that *GPet* differentiates between "the Jews and the elders and the priests" who beat themselves in 7:25 and "all the people" who beat their breasts in 8:28b. The former do so because by their sins they have made inevitable God's wrathful judgment and the end of Jerusalem, and thus they have done wrong to themselves. The latter do so, after they have murmured against the authorities, because the great signs have shown them how just Jesus was. In having this differentiation *GPet* is close to the twofold Lucan picture of reactions to Jesus before the crucifixion and after his death. (1190)

But that page invalidates all those other comments throughout *The Death of the Messiah,* given both before and after it in my list, about the anti-Jewish nature of the gospel of Peter. Even the very last mention of that motif is still inadequate, although better than most others:

> There is a strong antiJewish animus [in *GPet*], especially amongst the religious authorities. . . . Although there are instances of Jewish repentance. (1339)

Why does Brown give such an inaccurate description of Peter by alleging that its anti Judaism is the worst of all the gospels? Is it because that supports his argument that Peter is popular rather than official, heterodox rather than orthodox, and late rather than early? It is, to put the matter bluntly, a rather desperate ploy. Its invalidity can be seen most clearly by comparing the following two verses, one from Peter and the other from Matthew, both with almost the exact same Greek expression:

> All the people [*ho laos hapas*] were murmuring and beating their breasts, saying, "If at his death these exceeding great signs have come to pass, behold how righteous [*dikaios*] he was!" (Peter 8:28)

> The people as a whole [*pas ho laos*] answered, "His blood be on us and our children!" (Matthew 27:25)

Each verse concludes with an exclamation mark in English translation, but the former one asserts repentance and confession, the latter one asserts responsibility and condemnation. Each one, moreover, asserts those features for "all the people" or "the people as a whole." Compare Matthew's relocation of Peter to that earlier situation with Luke's adaptation, which retains it at exactly the same situation as in Peter:

> When the centurion saw what had taken place, he praised God and said, "Certainly this man was innocent [*dikaios*]. And when all the crowds who had gathered there for this spectacle saw what had taken place, they returned home, beating their breasts.

The repentance of "all the people" in Peter was accepted by Luke for "all the assembled multitudes" but was changed into the blood responsibility of "the people as a whole" in Matthew.

Furthermore, if increasing anti-Judaism is used as a norm for chronological progression and dating, the gospel of Peter comes out as the earliest rather than the latest of the five passion accounts. I did not even think of using that criterion until Brown himself proposed it, but, since he did, what happens if we use it? Speaking not of the Jewish authorities but of "Jewish group or groups collectively play[ing] a major role or roles in the Gospel narratives of the passion" (1421), Brown gives these conclusions:

> [*Mark*] "the crowd" . . . at the end of Mark . . . is not friendly to Jesus. To describe a collectivity hostile to Jesus Mark does not use in the PN "the people," "the nation," or "the Jews." (1421)
>
> [*Matthew*] Matt describes as hostile "all the people" (27:25), "the Jews" (28:15), and "the sons of Israel" (27:9). (1422)
>
> [*Luke*] in the Lucan Gospel taken by itself, one finds little emphasis on a collective group hostile to Jesus. (1422)
>
> [*Acts*] The reader of the whole work Luke-Acts . . . would come away with a strong sense that there was a Jewish collectivity very hostile to Jesus. (1423)
>
> [*John*] John 18:35 uses "nation" for those who with the chief priests gave Jesus over to Pilate. The phrase "the Jews" is used at least nine times in the PN to describe those hostile to Jesus and who want his death. The latter usage makes the Johannine picture of collective agency very strong. (1423)

I summarize those conclusions now and place Peter not as latest, where Brown locates it, but earliest, where it should be if one follows Brown's own principles of increasing anti-Judaism:

Peter:	Jewish authorities bad	and	Jewish people good
Luke (Gospel):	Jewish authorities bad	and	Jewish people good
Mark:	Jewish authorities bad	and	Jewish "crowd" bad
Luke (Acts):	Jewish authorities bad	and	Jewish people bad
Matthew:	Jewish authorities bad	and	Jewish people bad
John:	Jews (no distinction) bad		

I emphasize that Peter must be taken in its full narrative sweep from a beginning with Jewish authorities and Jewish people acting in concert against Jesus to an ending with those same authorities having to commit the greatest crime before God (that is, deny the resurrection that they had just seen) lest they be stoned by their own people. That bespeaks a situation in which a Christian author can still imagine *the Jewish people* as ready, willing, and able to accept Christianity if only *the Jewish authorities* had not lied, deceived, and misled them. That is an early rather than a late situation.

Such anti-Jewish animosity is, as I mentioned in the prologue section "Dependent and Independent Passion Stories," the bitterness of one group whose vision and program are *slowly but surely* being refused and they themselves, opposed, ostracized, and even persecuted by that wider population they had hoped to and failed to lead. But my present point is that if, with Brown, we use increasing animosity as a general index of sequence and progression, Peter comes out not at the end but at the beginning, not late but early. There, at least, the invective is not nearly as lethal as in Matthew and John. It would be nice to find the worst anti-Judaism outside the canon in unofficial Peter. It is unfortunately inside the canon in official Matthew, Acts, and John.

Caligula's Statue and Agrippa's Reign

In one sense, however, all that was but a very necessary aside. If Peter is a historicization based on Psalm 2, that explains why it has Jews and Gentiles, Herod and Pilate involved in trying Jesus. But, the question still presses: Why are the Jewish authorities so unbelievably bad, and why are the Roman authorities so unbelievably good? Jewish authority sees, ignores, and deceives. Roman authority sees (or even hears), confesses, and converts.

Let me emphasize both those points a final time before proceeding. You saw in the quotation from Peter 11:47–49 that the Jewish authorities, having actually witnessed the resurrection alongside the Roman soldiers guarding the tomb, request Pilate to command the soldiers' silence. They themselves accept the sin of hiding what they have seen and now know for, were the people to hear about it, they would stone their leaders to death for having crucified the Son of God. The Roman authorities, by contrast, are innocent of any participation in Jesus' condemnation and execution although Pilate does participate in the cover-up. But there is also this text:

> When those who were of the centurion's company saw this [the actual resurrection of Jesus], they hastened by night to Pilate, abandoning the sepulchre which they were guarding, and reported everything they had seen, being full of disquietude and saying, "In truth he was the Son of God." Pilate answered and said, "I am clean from the blood of the Son of God, upon such a thing have you decided." (Peter 11:45–46)

That is quite extraordinary and, of course, quite unhistorical. Jewish authority now confesses that Jesus is the Son of God but determines to hide it. Roman authority through Pilate the governor also confesses that Jesus is the Son of God. Rome is not only innocent, Rome is Christian (a little ahead of time). In what time and place, in what situation, might a Christian author have imagined such a scenario, at once profoundly in favor of Roman authority, profoundly against Jewish authority, and still hopeful for the Jewish people's conversion or, at least, blaming their authorities rather than themselves for its failure? I propose, in answer, the Jewish homeland in the 40s of the first century after the experience of *both* Caligula's statue and Herod Agrippa I's short reign as king of the Jews.

PETRONIUS AS SAINT

Recall the incident of Gaius Caligula's statue from chapter 1. Petronius, the Syrian governor, was ordered to place a statue of Caligula in Jerusalem's Temple. Faced with a massive readiness for unresisting martyrdom on the part of ordinary Jews, he decided to disobey his emperor's direct orders. Here are Josephus's two accounts of Petronius's decision, as he addresses the crowds:

> [Petronius responds in public:] "Either, God aiding me, I shall prevail with Caesar and have the satisfaction of saving myself as well as you, or, if his indignation is roused, I am ready on behalf of the lives of so many to surrender my own." (*Jewish War* 2.201)

> [Petronius thinks in private:] But if, after all, Gaius should turn some of his wrath against him, a man who made virtue his goal might well die on behalf of such a multitude of men. . . .

> [Petronius responds in public:] "If, however, Gaius is embittered and makes me the object of his inexorable wrath, I will endure every form of danger and every form of suffering that may be inflicted upon my body and my fortune rather than behold you who are so numerous destroyed for deeds so virtuous." (*Jewish Antiquities* 18.278, 282)

Petronius is here portrayed as himself ready for martyrdom to save the Jews. He is a Stoic saint. Indeed, in what follows, Josephus makes him almost a Jewish saint. First of all, and immediately:

> God, on His part, showed Petronius and He was with him and would lend His aid in all matters. For as soon as Petronius had finished delivering this speech before the Jews, God straightway sent a heavy shower that was contrary to general anticipation, for that day, from morning on, had been clear and the sky had given no indication of rain. (*Jewish Antiquities* 18.285)

But that shower was only a portent of God's concern for Petronius's fate. As I mentioned earlier, Caligula responded by ordering Petronius to commit suicide for disobeying an imperial command, but that letter arrived after another announcing Caligula's assassination:

God could never have been unmindful of the risks Petronius had taken in showing favour to the Jews and honouring God. No, the removal of Gaius in displeasure at his rashness in promoting his own claim to worship was God's payment of the debt to Petronius. . . . Petronius first received the letter which reported clearly the death of Gaius, and, not long afterwards, the one which ordered him to take his own life with his own hand. He rejoiced at the coincidence that Gaius' disaster came when it did, and marvelled at the providence of God, who swiftly and punctually had paid him his reward for showing honour to the temple and coming to the rescue of the Jews. (*Jewish Antiquities* 18.306, 308–9)

It is hard to imagine a moment in that first century when Jews or Jewish Christians would have felt more grateful for at least one Roman whose decency and humanity had saved a slaughter. Whether you were a Jew or a Jewish Christian, whether you were pro-Temple or anti-Temple, whether you were living in the Jewish homeland or even outside it, Petronius was alive, Gaius was dead, and Roman power looked very good indeed. (I leave it to personal taste to decide whether the Syrian governor's name, Petronius, and the Roman centurion's name, Petronius, in the gospel of Peter, is pure coincidence or deliberate allusion.) That is one-half of the background I propose for the writing of Peter, and it explains its almost rhapsodic pro-Roman stance. But the other half is just as important. Why is it so much against the Jewish and Herodian authorities?

HEROD AS VILLAIN

Herod the Great had more wives than Henry VIII and very many more children. The dynasty's generic name was Herod, and that could be used of many different individuals just as Caesar could be used of many different Roman emperors. In the New Testament, for example, three different men are called Herod without any further qualification. We distinguish them as Herod the Great, Herod Antipas, and Herod Agrippa I, but that is only because we know much more historical background from elsewhere. Those distinguishing individual names are never used anywhere in the New Testament itself. Figure 2 is a bare-bones family tree to show their relationship to one another.

Figure 2

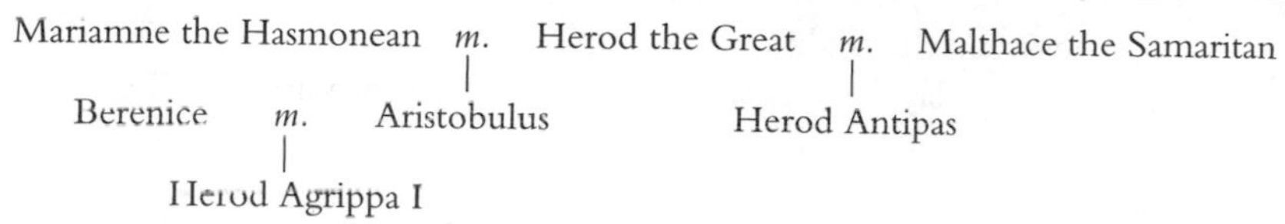

Mariamne the Hasmonean *m.* Herod the Great *m.* Malthace the Samaritan

Berenice *m.* Aristobulus   Herod Antipas

Herod Agrippa I

Herod the Great was officially given the title "King of the Jews" by the Roman Senate in 40 B.C.E. and walked out from the Senate House afterward with Antony on one side and Octavius (later Augustus) on the other, according to Josephus (*Jewish War* 1.282–85). Herod Antipas was not a king but a tetrarch, one ruling over *part* of a territory, in this case Galilee and Perea as part of the Jewish homeland. In the New Testament he is both correctly called a tetrarch and incorrectly called a king, for example, in the story about John the Baptist's execution (Matthew 14:1, 9). But the Romans were more careful about titles, and Caligula banished Antipas to Gaul for requesting the title of king in 39 C.E. Herod Agrippa I was, however, a titled king (*Jewish War* 2.181). He received that position from the emperor Caligula, but, after his assassination, the next emperor, Claudius,

> promulgated an edict whereby he both confirmed the rule of Agrippa, which Gaius had presented to him, and delivered a panegyric on the king. He also added to Agrippa's dominions all the other lands that had been ruled by King Herod [the Great], his grand-father, namely Judaea and Samaria. He restored these lands to him as a debt due to his belonging to the family of Herod. (*Jewish Antiquities* 19.274)

Herod Agrippa I was now, like Herod the Great before him, king of the Jews, and from 41 until his death in 44 C.E., there was no direct Roman rule in the Jewish homeland. In other words, immediately after the incident with Caligula's statue and Petronius's courage, a Jewish king was again and for the last time in charge of the whole Jewish homeland. And if Jewish Christians had been, like all other Jews, elated by the courage of Petronius, what did they think of Herod Agrippa I's accession? What did it mean for them?

We know, for example, that Herod Agrippa I appealed successfully to Petronius, still alive and well as governor of Syria, against certain pagans from the city of Dora who had

> brought an image of Caesar into the synagogue of the Jews and set it up. This provoked Agrippa exceedingly for it was tantamount to an overthrow of the laws of his fathers. (*Jewish Antiquities* 19.301)

And, at the end of his account of Herod Agrippa I, Josephus praises him quite lavishly in contrast with Herod the Great:

> He enjoyed residing in Jerusalem and did so constantly; and he scrupulously observed the traditions of his people. He neglected no rite of purification, and no day passed for him without the prescribed sacrifice. (*Jewish Antiquities* 19.331)

What would Herod Agrippa I have thought about dissident Jewish Christians and their attitudes toward the laws of his fathers, especially in Jerusalem? Here is what we have:

> About that time King Herod [Agrippa I] laid violent hands upon some who belonged to the church. He had James, the brother of John, killed with the sword. After he saw that it pleased the Jews, he proceeded to arrest Peter also. (This was during the festival of Unleavened Bread.) . . .
>
> [Peter is released miraculously.] Then Peter came to himself and said, "Now I am sure that the Lord has sent his angel and rescued me from the hands of Herod and from all that the Jewish people were expecting." (Acts of the Apostles 12:1–3, 11)

What is the point? The gospel of Peter puts "Herod the king" in charge of Jesus' crucifixion, and that phrase brings with it all the older and more general dislike for Herod the Great as well as the very recent and specific dislike by Jewish Christians for Herod Agrippa I. The author is not confused or unrealistic; it is not a case of bad *historicization* but of superb *actualization*, that is, bringing past history into conjunction with present actuality, and excellent *popularization*, that is, making past and present coalesce for popular consumption. In Peter's story, Jesus' past execution is described in terms of his followers' recent executions, and the villain is, as always, a royal Herodian. Rome (Pilate=Petronius) is innocent and even pro-Christian because that is how those Jewish Christians have most recently experienced it at the start of the 40s, and Herod (Antipas=Agrippa I) is responsible and anti-Christian because that is how they have experienced it as the 40s continued. For Jewish Christians who thought that way, the restoration of direct Roman rule over the Jewish homeland when Herod Agrippa I died after a very short reign in 44 C.E. must have been very good news indeed. I conclude, in summary, that the gospel of Peter was written against that background in the late 40s, and I emphasize again the three factors involved in its creation: historicization, actualization, popularization. Somebody, some anonymous genius, took those diverse scriptural fulfillments (for example, Psalm 2 on the trial) and *historicized* them into a story of what had happened to Jesus but did it so that those events were *actualized* in the most recent experiences of the Christian community, and that interaction of past and present was presented in *popularized* format. There is no historicization without actualization and popularization, not in Peter, and not in the canonical passion accounts either.

VERISIMILITUDE AND THEOLOGY

Brown emphasizes again and again throughout his commentary that the gospel of Peter could not have been written in the first century within the Jewish homeland. Here are the key passages:

> *GPet* 2:3–5, as part of its (unhistorical) portrait of Herod as judicially supreme in Jerusalem, has Joseph request Pilate and Pilate in turn request Herod for the body. (1175)

> *GPet* [is] skilled in popular drama but weak on details about 1st-cent. Jewish life. (1191)

> [*GPet* is] illustrative of the author's ignorance of the political realities of 1st-cent. Judea. (1232)

> *GPet* shows no reliable knowledge of 1st-cent. Palestine. (1281)

> Truly implausible behavior is found in what *GPet* has happen in the period of time about "when the Sabbath was dawning" (9:34). After the elders and scribes had joined in sealing the tomb, they pitched a tent there and along with soldiers safeguarded the tomb all through the sabbath into the night when the Lord's Day (Sunday) dawned (*GPet* 8:33–10:38). On the Sabbath they were joined by a crowd from Jerusalem who came out to see the sealed tomb (9:34). The picture of so many observant Jews spending the Sabbath at a tomb is another factor (along with chronological confusion about the Jewish calendar) that makes us doubt that *GPet* was written by a knowledgeable Jewish Christian. (1290)

> . . . a virtual certainty is that [*GPet*] could not have been composed in Palestine in the 1st cent. In a writing that involves a historical setting, whether that writing is 90 percent fact or 90 percent fiction, one expects at least minimum plausibility about circumstances with which everyone is familiar. . . . It is scarcely conceivable that a Palestinian of the 1st cent. A.D. could have imagined that Herod was the supreme ruler in Jerusalem and that the Roman governor Pilate was subject to him. . . . if one wishes to posit that *GPet* was written in the 1st cent., odds would have to favor its having been written outside Palestine by a nonJew with a good knowledge of the Jewish Scriptures and of Jesus. (1341–42)

All that is absolutely correct, and, indeed, one other major point should be added. Even if one could imagine Herod (Antipas) in charge of a crucifixion in Pilate's Jerusalem, it would have to be soldiers or at least police and not "the people" who carried it out. Stoning to death could be done by "the people," but crucifixion demanded brutal expertise particular to executioners.

I agree, therefore, that the gospel of Peter is riddled with historical implausibilities and that it repeatedly lacks, in Brown's term, factual verisimilitude. *The question is why.* And that question presses even more firmly on Brown's thesis than on mine. For, if, as Brown holds, the author of Peter had heard or read Matthew, Luke, and John, that author should have been educated about the basic political realities of early first-century life in the Jewish homeland. In my thesis, why does Peter not know them, or, in Brown's thesis, why does Peter forget them?

Brown himself gives us the general answer with sharp clarity: "Verisimilitude suggests that writers living in the 1st cent. A.D. would not describe a totally implausible scenario *without theological reason*" (963, my italics). And under that term *theological* I include, of course, apologetical and polemical purposes. In other words, the depths of theology quite properly override the surface of history. Consider the three most egregious examples cited by Brown.

First, Peter narrates a story of complete Jewish responsibility and complete Roman nonresponsibility for the condemnation and crucifixion of Jesus. Thereafter, it is the Jewish "people" and not the Roman soldiers who conduct the execution. That is totally implausible and false in terms of surface historicity. But what it does is actualize Jesus' execution, as just argued in the preceding sections, from early 30s to late 40s. It bespeaks a Christian experience and a Christian situation in which the enemy was more Herodian than Roman. It indicates why such a historicization, actualization, and popularization was necessary for ordinary Christians. It is written accordingly.

Second, when Pilate grants soldiers to guard the sepulchre, they are accompanied by "the elders and scribes . . . [who] rolled thither a great stone and laid it against the entrance to the sepulchre and put on it seven seals, pitched a tent and kept watch" in Peter 8:32–33. Absurd, of course. But how else can the Jewish authorities be there to witness the visible resurrection of Jesus? They must camp out at the tomb, no matter how historically implausible that is. And, in case you counter that they might have fallen asleep, there is this specific statement: "the soldiers awakened the centurion and the elders—for they were also there to assist at the watch. And . . . they saw . . . " in Peter 10:38–39. As we shall see in more detail in chapter 7 on the Resurrection, Peter's narrative demands that Jesus be vindicated visibly before his enemies, so their camp-out, no matter how historically implausible, is theologically necessary. It is written accordingly.

Finally, there is that statement that "early in the morning, when the Sabbath dawned, there came a crowd from Jerusalem and the country round about to see the sepulchre that had been sealed" in Peter 9:34. That would be most unlikely at any time, but especially on the Sabbath. We deal, once again, with apologetical or polemical override. The tomb was guarded, sealed, and *seen as sealed by a great crowd*. So, how can anyone claim that the body was stolen! Peter needs a crowd of witnesses, and there is only the Sabbath available for their advent. It is written accordingly.

Theological, apologetical, polemical, or just plain narrative override also occurs in the Synoptic and Johannine passion narratives.

First, the Synoptic tradition. Although the Synoptic gospels, for example, have Jesus celebrate the Last Supper as the Passover meal on the night he was arrested, we never hear of the Passover thereafter. Brown is very aware of this:

> Mark and Matt seem to forget that feast [Passover] once the supper is over. (156)

> There is not a single word in any Synoptic Gospel after the supper to remind readers that the night or day of the passion was Passover itself. (192 note 2)

> having mentioned that the Last Supper was a Passover meal, the Synoptics ignore the actual feast day in what follows. (283)

> the Synoptics themselves show not the slightest concern after the supper about any Passover details. (403)

> after the Last Supper the Synoptics never mention Passover or show consciousness that they are describing the feast day itself. (1027–28)

> No Synoptic Gospel ever mentions Passover or Unleavened Bread in its account of the hours of the arrest, trials, crucifixion, death, and burial of Jesus. (1353)

But because, after the Last Supper as Passover Eve meal, the next day must be Passover itself, whether mentioned explicitly or not, Brown can cite these implausibilities against the Synoptic tradition.

On the particular level, in Luke 22:52 it is "the chief priests, the officers of the temple police, and the elders" who come to arrest Jesus in the garden of Gethsemane. Brown comments:

> The idea that such dignitaries have come out carrying swords and wooden clubs (as Jesus' statement implies) in the night that is Passover to arrest a criminal amid armed resistance is simply staggering. (282)

But it makes for a better story to emphasize those who ordered the arrest and not just those who executed it. Call it narrative override.

On the general level, there is a tremendous amount of activity concerning Jesus on that not-noted Passover day in the Synoptic tradition.
Brown comments:

> the conglomeration of so much activity on a feast day has seemed highly
> implausible. Moreover, all this action against Jesus on the festal day seems to
> run against the expressed wish of the chief priests and the scribes that ar-
> resting Jesus and killing him should not take place on the feast lest there
> may be a disturbance among the people. (1358–59)

But in terms of their own interests, something like relative historical
plausibility or verisimilitude was all the Synoptics demanded. And that
demand was frequently overridden by theological, apologetical, polemical, or sheer narrative concerns.

Second, the Johannine tradition. Recall from chapter 2 on the Arrest
that the entire cohort of soldiers, and not Jesus, fell to the ground in the
garden across the Kidron valley in John 18:6. Brown comments:

> Is there historicity in this extraordinarily triumphal Johannine scene . . . ?
> Elsewhere when John has retold a scene in the light of his unique theo-
> logical outlook, he has rarely departed from verisimilitude. This seems to
> be a major exception. Even if John might be historical in indicating that
> Roman soldiers took part in the arrest of Jesus, critical standards would
> suggest that he has moved from history to parable in reporting that those
> soldiers plus the Jewish police attendants fell back to the ground when
> Jesus spoke to them. (262)

I agree with Brown on that judgment but have no idea why he made it
in this one case as distinct from any other. The entire Johannine passion
narrative lacks surface historical verisimilitude because it shows Jesus in
total control of the arrest, trial, crucifixion, and even burial. He is judging
Pilate, not Pilate him. John had no problem with that immediate implausibility because from a theological point of view, it was correct. Indeed,
from a long-term historical point of view, it was also correct. Jesus, eventually, was judging Rome, not Rome Jesus.

I think, however, that there is a *general* tendency to historicize more
plausibly in the Synoptic tradition than in the gospel of Peter. That ten
dency does not make that tradition more historically accurate, just more
historically plausible and, sometimes, less theologically profound. Matthew,
for instance, has Pilate in charge and Herod unmentioned. That is probably
both more plausible and more accurate. But he also wants Pilate innocent,
even though in charge, and that is, unfortunately, impossible. That is simply
a different implausibility. In Peter, Pilate is not in charge and is therefore

innocent. In Matthew, Pilate is in charge and therefore not innocent. You must choose between historical implausibilities.

One final point. Brown judges it most likely that Jesus was crucified on Passover Eve, as explicitly in John, rather than on Passover Day, as implicitly in the Synoptics (1373). I agree. But that is the same day as explicitly in the gospel of Peter 2:5b. In Brown's thesis, Peter knew Matthew, Luke, and John, so he would have remembered the Passover Eve crucifixion from John rather than the Passover Day crucifixion from the Synoptics. In my thesis, Peter got it right because he was first and had no reason to override the date theologically. In any case and in summary, all gospel writers, *precisely as such,* will let theology, apologetics, polemics, or sheer narrative force override surface historical plausibility in varying degrees. It is not just true for the gospel of Peter. To make too much of such implausibilities in historical verisimilitude while ignoring their profounder ideological purposes is, in Brown's apt and accurate phrase, to descend to the "low level" of the "village atheist" (174).

Mark's Literary Fingerprints

This is a crucial section for my entire reconstruction. Recall from the prologue section "Dependent and Independent Passion Stories" once again that, for Brown, Mark and Peter are *independent* versions of the passion narrative, and that, for me, John is *dependent* on Mark. I said there that my main argument would be presented in chapter 3; here it is.

How can you tell who, if anyone, copied from whom in two similar narratives? How can you tell if John, in the present debate, used or did not use Mark? There is no point in arguing from similar topics, themes, units, or even sequences, because those could simply be common traditions independently adopted by both. *What you must show is that something undeniably Markan in literary style is found in John.* That is what happens here at the start of Jesus' Jewish trial, and that is what convinces me that John is dependent on Mark.

One of the most peculiarly distinctive Markan compositional devices has been seen already and named an *intercalation,* or sandwich. I gave you an example in the section "Learn from the Fig Tree" in chapter 1. Take a moment, if you would, to reread that section. The device has two elements. First, literary presentation: Event 1 begins, then Event 2 begins and finishes, and finally, Event 1 finishes. Second, theological meaning: the purpose of the intercalation is not mere literary show; it presumes that those two events, call them the framing event and the insert event, are mutually interactive, that they interpret each other to emphasize Mark's theological intention. Thus, for example, the cursing and withering of the fruitless fig tree (the framing event) explains and is explained by the destruction of the Temple (the insert event). A Markan intercalation is never just a literary flourish but always an interactive theological process. I emphasize that point: a Markan intercalation is not just a juxtaposition of two events, or a literary flashback, or a move to another event to allow a former one to develop. It is, unlike those devices, a literary-theological technique, with both sides of the hyphen equally important. I will give you just two more examples here and point you elsewhere for more (see, for example, Donahue or Edwards listed in Sources).

In one example the *frames* concern opposition from Jesus' biological family that results in its rejection by Jesus in favor of a spiritual family, but the *insert* is the accusation that Jesus is possessed by the devil Beelzebul:

> *Event 1 begins:* Jesus' biological family moves to seize him as insane in Mark 3:19b–21
>
> *Event 2 begins and finishes:* Jesus is accused of demonic possession in Mark 3:22–30
>
> *Event 1 finishes:* Jesus rejects his biological for a spiritual family in Mark 3:31–35

That is a terribly brutal intercalation to think about, but frames and insert reverberate together theologically. Family insiders and accusing outsiders are lumped together.

The other example is two miracles involving women. In the framing story Jesus raises Jairus's unnamed daughter from the dead at twelve years of age, that is, at the age when she begins menstruation and becomes a woman. In the insert story he heals the woman with a permanent "menstrual" hemorrhage for twelve years:

> *Event 1 begins:* Jesus is asked to save Jairus's daughter and leaves to do so in Mark 5:22–24
>
> *Event 2 begins and finishes:* Jesus heals woman with hemorrhage in Mark 5:25–34
>
> *Event 1 finishes:* Jesus arrives and raises Jairus's daughter from the dead in Mark 5:35–43

Think about the theological implications of that intercalation, of a purity code in which menstruation is impure so that, from Mark's viewpoint, women start to die at twelve and are walking dead thereafter.

One of the surest indications that we are not just misreading those intercalations is the way Matthew and Luke handle them. We saw earlier in the section "Learn from the Fig Tree," that Matthew 21:18–19 had the cursed fig tree wither *immediately,* thereby ruining that event as frame for the Temple one, and Luke 19:45–46 just omitted the whole fig tree incident. Similarly, in the Family/Possession incident both Matthew and Luke omit completely the preceding frame in Mark 3:19b–21, so that the intercalation disappears. In the Daughter/Woman incident they both accept the intercalation, in Matthew 9:18–26 and Luke 8:40–56, but, though they keep the twelve years for the Woman, they both omit it for the Daughter. Really, Mark, that's intercalation with a hammer, not a pen.

When I come with all that background to the situation as Jesus' religious trial begins, I find the following structure:

> *Event 1 begins:* Peter follows Jesus into the courtyard of the High Priest in Mark 14:54
>
> *Event 2 begins and finishes:* Jesus is accused and tried but confesses in Mark 14:55–65
>
> *Event 1 finishes:* Peter is accused and denies Jesus thrice in Mark 14:66–72

That is a very deliberate model for Markan Christians of how (like Jesus) and how not (like Peter) to act under accusation, trial, and persecution. It has, in other words, Markan literary fingerprints all over its outsides and Markan theological DNA all over its insides. Furthermore, apart from that primary technique, distinctively or even exclusively Markan, there are also two secondary or subsidiary indications of Markan creativity involved in this presentation.

One minor indication is that when Mark creates an insert, he very often uses the same word or phrase to end what precedes and begin what succeeds it. A classic example is the healing of the paralytic in Mark 2:1–12:

> *Framing Phrase:* "Which is easier, to say to the paralytic, 'Your sins are forgiven,' or to say, 'Stand up and take your mat and walk'?" (Mark 2:9)
>
> *Insert Phrase:* "But so that you may know that the Son of Man has authority on earth to forgive sins" (Mark 2:10)
>
> *Framing Phrase:* —he said to the paralytic—"I say to you, stand up, take your mat and go to your home" (Mark 2:11)

That is certainly a minor matter of picking up the story after an interruption and is certainly not exclusively Markan, but Mark does a lot of it, and it appears here at the trial's opening within that intercalation under discussion:

> *Framing Phrase:* Peter is "warming himself" at the courtyard fire in Mark 14:54
>
> *Insert Phrase:* Jesus is accused and tried but confesses in Mark 14:55–65
>
> *Framing Phrase:* Peter is "warming himself" in Mark 14:54

The presence of that device strengthens the evidence that the passage is Markan, but because the device is not used exclusively by Mark, the intercalation itself remains the primary evidence.

The second subsidiary index of Markan creativity is also not in any way exclusively his own, but, once again, he does use it a lot. It is *triplication,* and we have seen two examples of it before in chapter 2: Jesus' threefold prophecy of his own fate in Mark 8:31; 9:31; 10:32–34, as well as the threefold interaction of Jesus praying and the disciples sleeping in Mark 14:32–42. If, in other words, you are creating an event, create it in triplicate both to emphasize its pattern and to establish its importance. Here, then, is the threefold denial of Jesus by Peter in Mark 14:66–72:

First Denial:

While Peter was below in the courtyard, one of the servant-girls of the high priest came by. When she saw Peter warming himself, *she stared at him and said,* "You also were with Jesus, the man from Nazareth."

But he denied it, saying, "I do not know or understand what you are talking about."

Second Denial:

And he went out into the forecourt. Then the cock crowed. And the servant-girl, on seeing him, *began again to say to the bystanders,* "This man is one of them."

But again he denied it.

Third Denial:

Then after a little while the *bystanders again said to Peter,* "Certainly you are one of them; for you are a Galilean."

But he began to curse, and he swore an oath, "I do not know this man you are talking about."

At that moment the cock crowed for the second time. Then Peter remembered that Jesus had said to him, "Before the cock crows twice, you will deny me three times." And he broke down and wept.

That is a much more elegant Markan triplication than the praying/sleeping one in Gethsemane. The accusations mount, as indicated by my italicized words, from server to Peter, server to bystanders, bystanders to Peter. And the denials also reach a climax from do not understand, am not one of them, do not know Jesus—that last denial enforced with a curse.

My conclusion is that the interaction of Jesus' confession and Peter's denials is a pure Markan creation as indicated by literary-theological *intercalation,* framing-word duplication, and internal-unit *triplication.* That intercalated Markan story is found just like that in Matthew 26:57–68. But Luke 22:54–71 destroys it by having first the denials in 22:54–62, then the abuse in 22: 63–65, and finally the trial at dawn in 22:66–71. John, however, accepts fully the Markan intercalation and even the "warming himself" duplication in John 18:18 and 18:25. In fact, he even intensifies the Markan purpose and effect because he puts the first denial *before* and the last two denials *after* Jesus' confession:

> *Event 1 begins:* Peter follows Jesus and denies him once in John 18:13–18
>
> *Event 2 begins and finishes:* Jesus is questioned and answers openly in John 18:19–24
>
> *Event 1 finishes:* Peter denies Jesus twice more in John 18:25–27

John accepts this story about Peter not just to compare him with Jesus, as Mark does, but also tacitly to compare him with the Other Disciple, presumably the Beloved Disciple, who is also there with Peter but who is never said to deny Jesus:

> Simon Peter and another disciple followed Jesus. Since that disciple was known to the high priest, he went with Jesus into the courtyard of the high priest, but Peter was standing outside at the gate. So the other disciple, who was known to the high priest, went out, spoke to the woman who guarded the gate, and brought Peter in. (John 18:15–16)

This is simply another example of the Johannine exaltation of the Beloved Disciple over Simon Peter, but it is inserted into a Markan source. My conclusion is that here is one unit that John took from Mark and in a fairly direct, literary manner. After that, my working hypothesis is that John's passion narrative itself is dependent on Mark. Brown, of course, knows everything I have just written about Markan sandwiches (119 note 4; 1356). He simply denies that it is a Markan intercalation, because "two simultaneous actions" are not characteristic of an intercalation (427). But, on the one hand, the withering of the fig tree and the Temple action, for example, *are* simultaneous, and, on the other, Mark never says whether Peter's and Jesus' actions are or are not simultaneous. For Brown, Mark and John simply want to show that these two events are "contemporaneous" (611), and John is not at all dependent on Mark. I find that argument, to be blunt, only slightly less biased than his argument on the anti-Judaism of the gospel of Peter.

One final question: what about the historicity of Peter's denials? Did they really happen? Recall that I already accepted the general flight of Jesus' followers as historical in chapter 2 on the Arrest. Peter would, of course, have been among those who fled, and I emphasized earlier that to lose your nerve is not necessarily to lose your faith. But, as Peter became more and more important as leader and model for the first Christians, his "flight" had to be highlighted even more than that of the rest. That might seem most inappropriate and indelicate from our point of view. But Peter alone was given the honor of walking on the waters with Jesus in Matthew 14:28–31 even though that honor meant that he sank from inadequate faith. He may have sunk and been saved by Jesus, but that happened only to Peter. And that underlines his importance, even when sinking.

Luke, for instance, never recorded Jesus' prophecy about the flight of all the disciples from Mark 14:27–28. Instead he has this unit:

"Simon, Simon, listen! Satan has demanded to sift all of you like wheat, but I have prayed for you that your own faith may not fail; and you, when once you have turned back, strengthen your brothers." (Luke 22:31–32)

That is the next step after Mark 14:27–28, which simply says that all will flee. Even though all, including Peter, may flee, his faith will not fail, and he will eventually "turn" to strengthen the others. Because all fled, Peter must be, as it were, first in flight.

I do not consider Peter's explicit denials to be historical and conclude that Mark created them as part of his own theological program for Christians who had to see an *ideal* model in Jesus and a *hopeful* model in Peter. Loss of nerve is not irrevocable, and even denial under persecution is not unforgivable. Markan Christians who had denied Jesus under duress could still be forgiven just as Peter had been before them.

From One to Two Trials

When Jesus was captured, his companions fled. They were not there to know what happened at any juridical proceedings against Jesus nor, indeed, whether any such proceedings ever took place. In seeking to understand what it all meant, some of them turned to texts such as Psalm 2. There they found a conspiracy or "coming together" of nations/peoples and kings/rulers against one who was entitled Messiah-Christ, King, and Son of God. Perfect! But searching the Scriptures was the prerogative of learned scholars and scribal exegetes, not ordinary Christians. For ordinary believers somebody had to historicize, actualize, and popularize exegesis into story and prophecy into narrative. That is what the gospel of Peter is all about. Hence, in making a first breakout from scholarly exegesis into popular story, Peter has a single composite trial with all those opponents from Psalm 2 together at one time in one place: Pilate ("rulers") and the Gentiles ("nations"), Herod ("kings") and the Jews ("peoples"). But, as we have seen, *historicization* does not just mean making this story *(popularization)* right for the past time of Jesus, it means, even more pointedly, making it right for the present time of its audience *(actualization)*. Jesus rises: Roman authority converts, Jewish authority lies to deceive its own people!

What I develop next is why Mark himself doubled that basic trial in Peter and how his duplication is evidenced by the amount of parallelism between the two trials.

A Creative Parallelism

Go back to the section on Mark in the prologue's "Dependent and Independent Passion Stories," and reread the quotation from Mark 13:9–13, in which Jesus "foretells" how Markan Christians have recently experienced persecution. Note the distinction made in Mark 13:9b:

> they will deliver you up to councils; and you will be beaten in synagogues
>
> and you will stand before governors and kings for my sake, to bear testimony before them

That is a distinction between Jewish religious authority and Roman civil authority, and Christians must be ready for both just as Jesus was ready before them. With every gospel, historicization is actualization, and Mark in the 70s, like Peter in the earlier 40s, is describing Jesus as present historical model, not just as past historical event. Gospel is always the past as present. So Mark wants and needs two quite separate trials, one religious and one civil, or maybe better in terms of *that* world, one religiopolitical

(Jewish) and the other politicoreligious (Roman). He also needs twin abuse-mockery situations: a religiopolitical one for Jesus *as Prophet* (Jewish) and a politicoreligious one for Jesus *as King* (Roman).

Mark's twin trials are composed in generally parallel presentations. On the widest level, each is a juridical process followed by physical abuse, as in Table 2.

On a more detailed level, each trial involves two key protagonists whose reactions and fates are played off against each other. In the Jewish Trial Peter's cowardly denials frame Jesus' brave confession. In the Roman Trial Jesus' innocent condemnation frames Barabbas's guilty release. That is outlined in Table 3.

Finally, on the most detailed level, there is a close parallelism between the interrogation of Jesus and his silence or responses at both trials. And, as in those preceding cases, Mark knows well how to double a unit without being too boringly obvious, as in Table 4.

What Mark did, in summary, was to create twin trials with strikingly similar overall constructions but with accusations, of course, quite appropriate for each venue. Mark, like all early Christians, knew with terrible

Table 2

	Jewish Process	Roman Process
Juridical process	14:53-64	15:1-15
Physical abuse	14:65	15:16-20a

Table 3

Jewish Trial and Abuse	Roman Trial and Abuse
[Opening verse in 14:53]	[Opening verse in 15:1]
Peter in 14:54	Jesus in 15:2-5
Jesus in 14:55-65	Barabbas in 15:6-15a
Peter in 14:66-72	Jesus in 15:15b-20

Table 4

Jewish Interrogation (High Priest)	Roman Interrogation (Pilate)
Question to Jesus in 14:60	Question to Jesus in 15:2a
No response by Jesus in 14:61a	Response by Jesus in 15:2b
Question to Jesus *again* in 14:61b	Question to Jesus *again* in 15:4
Response by Jesus in 14:62	No response by Jesus in 15:5

personal precision the different questions and accusations one heard from Jewish religious authorities and from Roman civil authorities. His newly created twin trials for Jesus are primarily based on the recent experiences of his own persecuted community. Jesus was "tried" as they were tried; they were tried as Jesus was "tried." Past is present in gospel.

Blasphemy and Rebellion

Josephus said, in that crucial text quoted early in the prologue section "Dependent and Independent Passion Stories," that Jesus was "accused by men of the highest standing amongst us" and then "condemned . . . to be crucified" by Pilate. Jesus' crime, in other words, had to be a capital one, not only from the viewpoint of the highest Jewish authorities, but also from that of the highest Roman authorities. Recall, for example, that the *word* of Jesus ben Ananias against the Temple was considered blasphemy worthy of death by the Jewish authorities, but, without any accompanying *deed,* he was judged to be but a raving lunatic by the Roman authorities. Jesus of Nazareth, in contrast, had done something against the Temple and had been arrested, and now the accusation should have been simple for both venues: he performed some sort of subversive act that could have engendered a riot in the Temple at Passover. Why, then, do we hear less about Jesus' *Temple actions* and more about Jesus' *title claims* during his twin trials? In what follows, always remember that, whether *we* like it or not, historicization of the past always meant actualization to the present for the gospel writers. Remember also those three titles from Psalm 2: Anointed (Messiah-Christ), King, and Son of God.

Mark's twin trials are not equally explicit on accusations about Jesus' Temple actions and Jesus' title claims. The outline is given in Table 5.

The trial before the Jewish authorities created by Mark has two clearly separate sections: one about the Temple in 14:55–61a and the other about titles in 14:61b–64—Messiah-Christ, Son of God, Son of Man. The former fails to achieve Jesus' condemnation; the latter does so immediately. The trial before the Roman authorities created by Mark is con-

Table 5

	Jesus' Temple Actions	Jesus' Title Claims
Jewish trial	14:55–61a	———
Roman trial	14:61b–64	15:2–5

cerned only with title claims: "King of the Jews." With titles such as Messiah-Christ, King, and Son of God, however, we are still working within the parameters of Psalm 2.

Here is the Temple accusation, accompanied by its later derisory repetition beneath the cross:

> Now the chief priests and the whole council were looking for testimony against Jesus to put him to death; but they found none. For many gave *false testimony* against him, and *their testimony did not agree.* Some stood up and gave *false testimony* against him, saying, "We heard him say, 'I will destroy this temple that is made with hands, and in three days I will build another, not made with hands.'" But even on this point *their testimony did not agree.* (Mark 14:55–59)

> Those who passed by derided him [Jesus on the cross], shaking their heads and saying, "Aha! You who would destroy the temple and build it in three days, save yourself, and come down from the cross!" (Mark 15:29–30)

Mark insists, by a double repetition of *falsity* and *disagreement,* that the Temple accusations are not true, yet, as we saw earlier, he knows that Jesus had destroyed the Temple in 11:15–17 as the tables were symbolically overturned and that God would confirm that action by abandoning the sanctuary in 15:38 as the veil was symbolically rent in two. How, then, are the accusations false?

Recall that Mark is writing in the aftermath of the terrible First Roman War, during which the Temple was actually and physically destroyed by Titus's legions in 70 C.E. In between his earlier 11:15–17 and later 15:38 Mark placed the long discourse by Jesus on the Temple's actual, physical destruction in 13:1–37. In that chapter he records that during those last awful days some Christians would equate the Temple's destruction and Jesus' return:

> Then Jesus began to say to them, "Beware that no one leads you astray. Many will come in my name and say, 'I am he!' and they will lead many astray. . . . "And if anyone says to you at that time, 'Look! Here is the Messiah!' or 'Look! There he is!'—do not believe it. False messiahs and false prophets will appear and produce signs and omens, to lead astray, if possible, the elect." (Mark 13:5–6, 21–22)

Some Christians must have expected the return of Jesus to have accompanied, or indeed effected, the Temple's actual, physical destruction. They were wrong, Mark says, and he has Jesus tell them that beforehand. It is their confusion between *past symbolical destruction,* in 30 C.E. by Jesus, and *present physical destruction,* in 70 C.E. but not by Jesus, that is false. Jesus never said that he would destroy the Temple in 70 C.E. (a Temple made with hands) and replace it with his own returning and triumphant presence (a Temple not made with hands). We already knew all of that by the end of 13:1–37, and yet Mark still repeats the Temple accusation twice more, once at the trial and again beneath the cross. Despite its layers of post-70 actualization, *something* about destroying the Temple, however misunderstood, was constitutive for the accusation against Jesus.

But if there was a historical link between Jesus' Temple action and his subsequent execution, it is now fast disappearing from the tradition. Mark is only interested in it because of Christian misunderstandings conjoining the Temple's physical destruction and Jesus' expected return. He had said he would destroy the Temple; the Temple was now destroyed; so he must be here, returned, present, and triumphant. He is primarily interested in Jesus' title claims because those were what Christians were questioned about during persecution. So here is what actually got Jesus condemned, for Mark:

> Again the high priest asked him, "Are you the Messiah, the Son of the Blessed One?" Jesus said, "I am; and 'you will see the Son of Man seated at the right hand of the Power,' and 'coming with the clouds of heaven.'"
> Then the high priest tore his clothes and said, "Why do we still need witnesses? You have heard his blasphemy! What is your decision?" All of them condemned him as deserving death. (Mark 14:61b–64)

The titles of "Messiah," or Christ, and "Son of the Blessed One," or Son of God, come in this trial context from Psalm 2, as we saw earlier. But here Mark corrects those titles with the one he prefers above all, Son of Man, the title for Jesus as the end-time judge of the world as foretold in prophecy:

> As I [Daniel] watched in the night visions, I saw one like a human being [literally, "like a son of man"] coming with the clouds of heaven. And he came to the Ancient One [God] and was presented before him. To him was given dominion and glory and kingship, that all peoples, nations, and languages should serve him. His dominion is an everlasting dominion that shall not pass away, and his kingship is one that shall never be destroyed. (Daniel 7:13–14)

All of that is Markan theology, not historical memory. It tells us accusations made against the Markan Christians by Jewish authorities, and it retrojects such accusations back onto Jesus himself. Similarly with the title claims before Pilate. Terms such as *Messiah, King of Zion,* or *Son of God* are translated from Jewish to Roman concerns and become *King of the Jews.* The former terms might indicate blasphemy and suffice for condemnation in a Jewish venue, but only rebellion, not blasphemy, would suffice for a Roman situation.

Not Jesus but Barabbas

In the Roman trial Mark introduces a scene of dreadful irony. In the Jewish trial he had created a contrast between Jesus and Peter by inventing, not Peter himself, but his triple denials, so now he creates a similar contrast between Jesus and Barabbas by inventing that very character itself:

> Now at the festival he used to release a prisoner for them, anyone for whom they asked. Now a man called Barabbas was in prison with the rebels who had committed murder during the insurrection. So the crowd came and began to ask Pilate to do for them according to his custom. Then he answered them, "Do you want me to release for you the King of the Jews?" For he realized that it was out of jealousy that the chief priests had handed him over. But the chief priests stirred up the crowd to have him release Barabbas for them instead. Pilate spoke to them again, "Then what do you wish me to do with the man you call the King of the Jews?" They shouted back, "Crucify him!" Pilate asked them, "Why, what evil has he done?" But they shouted all the more, "Crucify him!" So Pilate, wishing to satisfy the crowd, released Barabbas for them; and after flogging Jesus, he handed him over to be crucified. (Mark 15:6–15)

I judge that narrative to be absolutely unhistorical, a creation most likely of Mark himself, and for two reasons. One is that its picture of Pilate, meekly acquiescent to a shouting crowd, is exactly the opposite of what we know about him from Josephus. Brutal crowd-control was his specialty. Another is that *open* amnesty, the release of *any* requested prisoner at the time of the Passover festival. Such a custom is against any administrative wisdom. Philo, for example, writing about a decade later, described what decent governors did for crucified criminals on festival occasions: they postponed the execution until after the festival. Postponement, need it be said, is not amnesty, but postponement is as far as Philo's imagination can stretch. He is writing an indictment of A. Avillius Flaccus, Roman governor of Egypt from 32 to 38, because of the anti-Jewish attacks during the emperor Caligula's birthday on August 31 of 38 C.E.

> Rulers who conduct their government as they should and do not pretend to honour but do really honour their benefactors make a practice of not punishing any condemned person until those notable celebrations in

honour of the birthdays of the illustrious Augustan house are over. . . .
But Flaccus . . . ordered the crucifixion of the living, to whom the season
offered a short-lived though not permanent reprieve in order to postpone the punishment though not to remit it altogether. (*Against Flaccus*
81–84)

But if the Barabbas incident did not actually happen, why did Mark create such a story? What did its presence do for him or his audience?

Barabbas was a bandit, a rebel, an insurgent, a freedom fighter, depending always, of course, on your point of view. But Mark was written
soon after the terrible consummation of the First Roman War when
Jerusalem and its Temple were totally destroyed in 70 C.E. We saw earlier
how the Zealots, a loose coalition of bandit groups and peasant rebels,
swept into Jerusalem by the tightening Roman encirclement, fought
within the city for overall control of the rebellion in 68 C.E. There, says
Mark, was Jerusalem's choice: it chose Barabbas over Jesus, an armed
rebel over an unarmed savior. His narrative about Barabbas was, in other
words, a symbolic dramatization of Jerusalem's fate, as he saw it. The
Jewish authorities chose the (religiously) wrong person to release. The
Roman authorities chose the (politically) wrong person to crucify. Just
as Jesus versus Peter in the Jewish trial spoke to situations much later
than Jesus' actual execution, so did Jesus versus Barabbas in the Roman
trial.

Other Versions, Other Purposes

The hypothesis I am testing is that Jesus' companions knew he had been
arrested and executed but knew nothing at all about what, if anything,
had intervened. They had no details at all about any judicial process or,
indeed, any knowledge about whether any such event took place. At the
start of the trial narrative stands Psalm 2 and the scholarly application of
that text to Jesus' trial. At a first stage that was developed from scribal exegesis into popular narrative with but one single, composite trial as in the
gospel of Peter. This narrative was developed by Mark into two separate
trials, one before the religious authorities and another before the civil authorities, so that he could speak to his community's experience of both
religious and civil persecution. Finally, Luke expands his Markan source
to three trials, and John contracts it to one and a half. But each does so
for very specific purposes.

Pilate and Herod Become Friends

Recall that Mark's twin trials each involved juridical process followed by physical abuse. Luke extends Mark's two trials to three: one before the Jewish religious authorities (high priest), one before the Jewish civil authorities (Antipas), and one before the Roman authorities (Pilate). Here is that third trial:

> When Pilate heard this, he asked whether the man was a Galilean. And when he learned that he was under Herod's jurisdiction, he sent him off to Herod, who was himself in Jerusalem at that time. When Herod saw Jesus, he was very glad, for he had been wanting to see him for a long time, because he had heard about him and was hoping to see him perform some sign. He questioned him at some length, but Jesus gave him no answer. The chief priests and the scribes stood by, vehemently accusing him. *Even Herod with his soldiers treated him with contempt and mocked him; then he put an elegant robe on him, and sent him back to Pilate.* That same day Herod and Pilate became friends with each other; before this they had been enemies. (Luke 23:6–12, my italics)

Luke, in following his Markan source, associated physical abuse with the Jewish trial in 22:63–65 but not with the Roman trial in 22:25–26. Instead he relocated it here to the Herodian trial but more as mockery than as abuse (see my italics). I consider that incident to be pure Lukan creation with two major purposes. First, as seen earlier for the gospel of Peter, Jesus before Herod (not qualified as Antipas) serves to recall Christian persecution by that family. Second, that earlier conjunction of Roman governor (Pilate) *and* Herodian ruler (Antipas) both agreeing that Jesus was innocent in Luke 23:14–15 parallels the later situation in which Roman governor (Festus) *and* Herodian prince (Agrippa II) both agree that Paul is innocent in Acts 15:25 and 26:30–32. Remember that Luke always links the passion of Jesus in his first volume to that of followers such as Stephen and Paul in the second one. Finally, Luke emphasizes, as did the gospel of Peter but much more so, that Jesus' passion had immediate good or salvific results on some of those involved. Examples: Jesus heals the wounded ear of one arresting him in 22:51; finds "a great number of the people followed him, and among them were women who were beating their breasts and wailing for him" in 23:27; saves the good thief in 23:40–43; and, after his death, "when all the crowds who had gathered there for this spectacle saw what had taken place, they returned home, beating their breasts" in 23:48. Similarly with Herod and Pilate for

Luke. As Jesus moves from one to another, enmity departs and friendship begins. This specific Herodian trial is a pure Lukan creation.

What Is Truth? Who Is Judge?

Once the gospel of Peter had first given popular narrative form to the trial story, the other evangelists each developed it extensively, creatively, and quite deliberately. John, however, did so most brilliantly but, of course, in terms of his own theology. He has the twin trials from Mark but has changed them so that the Jewish one is much less emphasized and, correspondingly, the Roman one is much more important. What counts for John is, as seen before, that Jesus is in complete charge of the process. He, in fact, is judging Pilate, not the other way around.

For John the Jewish "trial" had taken place some time before this last night so that only a brief interrogation was necessary on that occasion. It was, as you may recall, the raising of Lazarus that led to Jesus' condemnation in John's gospel:

> Many of the Jews therefore, who had come with Mary and had seen what Jesus did, believed in him. But some of them went to the Pharisees and told them what he had done. So the chief priests and the Pharisees called a meeting of the council, and said, "What are we to do? This man is performing many signs. If we let him go on like this, everyone will believe in him, and the Romans will come and destroy both our holy place and our nation." But one of them, Caiaphas, who was high priest that year, said to them, "You know nothing at all! You do not understand that it is better for you to have one man die for the people than to have the whole nation destroyed." He did not say this on his own, but being high priest that year he prophesied that Jesus was about to die for the nation, and not for the nation only, but to gather into one the dispersed children of God. So from that day on they planned to put him to death. (John 11:45–53)

Later, after Jesus is arrested, he is taken first to the house of Annas, and it is there that the "interrogation" takes place. Thence he is taken to Caiaphas, and, without anything happening there, he is taken next to Pilate. Peter's triple denial, therefore, takes place in the courtyard of Annas, not Caiaphas, in John's account:

> First they took him to Annas, who was the father-in-law of Caiaphas, the high priest that year. Caiaphas was the one who had advised the Jews that it was better to have one person die for the people [*Peter's first denial*]....
> Then the high priest [Annas] questioned Jesus about his disciples and about his teaching. Jesus answered, "I have spoken openly to the world; I

have always taught in synagogues and in the temple, where all the Jews come together. I have said nothing in secret. Why do you ask me? Ask those who heard what I said to them; they know what I said." When he had said this, one of the police standing nearby struck Jesus on the face, saying, "Is that how you answer the high priest?" Jesus answered, "If I have spoken wrongly, testify to the wrong. But if I have spoken rightly, why do you strike me?" [*Peter's second and third denials*]. . . . Then Annas sent him bound to Caiaphas the high priest. . . .

Then they took Jesus from Caiaphas to Pilate's headquarters. It was early in the morning. (John 18:13–14, 19–24, 28)

Why does John mention Annas? Does he have special historical information not known to any of the other evangelists? Recall before proceeding that Mark never names the high priest who judged Jesus, that Matthew 26:3 and 26:57 name him as Caiaphas, that Luke 3:2 mentions "the high priesthood of Annas and Caiaphas," and that Acts 4:6 has "Annas the high priest, Caiaphas, John, and Alexander, and all who were of the high-priestly family." John, however, names Annas in 18:13, 24 and Caiaphas in 11:49; 18:13, 24, 28. It is John alone, therefore, who has Jesus and Annas confront each other during the passion narrative. Why?

One advantage of talking about Herod without any further specification was that, as seen above, the total Christian animosity to Herod the Great, Herod Antipas, and Herod Agrippa I could be encapsulated in one name. Herod, was, like Caesar, the enemy. Which Herod or which Caesar was secondary to that basic fact and possibly irrelevant for popular narrative in any case.

Similarly with the name or house of Annas (Theissen 1991:174). Figure 3 is a basic family tree of that house's control of the high priesthood up to the arrival of the Zealots in Jerusalem during the First Roman War (all rule dates are C.E.).

Figure 3

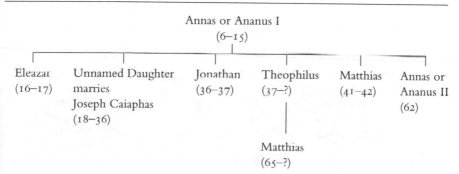

The house of Annas produced eight high priests between 6 and 65 C.E., and they ruled cumulatively for almost forty years. Besides Annas I himself, there were five sons, one son-in-law, and one grandson. Furthermore, the first three Christian martyrs mentioned in the Acts were all probably executed under the tenure of high priests from Annas's family:

Stephen: the high priest was Caiaphas? (Acts 6–7)

James, the brother of John: the high priest was Matthias? (Acts 12; *Jewish Antiquities* 19.316)

James, the brother of Jesus: the high priest was Annas II (*Jewish Antiquities* 20.197–203)

Here is another case of exemplary disagreement between myself and Brown. He knows all of the above just as well as I do. He knows the possibility that "every famous Christian who died violently in Judaea before the Jewish Revolt suffered in the tenure of a priest related to Annas" but still concludes that "even though only John gives Annas a role in the death of Jesus, there is no persuasive reason to doubt that memory, especially since no discernible theological reason would have caused the Johannine tradition to introduce this figure" (409). But just as the enemy for Christians is Caesar, or Herod, so also is it Annas. The enemy is imperial power (Caesar) or civil power (Herod) or high priestly power (Annas), and the individuals who exercised it are secondary to that fact. There is every reason for John to create an encounter with Annas, just as there was for Peter or Luke to create one with Herod.

Finally, the far more significant Johannine creation is the majestically balanced scenario in which he has Pilate run back and forth between Jesus inside and the Jewish authorities outside during the much, much longer Roman trial. Figure 4 shows the outline given by Brown (758):

Figure 4

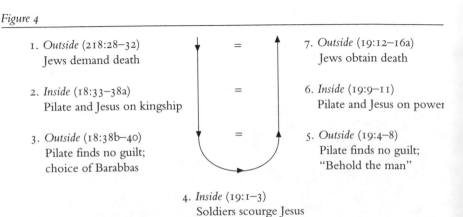

1. *Outside* (218:28–32)
   Jews demand death

2. *Inside* (18:33–38a)
   Pilate and Jesus on kingship

3. *Outside* (18:38b–40)
   Pilate finds no guilt;
   choice of Barabbas

7. *Outside* (19:12–16a)
   Jews obtain death

6. *Inside* (19:9–11)
   Pilate and Jesus on power

5. *Outside* (19:4–8)
   Pilate finds no guilt;
   "Behold the man"

4. *Inside* (19:1–3)
   Soldiers scourge Jesus

Brown admires the "dramatic quality," "deliberate artistry," and "dramatic purpose" of this "chef d'oeuvre of early Christian drama" (758–759). But he always presumes that such artistry, minimal in Mark, greater in Matthew and Luke, greatest in John, is but an expansion or rearrangement of received traditions based on a fairly detailed core of memory. For me, the received tradition is not a core of memory recalling what happened to Jesus under trial but a core of prophecy replacing memory's absence. The trial narrative was created from Psalm 2, and that prophecy's historicization, actualization, and popularization gave us the stories we now have in all five gospels.

In summary, unlike Crime and Arrest, for which, granted Execution, there was necessary historicity, the Trial is, in my best judgment, based entirely on prophecy historicized rather than history remembered. It is not just the *content* of the trial(s) but the very *fact* of the trial(s) that I consider to be unhistorical. It is, of course, always possible that there were trial(s) whose exact details are now lost forever. But, in historical reconstruction, I proceed minimally. I do not find trial(s) a necessary postulate. Imagine, for example, that Caiaphas and Pilate had standing agreements and orders concerning Passover whereby any subversive action involving the Temple and its crowds would beget instant punishment with immediate crucifixion as public warning and deterrent. There would be no need to go very high up the chain of command for a peasant nuisance nobody like Jesus, no need for even a formal interrogation before Caiaphas, let alone a detailed trial before Pilate. In the case of Jesus, there may well have been Arrest and Execution but no Trial whatsoever in between.

CHAPTER FOUR

Abuse

Scourging and Abuse

Flogging or scourging was usually part of the crucifixion process itself. It is mentioned as brutal prelude to execution by both the Jewish philosopher Philo and the Jewish historian Josephus.

Herod Agrippa I received from the new emperor, Gaius Caligula, the territories northeast of the Sea of Galilee along with the title of king. In the late summer of 38 he sailed for the Jewish homeland via Alexandria in Egypt. The popular reaction to his stopover in that city was a series of violent anti-Jewish attacks tolerated or even instigated by the governor, Flaccus, according to Philo's indictment. Note the conjunction of scourging and crucifixion in his descriptions:

> [Jews] were arrested, *scourged,* tortured and after all these outrages, which were all their bodies could make room for, the final punishment kept in reserve was the *cross.* . . . [Flaccus] ordered the *crucifixion* of the living. . . . And he did this after maltreating them with the *lash* in the middle of the theatre and torturing them with fire and the sword. (*Against Flaccus* 72, 84, my italics)

That same combination of scourging and crucifixion appears in Josephus, but now in the Jewish homeland itself. Three examples will suffice: first, under the Syrian monarch Antiochus IV Epiphanes in 167 B.C.E.; next, under the Roman procurator Gessius Florus between 64 and 66 C.E.; and finally under Titus, during the siege and fall of Jerusalem in 70 C.E.

> They were *whipped,* their bodies were mutilated, and while they were still alive and breathing, they were *crucified,* while their wives and the sons whom they had circumcised in despite of the king's wishes were strangled, the children being made to hang from the necks of their crucified parents. (*Jewish Antiquities* 12.256, my italics)

Many of the peaceable citizens were arrested and brought before Florus, who had them first *scourged* and then *crucified*. . . . Florus ventured that day to do what none had ever done before, namely, to *scourge* before his tribunal and nail to the *cross* men of equestrian rank, men who, if Jews by birth, were at least invested with that Roman dignity. (*Jewish War* 2.306, 308, my italics)

They were accordingly *scourged* and subjected to torture of every description, before being killed, and then *crucified* opposite the walls. . . . five hundred or sometimes more being captured daily. . . . The soldiers out of rage and hatred amused themselves by nailing their prisoners in different postures; and so great was their number, that space could not be found for the crosses nor crosses for the bodies. (*Jewish War* 5.446–451, my italics)

In summary, therefore, it may be taken for granted that torture and especially scourging were the ordinary concomitants of Roman crucifixion and that this derived not only from its inherent sadism but from its role as public deterrent. If you knew, therefore, that Jesus was crucified, you could presume that Jesus was scourged beforehand. Four of the five gospels record it, with Luke as the single omission: he is willing to have Jesus prophecy it in 18:33 but will not describe it in 23:24–25.

My present concern is not with scourging but with abuse, not with the terrible flagellation that preceded execution, but with that mocking abuse or abusive maltreatment recorded by all five evangelists. I use from now on that single term *abuse* for any or all of the full spectrum from theatrical mockery to minor maltreatment. On the one hand, theatrical mockery and/or minor maltreatment seems hardly worth mentioning or noting in one being scourged and crucified. On the other, then, why is it that everyone mentions it, even doubling it just as the trials are doubled when you move from the gospel of Peter to the canonical versions? Why is the mockery and/or abuse, apart from the scourging, of such significance?

Jesus as Scapegoat

This is the central chapter of the book in place and importance. It is here that I see most clearly the validity of the hypothesis that the passion narratives are prophecy historicized rather than history remembered. Furthermore, if I cannot persuade you in this chapter, I doubt if I can do it anywhere else.

First Stage: The Text

Imagine yourself as one of those learned followers of Jesus searching the Scriptures to understand his fate and your destiny. You know exactly what you need: texts, themes, or types that show *a dialectic of persecution and vindication,* that show human opposition, however lethal, as still under God's control, however postponed. You search for biblical places that show death not as end but as beginning, not as divine judgment but as divine plan, not as ultimate defeat but as eventual victory. You are especially looking for scriptural units with a certain duality, a certain hint of two stages, two moments, two phases, or two levels. We saw a beautiful example of that dialectic in Psalm 2 at the start of the last chapter: it began with conspiracy against God's Chosen One but ended with victory promised against that conspiracy. Shift now from prayer to liturgy, from prophecy read in a psalm to prophecy seen in a ritual. Think of Jesus in terms of the Day of Atonement, that great Jewish feast of purification in the early fall when, alone of all days, the high priest could enter the Holy of Holies itself. That ritual involved *two* goats to be differently sacrificed and *two* sets of clothing to be interchanged by the high priest. Here are the basic texts for those rituals:

> He shall take the two goats and set them before the Lord at the entrance of the tent of meeting; and Aaron shall cast lots on the two goats, one lot for the Lord and the other lot for Azazel [the desert demon?]. Aaron shall present the goat on which the lot fell for the Lord, and offer it as a sin offering; but the goat on which the lot fell for Azazel shall be presented alive before the Lord to make atonement over it, that it may be sent away into the wilderness to Azazel. . . . Then Aaron shall lay both his hands on the head of the live goat, and confess over it all the iniquities of the people of Israel, and all their transgressions, all their sins, putting them on the head of the goat, and sending it away into the wilderness by means of someone designated for the task. The goat shall bear on itself all their iniquities to a barren region; and the goat shall be set free in the wilderness. Then Aaron shall enter the tent of meeting, and shall take off the linen vestments that he put on when he went into the holy place, and shall leave them there. He shall bathe his body in water in a holy place, and put on his vestments. (Leviticus 16:7–10, 21–24)

It must be recalled that there are two goats, not just the single, better known scapegoat. None of that, however, looks very promising. There seems to be nothing as immediately obvious as was Psalm 2. So we continue, with a word of warning. If you find your head spinning a little as you follow this argument, you are getting the point. This was the work of scholarly exegetes, and it was precisely its somewhat impenetrable elitism that necessitated a translation or transformation from exegesis into story, from *passion prophecy* into *passion narrative*.

Second Stage: The Ritual

That rather schematic ritual for the two goats is expanded in the Mishnah, the code of Jewish law promulgated under Judah the Patriarch at the end of the second century of the common era. By then, of course, the Temple was gone forever, and the mishnaic legislation could only recall or imagine ancient custom before that destruction in 70 C.E. There are four points of present importance, and all are taken from the treatise on the Day of Atonement in the second of the Mishnah's six divisions, the one on Set Feasts (Danby 166–70).

First, there is the similarity preferred if not required between the two goats. In ideal theory they should be as alike as possible:

> The two he-goats of the day of Atonement should be alike in appearance, in size, and in value, and have been bought at the same time. Yet even if they are not alike they are valid, and if one was bought one day and the other on the morrow they are valid. (Day of Atonement 6:1)

Second, there is the scarlet wool attached differently to the two goats. The symbolism here is rather obvious if you recall Isaiah 1:18: "Come now, let us argue it out, says the Lord: though your sins are like scarlet, they shall be like snow; though they are red like crimson, they shall become like wool." Another text is already infiltrating this one, Isaiah is becoming an intertextual or even ritual part of Leviticus:

> [The high priest] bound a thread of crimson wool on the head of the scapegoat and he turned it towards the way by which it was to be sent out; and on the he-goat that was to be slaughtered [he bound a thread] about its throat. (Day of Atonement 4:2)

Third, there is a special ritual involving that crimson wool once the scapegoat has reached the wilderness and its place of death:

> What did he [the one who led the scapegoat to the wilderness] do? He divided the thread of crimson wool and tied one half to the rock and the other half between its horns, and he pushed it from behind; and it went rolling down, and before it had reached half the way down the hill it was broken in pieces. (Day of Atonement 6:6)

Fourth, there is the abusing of the scapegoat on its way to the wilderness, and this seems to represent a tension between Babylonian and Palestinian understanding of the ritual:

> They made a causeway for it [the scapegoat] because of the Babylonians who used to pull its hair, crying to it, "Bear [our sins] and be gone! Bear [our sins] and be gone!" (Day of Atonement 6:4)

That is not, of course, simple abuse. It allows some public participation in putting one's own sins on the poor scapegoat and hurrying it and them away to destruction. But all of that, even Bible and Mishnah combined, still does not seem very promising in terms of Jesus. Somebody, however, found it very promising. But before continuing, let me give you three other Old Testament texts that will be significant for what follows. The first two date from the sixth, the last from the fourth or third century. I give them without comment, for the moment:

> I gave my back to those who struck me, and my cheeks to those who pulled out the beard; I did not hide my face from insult and spitting [note *spitting*]. (Isaiah 50:6)

> Now [the high priest] Joshua was dressed with filthy clothes as he stood before the angel. The angel said to those who were standing before him, "Take off his filthy clothes [note *unrobing*]." And to him he said, "See, I have taken your guilt away from you, and I will clothe you with festal apparel." And I said, "Let them put a clean turban on his head." So they put a clean turban on his head [note *crowning*] and clothed him with the apparel [note *rerobing*]; and the angel of the Lord was standing by. (Zechariah 3:3–5)

> And I will pour out a spirit of compassion and supplication on the house of David and the inhabitants of Jerusalem, so that, when they look on [note *seeing*] the one whom they have pierced [note *piercing*], they shall mourn for him, as one mourns for an only child, and weep bitterly over him, as one weeps [note *mourning*] over a firstborn. (Zechariah 12:10)

Third Stage: The Exegesis

The Christian *Epistle of Barnabas* is outside the New Testament canon, but its method of Old Testament interpretation is very similar to that of the Epistle to the Hebrews inside the New Testament. Both are very interested in allegorical or typological exegesis linking the Day of Atonement with Jesus. The *Epistle of Barnabas*, which is neither an epistle nor by Barnabas, was probably composed under the emperor Nerva between 96 and 98 C.E. It shows no knowledge whatsoever of any New Testament texts, and, despite very great interest in finding prophetic foretellings or typological foreshadowings for Jesus' passion, it knows nothing at all about passion stories. It is, in other words, the classic example of *passion prophecy* before, apart from, and without *passion narrative*. That is what makes it so important for my present purpose. Here is the text divided into four parts corresponding to the four questions and answers that structure its argument:

[*Part 1*]

Note what was commanded: "Take two goats, goodly and alike, and offer them, and let the priest take the one as a burnt offering for sins." But what are they to do with the other?

"The other," he says, "is accursed." Notice how the type of Jesus is manifested: "And do ye all spit [note *spitting*] on it, and goad [note *piercing*] it, and bind the scarlet wool about its head, and so let it be cast into the desert." And when it is so done, he who takes the goat into the wilderness drives it forth, and takes away the wool, and puts it upon a [thorny] shrub [instead of a rock, as in the Mishnah]. . . .

[*Part 2*]

What does this mean?

Listen: "the first goat is for the altar, but the other is accursed," and note that the one that is accursed is crowned [note *crowning*] because then "they will see [note *seeing*] him on that day" with the long scarlet robe [note *robing*] "down to the feet" on his body, and they will say, "Is not this he whom we once crucified and rejected and pierced [note *piercing*] and spat [note *spitting*] upon? Of a truth it was he who then said that he was the Son of God."

[*Part 3*]

But how is he like the goat?

For this reason: "the goats shall be alike, beautiful, and a pair," in order that when they see [note *seeing*] him come at that time [that is, the parousia] they may be astonished at the likeness of the goat. See then the type of Jesus destined to suffer.

[*Part 4*]

But why is it that they put the wool in the middle of the thorns?

It is a type of Jesus placed in the Church, because whoever wishes to take away the scarlet wool must suffer much because the thorns are terrible and he can gain it only through pain. Thus he says, "those who will see me, and attain to my kingdom must lay hold of me through pain and suffering." (*Epistle of Barnabas* 7:6–11)

Before discussing those four sections individually, it may be helpful to indicate its dense intertextual weave in an outline diagram, as in Figure 5.

But how on earth did all that develop? Here is the general process, with details to follow in the next paragraph. The first move was to parallel the twin goats from the Day of Atonement with the twin comings of Jesus, the first coming for passion or persecution, the second coming for parousia or vindication. This is, of course, pushing it a bit, but the key point is that those two goats must be two-as-one, twin goats as much alike as possible, even to the price. That, you will recall, depends, not on Leviticus 16:7–10, 21–22, which never mentions such a similarity, but on traditions known from the Mishnah. The first goat represents Jesus' passion; the second represents Jesus' parousia. The next move links the disrobing and rerobing of the high priest in Leviticus 16:23–24 with a similar disrobing and rerobing (plus crowning) of the high priest in Zechariah 3:1–5. Once again, and rather more persuasively, the disrobing represents Jesus' passion; the rerobing (and crowning) represents Jesus' parousia. A further move brings in Zechariah 12:10, which speaks of Jerusalem seeing and mourning (at the parousia) over the one they pierced (at the passion). A final move introduces Isaiah 50:6, with its mention of spitting. The entire complex has arched beautifully from passion-persecution to parousia-vindication along an integrated triple trajectory of first goat/second goat, disrobing/rerobing, and piercing/seeing. Now for the details that are important for my continuing argument.

The most striking feature of the *Epistle of Barnabas* 7:6–12 is that its author has not just read Leviticus but knows some much more explicit

Figure 5

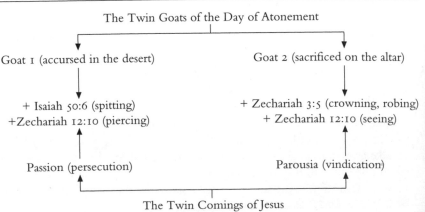

instructions for the ritual itself, details also reflected in the Mishnah but not identical with them.

Parts 1 and 2 explain in more detail how that abuse mentioned in the Mishnah took place. People were apparently spitting out their sins on the scapegoat and prodding (piercing, goading) it on its way toward the desert. That is obviously not just inhumane abuse but public participation in the ritual on a popular level. Spitting and goading come first from the scapegoat ritual and then, with links to Isaiah 50:6 (spitting) and Zechariah 12:10 (piercing), can readily be applied to Jesus.

Parts 1 and 3 mention that two-as-one feature that makes the twin goats and twin comings of Jesus at least a somewhat plausible parallelism.

Parts 1 and 4 cite the scarlet *wool* on the scapegoat's *head* that allows a double connection to the *robe* and *crown* of Zechariah 3:1–5. Instead of the Mishnah's rock we have here a thorny shrub, but already you can see in Part 4 that there is a conjunction of the scapegoat's head and the thorny shrub. You have already a crown *on* thorns, not yet, of course, a crown *of* thorns.

Finally, lest you think the *Epistle of Barnabas* 7 is some idiosyncratic creation of a very strange imagination, I give you another and independent version of that same *passion prophecy*. It is from Justin Martyr, born of pagan parents, converted to Christianity, and beheaded around 165 C.E. He wrote defenses of Christianity against both paganism and Judaism, and my quotation is from that latter work:

> And the two goats which were ordered to be offered during the fast, of which one was sent away as the scape [goat], and the other sacrificed, were similarly declarative of the two appearances of Christ: the first, in which the elders of your people, and the priests, having laid hands on Him and put Him to death, sent him away as the scape [goat]; and His second appearance, because in the same place in Jerusalem you shall recognize Him whom you have dishonoured [allusion to Zechariah 12:10], and who was an offering for all sinners willing to repent, and keeping the fast which Isaiah speaks of, loosening the terms of the violent contracts, and keeping the other precepts, likewise enumerated by him, and which I have quoted, which those believing in Jesus do. And further, you are aware that the offering of the two goats, which was enjoined to be sacrificed at the fast, was not permitted to take place similarly anywhere else, but only in Jerusalem. (*Dialogue with Trypho* 40; Roberts et al. 1.215)

I emphasize once again that *passion prophecy* is the work of erudite scholars and demands not only literacy but fairly high exegetical skills—at least for those who first did the work. Afterward, no doubt, others could copy or even memorize with more limited skills. But scholarly exegesis is a long way from popular narrative. The final stage manages that transition superbly.

Fourth Stage: The Story

How could you possibly get from an intricate exegetical treatise like *Epistle of Barnabas* 7 to a simple popular narrative that anyone could understand and remember? You would need some *framing structure,* similar to the one concerning David on the Mount of Olives from 2 Samuel 15–17 that controlled the overall story of Jesus' arrest. What similar framing structure could turn exegesis into story concerning Jesus' abuse?

Twice before, once on festal amnesty and once on scourging, I mentioned Philo's account of the anti-Jewish attacks in Alexandria brought on by the arrival there of Agrippa I as he traveled homeward with the title of king over the regions northeast of the Sea of Galilee in 38 C.E. Here is one more incident from Philo's indictment of the Roman governor of Egypt.

> For the lazy and unoccupied mob in the city, a multitude well practiced in idle talk, who devote their leisure to slandering and evil speaking, was permitted by him [Flaccus] to vilify the king [Agrippa I], whether their abuse was actually begun by himself or caused by his incitement and provocation addressed to those who were his regular ministers in such matters. Thus started on their course they spent their days in the gymnasium jeering at the king and bringing out a succession of jibes against him. In fact they took the authors of farces and jests for their instructors and thereby showed their natural ability in things of shame, slow to be schooled in anything good but exceedingly quick and ready in learning the opposite. . . . There was a certain lunatic Carabas, whose madness was not of the fierce and savage kind, which is dangerous both to the madmen themselves and those who approach them, but of the easy-going, gentler style. He spent day and night in the streets naked, shunning neither heat nor cold, made game of by the children and the lads who were idling about. The rioters drove the poor fellow into the gymnasium and set him up on high to be seen by all and put on his head a sheet of byblos spread out wide for a diadem, clothed the rest of his body with a rug for a royal robe, while someone who had noticed a piece of the native papyrus thrown away in the road gave it to him for his sceptre. And when in some theatrical farce he had received the insignia of kingship and had been tricked out as a king, young men carrying rods on their shoulders as spearmen stood on either side of him in imitation of a bodyguard. Then others approached him,

some pretending to salute him, others to sue for justice, others to consult him on state affairs. Then from the multitude standing round him there rang out a tremendous shout hailing him as Marin, which is said to be the name for "lord" in Syria. For they knew that Agrippa was both a Syrian by birth and had a great piece of Syria over which he was king. (*Against Flaccus* 32–34, 36–39)

The royal mockery of poor Carabas does not, of course, involve physical abuse or torture, but there is a theatrical mime involving throne, crown, robe, scepter, bodyguard, salutation and consultation, and especially his proclamation as Lord or King.

Suppose, now, that somebody with magnificent imagination took an exegesis such as that in *Epistle of Barnabas* 7 and a story such as that in *Against Flaccus* 32–39, put them together, and came up with this:

So they took the Lord and pushed him in great haste and said, "Let us hale the Son of God now that we have gotten power over him." And they put upon him a purple robe and set him on the judgment seat and said, "Judge righteously, O King of Israel!" And one of them brought a crown of thorns and put it on the Lord's head. And others who stood by spat on his face, and others buffeted him on the cheeks, others nudged him with a reed, and some scourged him, saying, "With such honour let us honour the Son of God." (Peter 3:6–9)

The abuse of the scapegoat and the mockery of Carabas have come together as the *abusive mockery* of Jesus in the gospel of Peter, created, as I claimed earlier, during or soon after the tenure of Agrippa I as king over all the Jewish homeland between 41 and 44 C.E. That abusive mockery is the paradigmatic example and strongest evidence I can offer for my hypothesis that the passion narratives are prophecy historicized rather than history remembered. In that one case you can see passion prophecy in the *Epistle of Barnabas* 7 turned into passion narrative in Peter 3:6–9 with some help from an incident like that in *Against Flaccus* 32–39.

Following the Trail of the Reed

The preceding section explains the origins of the Abuse in broad outline. This section confirms it by fine focus on one small detail. It will also establish one very important facet of those multiple layers of passion tradition noted above. Even when passion narrative had developed out of passion prophecy, that latter process continued on its own momentum and remained present as a permanent substratum. All the evangelists knew of its existence so that, no matter how dependent they were on one another for their narrative sequences, they all potentially had independent access to ongoing passion prophecy.

Look once more at that last verse in Peter 3:6–9, and compare its motifs with those given in the Greek text of Isaiah 50:6 (I use the same English terms where the Greek is similar), as in Table 6.

The same three motifs appear in each text, in reversed order: spitting, buffeting, scourging in Peter 3:9a and scourging, buffeting, spitting in Isaiah 50:6. There are two important details.

First, the scourging is tucked away almost incidentally among those other motifs of minor maltreatment. What dictates its presence and expression *(scourging)* here is Isaiah 50:6 rather than what might be expected in a normal Roman execution. That is very clear in comparison with the later Markan version. He separates the *flogging* of Jesus in 15:15, for which he uses a different and non-Isaian Greek expression, from the subsequent abuse in 15:16–20, which has no mention of the Isaian *scourging:*

> So Pilate, wishing to satisfy the crowd, released Barabbas for them; and after flogging Jesus, he handed him over to be crucified.
>
> Then the soldiers led him into the courtyard of the palace (that is, the governor's head-quarters); and they called together the whole cohort. And they clothed him in a purple cloak; and after twisting some thorns into a crown, they put it on him. And they began saluting him, "Hail, King of the Jews!" They struck his head with a reed, spat upon him, and knelt down in homage to him. After mocking him, they stripped him of the purple cloak and put his own clothes on him. Then they led him out to crucify him. (Mark 15:15–20)

As you move, in other words, from Peter to Mark, the process of historicizing prophecy is much improved, and the *scourging* of Isaiah 50:6 has yielded place to normal Roman *flogging.*

Table 6

And others who stood by spat on his face, and others buffeted him on the cheeks, others nudged him with a reed, and some scourged him. (Peter 3:9a)	I gave my back to those who scourged me, and my cheeks to buffetings; I did not hide my face from . . . spitting. (Isaiah 50:6)

Second, and more important for now, is how doubly strange is that *nudging* with a reed. It does not come from Isaiah 50:6 but is now included within it, and it is rather anomalous to be both scourged with whips and nudged with a reed at the same time. Watch closely as I follow that clue.

In the *Epistle of Barnabas* 7:6–11 spitting one's sins upon the scapegoat and then goading it swiftly toward the desert made clear ritual sense. But the Greek term used for that goading process is actually *piercing,* a rather strong term for what the people were doing but one entirely appropriate for a combination with Zechariah 12:10 ("the one whom they have pierced"). We are not told, however, how the people goaded/pierced the scapegoat as they ritually hurried it and their sins away into the desert. My proposal is that what they actually did (apart from any adaptation to Zechariah 12:10) is nudged it with reeds. In other words, Peter 3:9a got that strange "nudging with reeds" from the scapegoat ritual, not from Isaiah 50:6 or Zechariah 12:10 or anywhere else. The scapegoat ritual gave us spitting and nudging with a reed. That former motif could be easily combined with the *spitting* from Isaiah 50:6; that latter could be less easily combined with Zechariah 12:10's *piercing.* In Greek, nudging and piercing are quite separate verbs. So what happened, after Peter 3:9a, to that telltale "nudging with reeds"?

Peter's single trial and single abuse were doubled, as seen already, into two trials and two abuses, one Jewish and one Roman, in Mark. I give the motifs in set translation for the same Greek terms:

> Some began to spit on him [*spitting*], to blindfold him, and to *strike* him, saying to him, "Prophesy!" The guards also took him over and beat him [*buffeting*]. . . .
>
> Then the soldiers led him into the courtyard of the palace (that is, the governor's head-quarters); and they called together the whole cohort. And they clothed him in a purple cloak; and after twisting some thorns into a crown, they put it on him. And they began saluting him, "Hail, King of the Jews!" They *struck* his head with a reed, spat upon him [*spitting*], and knelt down in homage to him. After mocking him, they stripped him of the purple cloak and put his own clothes on him. Then they led him out to crucify him. (Mark 14:65; 15:16–20a, my italics)

Mark doubled that single abuse story from Peter into twin versions of his own. In the Jewish version he had both spitting and striking. In the Roman version he also used spitting and striking, and that gave him this solution to the reed problem: they struck Jesus on his head with a reed.

That is not, to be blunt, a very good solution. What is the point of striking somebody on the head with a reed?

Matthew saw the problem and, in turning his Markan source into an elegant chiasm, he mentions the reed twice:

> They put a reed in his right hand and knelt before him and mocked him, saying, "Hail, King of the Jews!" They spat on him, and took the reed and struck him on the head. (Matthew 27:29b–30)

Matthew keeps Mark's reed-struck head in the latter verse, but his solution in the former one is very good. In effect, the reed becomes a mock scepter just like the papyrus for poor Carabas. Luke's solution is even better, if a little drastic. He omits all mention of the reed.

Finally, there is John, who is, as usual, the most creative with his sources. He too has the twin abuse situations of Mark:

> When he had said this, one of the police standing nearby struck Jesus on the face [*buffeting*], saying, "Is that how you answer the high priest?" . . .
>
> And the soldiers wove a crown of thorns and put it on his head, and they dressed him in a purple robe. They kept coming up to him, saying, "Hail, King of the Jews!" and striking him on the face [*buffeting*]. (John 18:22; 19:2–3)

No mention of reed there at all. That is one half of John's solution. The other half is even more brilliant:

> Since it was the day of Preparation, the Jews did not want the bodies left on the cross during the sabbath, especially because that sabbath was a day of great solemnity. So they asked Pilate to have the legs of the crucified men broken and the bodies removed. Then the soldiers came and broke the legs of the first and of the other who had been crucified with him. But when they came to Jesus and saw that he was already dead, they did not break his legs. Instead, one of the soldiers pierced [*nudging*] his side with a spear, and at once blood and water came out. (He who saw this has testified so that you also may believe. His testimony is true, and he knows that he tells the truth.) These things occurred so that the scripture might be fulfilled, "None of his bones shall be broken." And again another passage of scripture says, "They will look on the one whom they have pierced [*piercing*]" [=Zechariah 12:10]. (John 19:31–37)

The reed has become a spear, and the *nudging* in 19:3 becomes *piercing* in 19:7 accompanied with an explicit allusion to Zechariah.

Go back to imagine the scapegoat ritual's popular expansion as the people spat their sins upon it and nudged it with reeds toward its desert fate. Where would they have poked it? Probably on its sides. So the full tradition would be *nudged on the side(s) with reed(s)*. John 19:31–37 has picked up another element from that underlying and continuing substratum of passion prophecy. So far he is the only one who has mentioned the word "side." Is that just coincidence?

There are two texts from outside the New Testament that indicate the scapegoat-derived tradition of nudging side(s) with reed(s) did not disappear quite so easily as the Synoptic gospels seem to indicate and that John 19:31–37 knows precisely that three-point unit of passion prophecy even as he turned the reed into a spear.

The first texts are from the Christian Sibylline Oracles. Both Jewish and Christian authors created poetic prophecies modeled on the ancient Greek Sibylline Oracles. And Christian writers also adapted Jewish ones to their own purposes. My quotations are from texts dated before the middle of the second century and therefore later than all five passion narratives. They seem, however, to be more dependent on passion prophecy than on passion narrative, and they testify to the abiding presence of that tradition even after the gospels were written:

> They shall pierce [*nudge*] his sides with a reed because of their law. (*Sibylline Oracles* 8:296; Collins)

> and his side
> They pierce [*nudge*] with reeds [for the sake of the law].
> (*Sibylline Oracles* 1:373–74; Collins)

The verb, once again, is nudging rather than piercing, and one has both sides/reed and side/reeds. But most significant is the phrase "because of their law" present in the Greek of the first but not the second citation. That points the phrase back to its scapegoat origins in the law of the Day of Atonement.

The second text is also from a Christian adaptation of a pagan genre of writing, not that of poetic oracle as in the last instance, but that of narrative romance. My quotation is from a section dating to the early second century, once again later than the five passion narratives. In it the real, true Jesus is not the one crucified on the cross but is commenting on it to his disciples quite apart from that scene:

> My Lord stood in the middle of the cave and giving light to me said:
> "John, for the people below in Jerusalem I am being crucified and pierced [*nudged*] with lances and reeds and given vinegar and gall to drink." (*Acts of John* 97; Schäferdiek 184)

There, finally, the scapegoat's reed and the Johannine spear come to-gether. My point is that the tradition of *nudging side(s) with reed(s)* derives originally from the popular scapegoat ritual and is explicable only in terms of that process. It came originally into passion tradition as prophecy historicized and hung on steadily or left and returned as pas-sion prophecy continued to interact with passion narrative. It is one of those tiny, delicate strands of tradition whose perdurance reveals an entire procedure.

My historical reconstruction is already quite clear. Jesus may well have been *flogged* as part of the regular brutality preparatory to Roman crucifixion. That was possibly a good guess. But any mention of *spitting* and *nudging* comes from the popular scapegoat ritual; any mention of *scourging, buffeting,* and *spitting* comes from Isaiah 50:6; any mention of *piercing, seeing, mourning* comes from Zechariah 12:10; any mention of *dis-robing, rerobing,* or *crowning* comes from Zechariah 3:1–5. Above all, there-fore, it is the abused scapegoat ritual and the mocked king theater that created the abusive mockery of Jesus. Nowhere can you see the process of historicizing prophecy so obviously as here. And if you do not believe it here, you will probably not believe it anywhere else.

CHAPTER FIVE

Execution

A Thief on Either Side

Christian tradition has always talked in English of the two *thieves* or of the good *thief* and the bad *thief.* The Greek, however, never uses *thief* in any of the five accounts. The term is *malefactors* in Peter and Luke, *bandits* in Mark and Matthew, and simply *others* in John. I use those three terms as standard translations for the three Greek expressions, but I retain the term *thieves* for general purposes. Here are the five accounts:

> And they brought two malefactors and crucified the Lord in the midst of them. (Peter 4:10a)

> And with him they crucified two bandits, one on his right and one on his left. (Mark 15:27)

> Then two bandits were crucified with him, one on his right and one on his left. (Matthew 27:38)

> They crucified Jesus there with the criminals [malefactors], one on his right and one on his left. (Luke 23:33)

> There they crucified him, and with him two others, one on either side, with Jesus between them. (John 19:18)

Everyone is in general agreement so far, but is this historical memory or prophetic fulfillment? Luke had Jesus cite Isaiah 53:12b about himself just before the arrest:

> "For I tell you, this scripture must be fulfilled in me, 'And he was counted among the lawless' and indeed what is written about me is being fulfilled." (Luke 22:37)

But there is an even more likely origin for this tradition in Psalm 22, which, more than any other Old Testament text, was a virtual quarry for passion prophecy concerning the crucifixion. At least, therefore, within that general using of Psalm 22 to create crucifixion details, the statement in 22:16 that "a company of evil-doers encircles me" best explains that fivefold agreement on the presence of the two thieves. But what happens next is even more significant.

After that initial mention of the thieves, all five accounts move on to other details but then return to them at a later point in their narratives. They return, however, for very different purposes. Here is Mark 15:27–32, which is closely copied into Matthew 27:38–44:

> Those who passed by derided him, *shaking their heads* and saying, "Aha! You who would destroy the temple and build it in three days, save your-self, and come down from the cross!" In the same way the chief priests, along with the scribes, were also mocking him among themselves and *say-ing,* "He saved others; he cannot save himself. Let the Messiah, the King of Israel, come down from the cross now, so that we may see and believe." Those who were crucified with him also *taunted* him. (Mark 15:29–32, my italics)

That triple derision, from the passersby, from the authorities, and even from the co-crucifieds, picks up and continues the references to Psalm 22 from passion prophecy:

> I am a worm, and not human; scorned [*taunted*] by others, and despised by the people. All who see me mock at me; they make mouths at me, *they shake their heads;* [*saying*] "Commit your cause to the Lord; let him de-liver—let him rescue the one in whom he delights!" (Psalm 22:6–8, my italics)

But something very different from Peter happens in Luke and John. Mark, in effect, has two bad thieves; Peter has one explicitly good (and the other ignored), but Luke combines those traditions into one explic-itly bad and one explicitly good thief. John, as usual, is something else again. Here is Peter's version:

> (1) But one of the malefactors rebuked them, saying, "We have landed in suffering for the deeds of wickedness whch we have committed, but this man, who has become the saviour of men, what wrong has he done you?"

> (2) And they were wroth with him and commanded that his legs should not be broken, so that he might die in torments. (Peter 4:13–14)

This gives us a good thief but, as yet, no corresponding bad one. More important, it effects what it proclaims: Jesus, even on the cross, becomes "the saviour of men." This good thief is a first and individual sign of Jewish repentance that will later become more general and corporate among the Jewish *people* but not the Jewish *authorities,* even though people and authorities started out in agreement and collaboration on Jesus' crucifixion in the gospel of Peter.

A word about leg breaking: The exact mode of death in crucifixion depends ultimately on how exactly the person is affixed to the cross, but leg breaking was considered a merciful act that somehow speeded that death. It might, for example, have removed any support from the legs and rendered breathing impossible so that one died swiftly of asphyxiation or shock. The martyrdom of Andrew, for instance, is told as follows, in a text from before 200 C.E.:

> He [the proconsul Aegeates] commanded that Andrew be flogged with seven whips. Then he sent him off to be crucified and commanded the executioners not to impale him with nails but to stretch him out tied up with ropes, [and] to leave his knees uncut, supposing that by so doing he would punish Andrew even more severely. . . . The executioners . . . tied up only his feet and armpits, without nailing up his hands or feet nor severing his knees because of what the proconsul had commanded them, for Aegeates intended to torment him by his being hung and his being eaten by dogs if still alive at night. (*Acts of Andrew: The Passion of Andrew* 51.1; 54.4; MacDonald 395, 407)

(Remember those dogs for later.) The absence of leg breaking was, therefore, an added punishment intended to prolong the agony of dying on the cross. In Peter 4:13–14 above it is "his" legs that are not broken. That could refer to Jesus' legs, but, apart from thinking about John's later interpretation, the more obvious meaning is that the good thief was punished for his impudence by being left to die as slowly as possible. Watch, now, as Luke and John develop that compact unit in two very different directions. Luke picks up and develops the motif of the good thief's confession. John picks up and develops that of his legs not being broken.

Luke knows two stories: that of the one good thief from Peter and that of the two bad thieves from Mark. He combines them to give us a contrast of one bad (from Mark) and one good thief (from Peter). The gospel of Peter had a simple double interaction: first, good thief to crucifiers; then, crucifiers to good thief. Luke expands that to a fourfold interaction: first, bad thief to Jesus; then, good thief to bad thief; next, good thief to Jesus; finally, Jesus to good thief:

> (1) One of the criminals who were hanged there kept deriding him and saying, "Are you not the Messiah? Save yourself and us!"

(2) But the other rebuked him, saying, "Do you not fear God, since you are under the same sentence of condemnation? And we indeed have been condemned justly, for we are getting what we deserve for our deeds, but this man has done nothing wrong."

(3) Then he said, "Jesus, remember me when you come into your kingdom."

(4) He replied, "Truly I tell you, today you will be with me in Paradise." (Luke 23:39–43)

In Luke, the bad thief's taunting "save yourself" summarizes Mark 15:29–32 with its "save yourself" in 15:30. But now the good thief "rebukes" (different Greek verbs) him rather than the crucifiers, as in Peter. Finally, the beautiful dialogue between the good thief and Jesus is Luke's own creation, but it does no more than spell out explicitly what is already implicit in the good thief's repentance and confession in Peter. For both Peter and Luke, the crucified Jesus is already salvific.

We saw earlier how John changed Peter's *nudging with a reed* from the abused scapegoat background of Jesus' abusive mockery into *nudged/ pierced with a spear* in 19:34. Here is that text once more:

> Since it was the day of Preparation, the Jews did not want the bodies left on the cross during the sabbath, especially because that sabbath was a day of great solemnity. So they asked Pilate to have the legs of the crucified men broken and the bodies removed. Then the soldiers came and broke the legs of the first and of the other who had been crucified with him. But when they came to Jesus and saw that he was already dead, they did not break his legs. Instead, one of the soldiers pierced [*nudged*] his side with a spear, and at once blood and water came out. (He who saw this has testified so that you also may believe. His testimony is true, and he knows that he tells the truth.) These things occurred so that the scripture might be fulfilled, "None of his bones shall be broken" And again another passage of scripture says, "They will look on the one whom they have pierced." (John 19:31–37)

For John, both the nudging/piercing of Jesus' side and the nonbreaking of Jesus' legs explicitly fulfill discrete scriptural prophecies. That first one refers to the unbroken bones of the paschal lamb in Exodus 12:46 ("you shall not break any of its bones") or Numbers 9:12 ("nor break a bone of it") and/or to God's protection for the innocent sufferer in Psalm 34:20 ("He keeps all their bones; not one of them will be broken"). The second one, as already seen, stems from Zechariah 12:10.

Two conclusions: First, the twin thieves are not history remembered but prophecy historicized. Their presence comes originally from Psalm 22 as the basic prophetic background for crucifixion details. In Mark and Matthew the thieves are both bad, both part of the negative and taunting background from Psalm 22. Peter, Luke, and especially John insist, however, on the salvific power of the crucified Jesus even while on the cross. In Peter one thief is good, repents, confesses Jesus, and is persecuted for that confession. Luke, combining Peter and Mark, has one good and one bad thief: one taunting and one confessing Jesus. And the good thief is explicitly promised heaven that very day. John, finally, downplays the thieves as simply those "others" crucified with Jesus, but he then has streams of salvation flowing out from the pierced side of Jesus and underlines that theological (not historical) point with solemn and emphatic witness.

Second, if, as in Brown's explanation, Peter had read Luke and John and later recalled those magnificent stories in Peter 4:13–14, I know no theory of memory that would explain such a phenomenon. It is, of course, never possible to predict how somebody will remember a story, but it is usually possible, after hearing their memory, to describe how they did it: why they omitted, maintained, changed, and created details. I find it far easier to put Peter 4:13–14 (good thief's legs unbroken because he was impudent) at the start of the process and Luke 23:39–43 (bad versus good thief) or John 19:31–37 (Jesus' legs unbroken because he was dead) at the end of the development from that original unit.

The Two Thieves as a Test Case

The incident of the "good thief" is a very useful text case of that third fundamental difference between Brown and myself, namely, whether the Cross Gospel within Peter is dependent on and derived from the canonical versions (Matthew, Luke, John) or whether, in the opposite direction, the canonical versions (Mark, Matthew, Luke, John) are dependent on and derived from it.

In the prologue under "Sources and Theories" I mentioned in passing the most important objection to my theory that the canonical gospels used the Cross Gospel as their basic source for the passion narrative. There are several units in the Cross Gospel that are not found in Mark: if Matthew, Luke, and John knew the Cross Gospel (as well as Mark) why did each of them pick so differently from among those units in copying from it? To make the point sharp and clear, I give three key examples for each of those three canonical gospels in Table 7. More could be added, but these are the major ones and serve well enough to make the objection extremely significant (Brown 1987:333; 1994:1328–32).

It is exceedingly strange that Matthew, Luke, and John each chose different units to copy from the Cross Gospel and none of them chose the same unit. That is a serious problem for my theory, and I have no explanation for it beyond that it just happened that way. But now recall Brown's contrary theory:

> GPet . . . draws on the canonical Gospels (not necessarily from their written texts but often from memories preserved through their having been heard and recounted orally). (1001)

> GPet may have heard a reading of Matt or of Mark and have written from memory of that oral communication rather than from a written copy. (1057)

> GPet is best explained in terms of the author's knowing the canonical gospels (perhaps by distant memory of having heard them). (1306)

> GPet had [no] written Gospel before him, although he was familiar with Matt because he had read it carefully in the past and/or had heard it read several times in community worship on the Lord's Day, so that it gave the dominant shaping to his thought. Most likely he had heard people speak who were familiar with the Gospels of Luke and John—perhaps traveling

Table 7

Elements in the Cross Gospel within the Gospel of Peter but not in Mark	also only in Matthew	also only in Luke	also only in John
1. Pilate washes his hands & claims innocence (1:1; 11:46)	27:24		
2. Guards at the tomb (8:29-11:49)	27:62-66 28:2-4, 11-15		
3. Earthquake and raising of those "asleep" (6:21b; 10:41-42)	27:51B-53		
4. Herod during the passion (1:1-2; 2:5b)		23:6-12	
5. Good "evildoer" (4:13-14)		23:39-43	
6. Jewish *people* repentant (8:28; 11:48)		23:27, 35, 48	
7. Crucifixion on Passover Eve (2:5b) 18:28b			
8. No leg breaking (4:14)			19:31-37
9. Nails in Jesus' hands (6:21)			20:25

preachers who rephrased salient stories—so that he knew some of their contents but had little idea of their structure. . . . I see no compelling reason to think that the author of *GPet* was directly influenced by Mark. (1334–35)

Think of that same objection but now turned against his own theory. Why did Peter remember, from distant scribal reading and/or oral hearing, precisely what was distinctive to Matthew, Luke, and John as given in Table 7? If you claimed, which Brown would definitely *not* do, that Peter was drawing directly on those written gospels and trying to integrate all their special materials into one more-or-less harmonized whole, you might have an explanation. But that claim would, unfortunately, raise all sorts of other problems: for instance, why are there no indications of the individual vocabulary or style of Matthew, Luke, or John on Peter?

It seems to me that those peculiarities outlined in Table 7 strike equally against either theory or direction of dependence. Against myself: Why did the canonical versions choose those separate and distinct units to copy from the Cross Gospel? It just happened that way? Against Brown: Why did Peter "choose" those separate and distinct units to remember? It just happened that way? None of that reasoning intends to dismiss the objection but to emphasize that it is a two-edged sword. And, in general, I still prefer my explanation because, to put it bluntly, the memory of the Gospel of Peter's author as imagined by Brown seems to me unique in all the world. Memory, especially oral memory, has its own logic, seldom predictable beforehand but usually explicable afterward. I cannot, however, fathom Peter's memory as proposed by Brown.

As an attempt to move beyond this general impasse, I use the case of the two thieves as a test case to compare the twin theories of Brown and myself in a concrete instance. Maybe it is just another impasse, but the reader can decide. I give the texts in parallel columns in Table 8.

Each text makes eminent sense by itself. Each has its own theological profundity. Longer or shorter proves nothing because authors can always move in either direction with a source. But I have specifically chosen this example as a test, not because it suits me more than any other, but because of this comment by Brown:

Are we to think that Luke and John read *GPet* 4:13–14, and that Luke excerpted and developed the element of no leg-breaking, without ever giving the slightest indication of being aware of the other element in this two-verse passage—a silence even more incomprehensible in Crossan's theory where John knew Luke as well as *GPet*! (1333).

If you read the texts within my theory, you must, as Brown says, imagine Luke expanding the good thief part and ignoring the no leg breaking part, while John, on the contrary, expands the no leg breaking part and ignores the good thief part. If you read the texts within Brown's own theory, you must imagine Peter's forgetting or ignoring the specific Lukan and Johannine versions while coming up with that summary. I do not find absurdity in either theory or either explanation. Still, I can at least understand why Luke would have so expanded the Cross Gospel unit: he thereby emphasizes something he had learned directly from it, what Brown calls "the special Lucan theology of Jesus acting as savior during the passion itself" (281). The good thief in Peter 4:13–14 both proclaims

Table 8

Peter 4:13–14	Luke 23:39–43
But one of the malefactors rebuked them saying, "We have landed in suffering for the deeds of wickedness which we have committed, but this man, who has become the saviour of men, what wrong has he done you?"	One of the criminals who were hanged there kept deriding him and saying, "Are you not the Messiah? Save yourself and us!" But the other rebuked him, saying, "Do you not fear God, since you are under the same sentence of condemnation? And we indeed have been condemned justly, for we are getting what we deserve for our deeds, but this man has done nothing wrong." Then he said, "Jesus, remember me when you come into your kingdom." He replied, "Truly I tell you, today you will be with me in Paradise."
	John 19:31–37
And they were wroth with him and commanded that his legs should not be broken, so that he might die in torments.	Since it was the day of Preparation, the Jews did not want the bodies left on the cross during the sabbath, especially because that sabbath was a day of great solemnity. So they asked Pilate to have the legs of the crucified men broken and the bodies removed. Then the soldiers came and broke the legs of the first and of the other who had been crucified with him. But when they came to Jesus and saw that he was already dead, they did not break his legs. Instead, one of the soldiers pierced his side with a spear, and at once blood and water came out. (He who saw this has testified so that you also may believe. His testimony is true, and he knows that he tells the truth.) These things occurred so that the scripture might be fulfilled, "None of his bones shall be broken." And again another passage of scripture says, "They will look on the one whom they have pierced."

and exemplifies Jesus as "saviour" even or especially during his passion. I also understand why Luke would prefer to avoid any mention of no leg breaking; he also preferred to avoid any mention of spitting on Jesus during his trials. I presume both omissions are examples of what Brown calls, speaking of the no spitting, "Luke's sensitivities" (584 note 19). I can also understand why John would want to include nothing about the thieves. Though he admits their existence, it is only as "two others" in John 19:18. In the transcendental scenario of John's passion account, bandits or malefactors on either side of Jesus are not mentioned. Neither are there any mockeries from anyone. Neither should there be even a good "other" who addresses Jesus. It is Jesus, for John, who was in charge of the passion just as he was in charge of the trial. It is Jesus, for John, who speaks as in 19:28–30 and others who respond and obey.

Theories are seldom perfect. It is enough if they are better than their nearest alternatives. Then they can become working hypotheses and be tested to see if they falter or fail. It is hard, as a general problem, to know whether and why the canonical versions each chose divergent units from Peter (myself) or whether and why Peter recalled those divergent units from them (Brown). As a specific example, it is hard to know whether and why Luke and John each chose divergent parts of Peter 4:13–14 (myself) or whether and why Peter 4:13–14 recalled those divergent parts of Luke and John so differently (Brown). But, given those twin theories or explanations for the facts, I still prefer my own. I can understand how to get from Peter 3:13–14 to both Luke 23:39–43 and John 19:31–37 better than I can understand how to get from those twin canonical texts to Peter 4:13–14.

Casting Lots for His Garments

The next unit is not quite as complicated as the preceding or succeeding ones. We are back once again in the prophetic quarry of Psalm 22. That prayer begins with individual supplication from the depths of anguish in 22:1–21 and then soars into communal rejoicing at divine deliverance in 22:22–31. It is difficult to imagine a more appropriate quarry for the crucifixion *and* vindication of Jesus. Like Psalm 2 (see earlier), Psalm 22 is not just about persecution and death but also and equally about deliverance and vindication. Here is the text, in twin lines of Hebrew poetic parallelism more or less describing the same event twice:

> They divide my clothes among themselves,
> and for my clothing they cast lots.
> (Psalm 22:18)

The *Epistle of Barnabas* 6:6 applies that verse to Jesus' passion as part of the following three-part sequence of prophecies:

> What then does the Prophet say again? "The synagogue of the sinners compassed me around [=Psalm 22:16a], they surrounded me as bees round the honeycomb" [=Psalm 118:12a], and "They cast lots for my clothing" [=Psalm 22:18].

But, as with the scapegoat earlier, that is passion prophecy. Here is passion narrative, in all five versions of the crucifixion, with only John significantly different:

> And they laid down his garments before him and divided them among themselves and cast the lot upon them. (Peter 4:12)

> They . . . divided his clothes among them, casting lots to decide what each should take. (Mark 15:24)

> They divided his clothes among themselves by casting lots. (Matthew 27:35)

> And they cast lots to divide his clothing. (Luke 23:34b)

> The soldiers . . . took his clothes and divided them into four parts, one for each soldier. They also took his tunic; now the tunic was seamless, woven in one piece from the top. So they said to one another, "Let us not tear it, but cast lots for it to see who will get it." This was to fulfill what the scripture says, "They divided my clothes among themselves, and for my clothing they cast lots." And that is what the soldiers did. (John 19:23–25a)

In those first four cases, Psalm 22:18 lies latent behind the story. In John its presence is again rendered explicit. What is John's purpose?

The text of Psalm 22:18, of the *Epistle of Barnabas* 6:6, of Peter, Mark, Matthew, and Luke all speak of garments, clothes, or clothing. Only John speaks of a *tunic,* and that probably reveals his intention. After having described the robes of the Temple priests, Josephus says,

> The high-priest is arrayed in like manner, omitting none of the things already mentioned, but over and above these he puts on a *tunic* of blue material. . . . But this *tunic* is not composed of two pieces, to be stitched at the shoulders and at the sides: it is one long woven cloth, with a slit for the neck, parted not crosswise but lengthwise from the breast to a point in the middle of the back. A border is stitched thereto to hide from the eye the

unsightliness of the cut. There are similar slits through which the hands are passed. (*Jewish Antiquities* 3.159–61, my italics)

Although John is much more interested in royal than in priestly symbolism during Jesus' passion, and although the connection to the Temple is rather through the paschal lamb than the high priest, his emphasis on the seamless robe in 19:23b must be an allusion to the seamless tunic of the high-priest. But, once again, in the beginning the details came not from history but from prophecy.

Gall and Vinegar to Drink

The next case is as complicated as it is instructive. The background is now Psalm 69, which, like Psalm 22, begins with an anguished individual prayer from the depths of persecution in 69:1–19 and then ends with a corporate hymn of praise for deliverance in 69:30–36. Once again, this is extremely appropriate as prophecy for the execution and vindication of Jesus. Here is the verse in question, once again in Hebrew poetic parallelism:

They gave me poison for food,
and for my thirst they gave me vinegar to drink.
(Psalm 69:21)

The persecuted one receives poison (or gall) and vinegar instead of food and drink. Originally, therefore, there is a double dualism of poison/food and vinegar/drink. We also know, again from the *Epistle of Barnabas,* that Psalm 69:21 was used in passion prophecy concerning the death of Jesus:

But moreover when he was crucified "he was given to drink vinegar and gall. . . ." Why? Because you are going "to give to me gall and vinegar to drink" when I am on the point of offering my flesh for my new people. (*Epistle of Barnabas* 7:3–5)

That prophetic passage is then turned into story in all five crucifixion accounts but in very different ways.

In the gospel of Peter it is the Jewish people who crucify Jesus and then repent when they see the miracles that accompany his death. But here is what happens before that moment:

Now it was midday and a darkness covered all Judaea. And they became anxious and uneasy lest the sun had already set, since he was still alive. [For] it stands written for them: the sun should not set on one that has been put to death. And one of them said, "Give him to drink gall with vinegar." And they mixed it and gave him to drink. And they fulfilled all things and completed the measure of their sins on their head. (Peter 5:15–17)

Here at least somebody seems to notice that three-hour darkness! The biblical reference is to the law requiring burial of crucified people by sunset:

When someone is convicted of a crime punishable by death and is executed, and you hang him on a tree, his corpse must not remain all night upon the tree; you shall bury him that same day, for anyone hung on a tree is under God's curse. You must not defile the land that the Lord your God is giving you for possession. (Deuteronomy 21:22–23)

We will look at that text in greater detail in the next chapter, on Jesus' Burial. For now it suffices to take it as an explanation for what happens in the gospel of Peter. When the darkness starts, the people think it is night and fear lest they have broken the law by leaving a crucified body on the cross after sunset. So they plan to finish the crucifixion speedily by poisoning Jesus. The food/poison (or gall) and vinegar/drink is simply and necessarily collapsed into gall and vinegar or, in other words, poisoned vinegar. It is that act that both "fulfilled all things and completed the measure of their sins on their head." For Peter, the drink of vinegar and gall poisons the crucified Jesus to a quicker death.

Mark's usage is very, very different. We saw before that, where Peter had one trial and one abuse, Mark had doubled those to twin trials and twin abuses. So also with the drink. He doubles it to frame the start and end of the crucifixion:

They offered him wine mixed with myrrh; but he did not take it. (Mark 15:23)

At three o'clock Jesus cried out with a loud voice, "Eloi, Eloi, lema sabachthani?" which means, "My God, my God, why have you forsaken me?" When some of the bystanders heard it, they said, "Listen, he is calling for Elijah." And someone ran, filled a sponge with sour wine, put it on a stick, and gave it to him to drink, saying, "Wait, let us see whether Elijah will come to take him down." (Mark 15:34–36)

Those twin drinks in Mark have very different meanings from the single poisoned drink in Peter. The first drink was an act of mercy. It uses the ordinary word for *wine*, and such a drink of heavy, perfumed wine was intended as a narcotic, a soporific to dull the pain of the impending crucifixion. Since that is its purpose, Mark has Jesus refuse it because, after the agony in Gethsemane, he is now determined to drink the cup of suffering decreed by his Father. That first drink, therefore, has nothing about poison-gall or vinegar.

The second drink was an act of mockery. Jesus' cry cites the opening verse of Psalm 22:1 in Aramaic dialect. Bystanders hear him cry out "Eloi, Eloi," that is, "My God, my God," but misunderstand it or mock it as calling out "Elijah, Elijah." So they say, in effect, let's keep him alive to see if the prophet Elijah comes to help him. The drink is now the *vinegar* of Psalm 69:21 but, of course, with no poison-gall mentioned, because its purpose is to keep Jesus alive a little longer. Here Mark's drink has exactly the opposite purpose of Peter's. The latter hurries death, the former delays it. Mark may not recognize the Psalm 69:21 reference, or, more likely, he simply intends to eliminate the meaning Peter has given it. The duplication and its content seem his own particular creation.

Matthew follows Mark in having two drinks, one at the start and the other at the end of the crucifixion. The second one, in Matthew 27:46–49, is exactly like Mark's second one, but the first drink has the differences shown in italics:

> They offered him wine to drink, *mixed with gall; but when he tasted it,* he would not drink it. (Matthew 27:34, my italics)

Matthew recognized the allusion to Psalm 69:21 and changed Mark accordingly. The wine now contains poison-gall rather than perfume-myrrh. So, with *poison-gall* in Matthew 27:34 and *vinegar* in Matthew 27:46–49, the poison-gall and vinegar of Psalm 69:21 are back again, even if now split over two drinks.

Luke's solution is, once again, simpler but more drastic. In 23:33 he completely eliminates Mark's first drink and then rephrases the second one like this:

> The soldiers also mocked him, coming up and offering him sour wine [*vinegar*]. (Luke 23:36)

There is now no mention of Eloi/Elijah, and the *vinegar* is just some form of unexplained mockery. Still, even in Luke, the vinegar is there in residual memory of Psalm 69:21.

John, as always, presents the most creative solution to the drink problem. First, like Luke, he omits completely any mention of Mark's first drink. Next, he records the second drink but in the context of a very different death for Jesus. In Mark, as seen earlier, Jesus was mocked on the cross by "those who passed by" in 15:29–30, by the "chief priests . . . with the scribes" in 15:31–32, and by the two thieves "who were crucified with him" in 15:32. Finally, as just seen, he is mocked by the "bystanders" with the vinegar drink in 15:34–36. After that sustained chorus of derision,

> Jesus uttered a loud cry, and breathed his last. (Mark 15:37)

Mark offers no mitigation to the terrible isolation of Jesus' death. He dies amidst a chorus of universal mockery because, as Mark's community knows full well, that is how their persecuted members were executed during and after the terrible First Roman War. But Jesus' death in John is absolutely different because, as seen so often already, the Johannine Jesus always remains completely in control of events and acts with royal mastery from the garden of the arrest to the garden of the burial. Just as John included no agony in the garden and no cry of dereliction on the cross, so also will there be no mockery before or during his death. Here is how John connects drink and death:

> After this, when Jesus knew that all was now finished, he said (in order to fulfill the scripture), "I am thirsty." A jar full of sour wine [*vinegar*] was standing there. So they put a sponge full of the wine [*vinegar*] on a branch of hyssop and held it to his mouth. When Jesus had received the wine, he said, "It is finished." Then he bowed his head and gave up his spirit. (John 19:28–30)

It is now Jesus who initiates the drink episode, and he does so to fulfill Scripture. The phrase "I *thirst*" connects with Psalm 69:2, "They gave me poison for food, and for my *thirst* they gave me vinegar to drink." They offer Jesus vinegar-wine not as poison (Peter) or as mockery (Mark) but as servants obeying Jesus' demand. John's hyssop is, once again, not history but prophecy. It is another contact between Jesus and the paschal lamb, recalling the use of hyssop for sprinkling the protective blood of the first Passover lambs on the doorposts of the Israelite houses in Egypt:

> Take a bunch of hyssop, dip it in the blood that is in the basin, and touch the lintel and the two doorposts with the blood in the basin. None of you shall go outside the door of your house until morning. (Exodus 12:22)

After receiving the drink, Jesus, in his own good time, gives up his spirit, in control to the very end.

Two conclusions, in parallel with those concerning the thieves in the first part of this chapter: First, the whole gall and vinegar episode is not history remembered but prophecy historicized. At its origins stands Psalm 69:21. Second, if Peter, as Brown proposes, is recalling the canonical accounts, he has managed to make eminent and single sense out of very varied and disparate sources. In Peter, and only in Peter, the poison-gall and vinegar-wine of Psalm 69:21 make full and complete sense. Poisoned vinegar is given to Jesus to hasten his death lest he remain on the cross after sunset. All the other accounts make better sense as derived from that initial usage rather than as the sources for it. The canonical accounts, in other words, come from Peter rather than Peter from them. Mark does not want the soldiers (and their centurion!) to poison Jesus to death, so he doubles the drink story into one of mercy (from the soldiers) and one of mockery (from bystanders not soldiers) and omits the poison-gall completely. Matthew puts it back into the mercy drink, which hardly improves the situation. Luke and John simplify back to a single drink, with Luke leaving it as a minimal situation and John using it as masterful conclusion to Jesus' control of the crucifixion. But, just as following the trail of the reed in the Abuse led back to Peter as the earliest and most original version, so also here. Following the trail of the poison-gall and vinegar-wine leads back to the same conclusion. In the beginning was passion prophecy, not passion narrative. And in the beginning of passion narrative was Peter.

Pilate, the Crowd, and the Crucifixion

I held this next section for here because it touches on many of the preceding chapters. All five passion narratives agree that the Roman governor Pilate judged Jesus to be innocent and that his death was due to Jewish insistence. That cannot be explained as prophecy historicized because it fulfills nothing from the Old Testament. Is it, then, history remembered?

The Longest Lie

Josephus said, as you will recall from earlier, that "Pilate . . . hearing him [Jesus] accused by men of the highest standing amongst us . . . condemned him to be crucified" (*Jewish Antiquities* 18.63). Because I can see no reason for Josephus to have created that Jewish responsibility, I take it as historical that Jesus was executed by some conjunction of Jewish and Roman authority. That places the focus, in terms of personalities, on Joseph Caiaphas and Pontius Pilate. In the vagaries of archaeological recovery we have, since 1961, "Pontius Pilate, prefect of Judea" in Latin on a dedicatory stone from the amphitheater at Caesarea, the Roman capital northwest of Jerusalem on the Mediterranean coast, and, since 1990, "Joseph son of Caiaphas" in Aramaic on his ossuary, or bone-box, in the family tomb at Abu Tor just south of Jerusalem.

Caiaphas was the Jewish high priest from 18 to 36 C.E. In a century when such officials averaged four years at best, he lasted for eighteen years. That was twice the tenure of Annas I, the founder of the high priestly dynasty into which Caiaphas married, who ruled from 6 to 15 C.E. Pilate was Roman prefect of Judea from 26 to 36 C.E. We must presume that the Romans and Caiaphas worked well together because, while Valerius Gratus, Pilate's predecessor as governor, began by dismissing Annas I as high priest and then appointing four others between 15 and 18 C.E., Caiaphas lasted not only for eight years under Gratus but for ten more under Pilate. But it is equally significant that both Caiaphas and Pilate were themselves dismissed around the same time in late 36 and early 37 C.E.:

> [The Syrian governor, Vitellius] ordered Pilate to return to Rome to give the emperor his account of the matters with which he was charged . . . [and] he removed from his sacred office the high priest Joseph surnamed Caïaphas, and appointed in his stead Jonathan, son of Ananus the high priest. (*Jewish Antiquities* 18.89, 95)

It is not unfairly cynical to presume that there was close cooperation between Caiaphas and Pilate, that it often offended Jewish sensibilities, and that eventually it became necessary to break up that cooperation in Rome's best interests.

Pilate was neither a saint nor a monster but compared with some of Judea's other early governors we know a lot about him from both Philo and Josephus. Philo is writing around 41 C.E. about the attempt to place Gaius Caligula's statue in Jerusalem's Temple, and he inserts this description of Pilate into a letter sent during that crisis from King Agrippa I to Caligula himself:

> [Pilate used] briberies, insults, robberies, outrages, wanton injuries, constantly repeated executions without trial, ceaseless and supremely grievous cruelty. (*Embassy to Gaius* 302)

That is probably rhetorical overkill, but two stories about Pilate from Josephus show him as lacking in concern for Jewish religious sensibilities and as capable of rather brutal methods of crowd control.

The first story is that of the iconic standards. Josephus tells it twice, and it is probably the same story as the one about the aniconic shields in Philo's

Embassy to Gaius 199–305. The differences between Josephus's and Philo's accounts are the expected ones between twin versions of the same situation, especially in a rhetorical context in which Philo is contrasting a villainous Pilate with an idealized Tiberius. Here are Josephus's two versions.

> Pilate, being sent by Tiberius as procurator to Judaea, introduced into Jerusalem by night and under cover the effigies of Caesar which are called standards. This proceeding, when day broke, aroused immense excitement among the Jews . . . considering their laws to have been trampled under foot, as those laws permit no images to be erected in the city. (*Jewish War* 2:169)

> Now Pilate, the procurator of Judaea, when he brought his army from Caesarea and removed it to winter quarters in Jerusalem, took a bold step in subversion of the Jewish practices by introducing into the city the busts [embossed medallions] of the emperor that were attached to the military standards, for our law forbids the making of images. It was for this reason that the previous procurators, when they entered the city, used standards that had no such ornaments. Pilate was the first to bring the images into Jerusalem and set them up, doing it without the knowledge of the people, for he entered at night. (Josephus, *Jewish Antiquities* 18.56)

The ordinary people of Jerusalem went to Caesarea, gathering country reinforcements as they went, and implored Pilate to remove the offending emblems. He refused and "they fell prostrate around his house and for five whole days and nights remained motionless in that position" (*Jewish War* 2.171). Pilate hid his soldiers in the stadium, had the demonstrators come there for an audience, and then threatened them with immediate death unless they submitted. When all simultaneously offered to accept martyrdom, Pilate was himself forced to submit rather than massacre so many.

The second story is that of the Temple funds. Josephus makes it, from a literary point of view, almost a parallel companion piece to the preceding episode. Indeed, the demonstrations at Caesarea and Jerusalem form a diptych in Josephus, and one may wonder if literary harmony may have overcome historical accuracy in the details.

> He provoked a fresh uproar by expending upon the construction of an aqueduct the sacred treasure known as Corbonas; the water was brought from a distance of 400 furlongs. . . . He, foreseeing the tumult, had interspersed among the crowd a troop of his soldiers, armed but disguised in civilian dress with orders not to use their swords, but to beat any rioters with cudgels. (*Jewish War* 2.175–76)

> He spent money from the sacred treasury in the construction of an aque-
> duct to bring water into Jerusalem, intercepting the source of the stream at
> a distance of 200 furlongs. . . . Tens of thousands assembled. . . . Some too
> even hurled insults and abuse of the sort that a throng will commonly en-
> gage in. He thereupon ordered a large number of soldiers to be dressed in
> Jewish garments, under which they carried clubs. . . . They, however, in-
> flicted much harder blows than Pilate had ordered, punishing alike both
> those who were rioting and those who were not. (*Jewish Antiquities*
> 18.60–62)

The logic of that tactic derives from Pilate's previous experience. In the
iconic standards incident he had suddenly confronted a Jewish crowd
with armed soldiers and, confronted with mass unresisting martyrdom,
had been forced to back down. In the Temple funds case he planned to
stampede the crowd either into violent action or headlong flight. I presume, therefore, that both events happened in relatively close proximity
to each other, soon after Pilate first became governor.

Although both incidents involve the sanctity of Jerusalem and its
Temple, nothing is said about any reaction from Caiaphas, who was, presumably, ready to accept both situations.

In the five passion accounts we meet a very different Pilate. In Peter
he removes himself completely from the condemnation and crucifixion
of Jesus. I presume that he washed his hands in the lost verses before the
present opening of that gospel:

> But of the Jews none washed their hands, neither Herod nor any one of his
> judges. And as they would not wash, Pilate arose. . . . Pilate answered and
> said, "I am clean from the blood of the Son of God, upon such a thing have
> you decided." (Peter 1:1; 11:46)

In Peter, Pilate believes that Jesus is innocent, and he himself is absolutely
innocent of his execution.

In Mark Pilate is more ambiguous but also more believable. He
knows Jesus is innocent but crucifies him to please the crowd.

> He realized that it was out of jealousy that the chief priests had handed
> him over. . . . Pilate asked them, "Why, what evil has he done?" But they
> shouted all the more, "Crucify him!" (Mark 15:10, 14)

He knows that Jesus is innocent, but "the chief priests stirred up the
crowd" (15:11) and, after they have twice demanded to "crucify him"
(15:13,14), Pilate crucifies Jesus "wishing to satisfy the crowd" (15:15).

In Luke Pilate thrice announces that Jesus is innocent, and, in case you miss it, Luke spells out that number explicitly:

> (1) Pilate said to the chief priests and the crowds, "I find no basis for an accusation against this man." (23:4)

> (2) Pilate . . . said to them [the chief priest and the rulers and the people], "You brought me this man as one who was perverting the people; and here I have examined him in your presence and have not found this man guilty of any of your charges against him. Neither has Herod, for he sent him back to us. Indeed, he has done nothing to deserve death. I will therefore have him flogged and release him." (23:13–16)

> (3) A third time he said to them, "Why, what evil has he done? I have found in him no ground for the sentence of death; I will therefore have him flogged and then release him." (23:22)

Once again, Pilate is constrained by twice-repeated cries: "crucify him, crucify him" (23:21) and "they were urgent, demanding with loud cries that he should be crucified" (23:23a), until, in Luke's terribly laconic phrase, "their voices prevailed" (23:23b).

John has a similar triadic insistence by Pilate on Jesus' innocence.

> (1) Pilate . . . went out to the Jews again and told them, "I find no case against him." (18:38b)

> (2) Pilate went out again and said to them, "Look, I am bringing him out to you to let you know that I find no case against him." (19:4)

> (3) Pilate said to them [the chief priests and the police], ". . . I find no case against him." (19:6)

What finally prevails upon Pilate in John is not just the doubly repeated cries of "crucify him, crucify him" (19:6) and "away with him, away with him, crucify him" (19:15) but also the political threat "If you release this man, you are no friend of the emperor. Everyone who claims to be a king sets himself against the emperor" (19:12).

Brown's conclusion on the preceding data is, "Both John and Luke are stylized in having Pilate three times declare Jesus innocent. With those exceptions, however, the NT [New Testament] descriptions of Pilate are not patently implausible. (The subsequent canonization of him is!) That does not mean any one of them is historical, but the theory that the Gospels exculpate the Romans by creating a totally fictional, sympathetic Pilate has been overdone" (704). I do not speak of absolute but of relative implausibility. I use the same discrimination here that I use in watching a modern movie like Oliver Stone's *JFK*. I do not ask if it is plausible in an absolute sense, or "patently implausible." I simply ask if it is more plausible than the next best alternative. Knowing, on the one hand, what I do about Pilate as an ordinary second-class governor, of his ten-year tenure and his eventual removal, of his attitude toward Jewish religious sensitivities and his tactics toward unarmed but demanding crowds, and, on the other hand, of Christian reasons for increasing the responsibility of Jewish and decreasing that of Roman participants in the crucifixion, there can be only one *relatively plausible* conclusion. That reiterated juxtaposition of Jewish demands for Jesus' crucifixion and Roman declarations of Jesus' innocence is not prophecy, and neither is it history. It is Christian propaganda.

Let me be very clear about what I am saying. For Christians the New Testament texts and the gospel accounts are inspired by God. But divine inspiration necessarily comes through a human heart and a mortal mind, through personal prejudice and communal interpretation, through fear, dislike, and hate as well as through faith, hope, and charity. It can also come as inspired propaganda, and inspiration does not make it any the less propaganda. In its origins and first moments that Christian propaganda was fairly innocent. Those first Christians were relatively powerless Jews, and compared to them the Jewish authorities represented serious and threatening power. As long as Christians were the marginalized and disenfranchised ones, such passion fiction about Jewish responsibility and Roman innocence did nobody much harm. But, once the Roman Empire became Christian, that fiction turned lethal. In the light of later Christian anti-Judaism and eventually of genocidal anti-Semitism, it is no longer possible in retrospect to think of that passion fiction as relatively benign propaganda. However explicable its origins, defensible its invectives, and understandable its motives among Christians fighting for survival, its repetition has now become the longest lie, and, for our own integrity, we Christians must at last name it as such.

Responsibility for Innocent Blood

What follows is the last of those six fundamental disagreements between Brown and myself on the passion narratives. It concerns the existence of independent, popular passion traditions. As mentioned often before, he considers Mark and John to have independent passion narratives. But, even apart from them, he finds another and also independent stream of passion tradition. He describes this passion tradition in various places as

> a body of popular and imaginative tradition (92)
>
> a vein of popular material characterized by vivid imagination (287 note 10)
>
> popularly preserved oral tradition about minor incidents of the passion that could be historical (784)
>
> popular reflection (which probably already existed as romanticized characterization) (860)
>
> vivid popular tales of the passion (1118)
>
> collection of popular tradition (1287)
>
> popular circles (1288)
>
> stories that bore the stamp of popular, imaginative reflection on the events surrounding the death of Jesus (1304)
>
> vivid popular material (1304)
>
> popular material (1345)

By that term "popular" Brown intends "nothing pejorative historically, theologically, or intellectually" but simply means "a transmission of Jesus material" other than by the more official channels that marked and shaped the Synoptic or Johannine material (1304 note 41). I also have been using the term "popular" throughout this book, but it means for me not works composed *by* popular creation but works composed *for* popular consumption. When Brown, for example, says that "in part *GPet* is a folk-gospel" (1118 note 47) or speaks of "the popular storytelling facet" of that document, I presume he means created *by* and not just *for* the folk. A folk-gospel in Brown's sense would have been created orally (because "folk" did not write in the ancient world) and eventually written down by "nonfolk." I find neither the slightest evidence nor the slightest need for such a hypothesis.

Furthermore, Brown continues, those popular traditions appear only in Matthew and Peter, but at an earlier stage in Matthew and at a more developed stage in Peter. As Brown puts it, "Intermingled in the *GPet* author's mind were also popular tales about incidents in the passion, the very type of popular material that Matt had tapped in composing his Gospel at an earlier period," (1335) and again, "I would see the ethos of *GPet* as later but not far removed from the ethos that Matt had tapped in the 80s–90s for what I have called the popular material" (1345). I argue strongly against both those points.

A COLLECTION OF POPULAR TRADITION?

My objection to Brown's first point concerns the very existence of such popular reflection, material, or tradition. As an example of it, Brown cites from Matthew, "the suicide of Judas and the blood money (27:3–10); the dream of Pilate's wife (27:19); Pilate's washing his hands of Jesus' blood while the people accepted responsibility for it (27:24–25)" (1287). I see absolutely no reason to distinguish those items as "popular" over against other items as somehow more official in the passion narrative. They are very good story elements, to be sure, but so is item after item in the passion story, from Judas's kiss and Malchus's ear through Peter's denials and Jesus' abuse and on to the two thieves, lots for garments, and merciful, mocking, or poisoned drink. In fact, as Christian art has known since Constantine, what element in the passion is not a brilliant video shot? The passion narratives are, to put it bluntly, *all* popular storytelling. They represent the popularization, under communal control, of the prophetic passion that, without that narrativization, would have remained as popularly impenetrable as was the *Epistle of Barnabas* when we were reading it earlier. That is a general objection, but there is also a more specific one. Is concern with responsibility for blood popular or official, is it derived from popular story or from biblical law?

What if a murdered body is found and nobody knows who killed the person? Will not that blood pollute the land and its inhabitants unless those nearest to the discovered corpse assume responsibility to atone for it? There is, of course, no question that they are in any way guilty or even responsible for the crime. They are only responsible for purging the unpunished evil from their midst:

> If, in the land that the Lord your God is giving you to possess, a body is found lying in open country, and it is not known who struck the person down, then your elders and your judges shall come out to measure the distances to the towns that are near the body. The elders of the town nearest the body shall take a heifer that has never been worked, one that has not pulled in the yoke; the elders of that town shall bring the heifer down to a wadi with running water, which is neither plowed nor sown, and shall break the heifer's neck there in the wadi. Then the priests, the sons of Levi, shall come forward, for the Lord your God has chosen them to minister to him and to pronounce blessings in the name of the Lord, and by their decision all cases of dispute and assault shall be settled. All the elders of that town nearest the body shall wash their hands over the heifer whose neck was broken in the wadi, and they shall declare: "Our hands did not shed

this blood, nor were we witnesses to it. Absolve, O Lord, your people Israel, whom you redeemed; do not let the guilt of innocent blood remain in the midst of your people Israel." Then they will be absolved of bloodguilt. So you shall purge the guilt of innocent blood from your midst, because you must do what is right in the sight of the Lord. (Deuteronomy 21:1–9)

The symbolism of the slain heifer is somewhat ambiguous: it could represent the murdered man and/or the fate of the speakers should they lie. But the symbolism of the hand washing is quite clear. The entire ritual is a cultic act performed in the presence of the priests. They wash their hands to show their innocence not, like Lady Macbeth, to remove their guilt. The full ritual involved both word and deed, both statement and action, both declaration of innocence and symbolism of hand washing.

It was also possible to refer to that double ritual in more compact form as "washing your hands in (or as) innocence":

> I do not sit with the worthless,
>> nor do I consort with hypocrites;
> I hate the company of evildoers,
>> and will not sit with the wicked.
> I wash my hands in innocence,
>> and go around your altar, O Lord.
> (Psalm 26:4–6)

> Such are the wicked;
>> always at ease, they increase in riches.
> All in vain I have kept my heart clean
>> and washed my hands in innocence.
> (Psalm 73:12–13)

It was also possible to declare one's innocence of blood unjustly shed without mentioning hand washing at all. That is what happens in a popular story, that of Susanna and the Elders, added at the start or end of the book of Daniel in some Bibles.

> Susanna [was] a very beautiful woman and one who feared the Lord. . . . That year two elders from the people were appointed as judges. . . . Susanna would go into her husband's garden to walk. Every day the two elders used to see her, going in and walking about, and they began to lust for her. . . . Then together they arranged for a time when they could find her alone. . . . When the maids had gone out, the two elders . . . said, . . . "Give your consent, and lie with us. If you refuse, we will testify against you that a young man was with you, and this was why you sent your maids away." Then Susanna cried out with a loud voice, and the two elders shouted

against her. . . . Because they were elders of the people and judges, the assembly believed them and condemned her to death. . . . Just as she was being led off to execution, God stirred up the holy spirit of a young lad named Daniel, and he shouted with a loud voice, "I want no part in shedding this woman's blood!" (Susanna 2–46)

Against that entire biblical background, a concern for the biblical ritual wherein one's innocence is declared orally *and* displayed symbolically pertains more to the domain of learned biblical law than to popular oral story, and, where it appears in the latter, it comes from the former.

PETER MORE DEVELOPED THAN MATTHEW?

My objection to Brown's second point is that Peter is less, not more, developed than Matthew and that Matthew is more, not less, developed than Peter on those allegedly "popular" contents. Compare, first, the content of their texts.

Peter's present fragmented state begins at the end of a single, composite trial with all the authorities present in one place at one time. It seems *most probable* that Pilate has just washed his hands and it might be *just possible* that he did so because of a message from his wife. But his declaration of personal innocence for Jesus' death comes much later, after the resurrection, where it is accompanied, as it were, by a statement of Christian confession:

> But of the Jews none washed their hands, neither Herod nor any one of his judges. And as they would not wash, Pilate arose. . . . Pilate answered and said, "I am clean from the blood of the Son of God, upon such a thing have you decided." (Peter 1:1; 11:46)

I emphasize one point. *Only in Peter is Pilate really innocent.* Only in Peter could his hand washing and his declaration of innocence ring true. He withdrew completely from the condemnation and crucifixion of Jesus. He was as innocent as possible while still being the governor. In Matthew, by contrast, his hand washing and declaration of innocence ring hollow, because he goes on to crucify Jesus in any case, *even though he knows Jesus is innocent.* To my mind, Peter is clearly earlier and more original on this point than Matthew. It is not, of course, historical, but at least Peter's "innocent" Pilate makes more sense than does Matthew's.

Contrast, then, these units from Peter with the following excerpts from Matthew, which raise the same question of innocence and responsibility for Jesus' death in terms of Judas, Pilate, and the people:

(1) When Judas, his betrayer, saw that Jesus was condemned, he repented and brought back the thirty pieces of silver to the chief priests and the elders. He said, "I have sinned by betraying innocent blood." But they said, "What is that to us? See to it yourself." Throwing down the pieces of silver in the temple, he departed; and he went and hanged himself. But the chief priests, taking the pieces of silver, said, "It is not lawful to put them into the treasury, since they are blood money." (27:3–6)

(2) While he [Pilate] was sitting on the judgment seat, his wife sent word to him, "Have nothing to do with that innocent man, for today I have suffered a great deal because of a dream about him." (27:19)

(3) So when Pilate saw that he could do nothing, but rather that a riot was beginning, he took some water and washed his hands before the crowd, saying, "I am innocent of this man's blood; see to it yourselves." Then the people as a whole answered, "His blood be on us and on our children!" (27:24–25)

Contrary to Brown, I see Peter as less developed rather than more developed in comparison with Matthew. Both *certainly* have Pilate's declaration of personal innocence. Both *most probably* had Pilate's hand washing. Both *may* even have had Pilate's wife's dream. But Matthew, and Matthew alone, has Judas say anything about Jesus' innocent blood. Recall and compare the other version of the death of Judas in Acts 2:16–20, which never mentions that point. And above all, Matthew, and Matthew alone, has "the people as a whole" accept full and explicit responsibility for Jesus' death on behalf of both themselves and their descendants. The anti-Judaism of Matthew is more bitter than that in Peter, since, as seen before, Peter 8:28 has "all the people [*ho laos hapas*]" repent upon seeing the miracles attendant upon Jesus' death while Matthew 27:25 has "the people as a whole [*pas ho laos*]" demand his crucifixion and assume responsibility for his condemnation. The development of the *blood* theme is much more advanced and virulent in Matthew than in Peter. It bespeaks the concerns of Matthew as a learned scribe, skilled and knowledgeable in biblical law. It bespeaks the bitterness of Matthew as a learned scribe whose vision was slowly, steadily, but surely being refused by his people. Judaism would not become Christian Judaism but rabbinic Judaism.

BLOOD REMEMBERED BUT FORGIVENESS FORGOTTEN

In my historical reconstruction, Matthew *created* that saying in which "the people as a whole" accept responsibility for Jesus' death, and it has had, as Brown says, a "tragic history in inflaming Christian hatred for

Jews" (833). But I find it unnecessary to postulate, as Brown does, that it "represents Matthean composition on the basis of a popular tradition" nor that "there may have been a small historical nucleus; but the detection of that nucleus with accuracy is beyond our grasp" (833). In that verse Matthew speaks for the Jewish people from whom he is ultimately alienated. They do not speak for themselves.

One final point as long as we are focusing on specific verses: The "blood be upon us" text in Matthew 27:25 is found only in Matthew, and, pending alternative evidence, I judge that he *created* it all by himself. Here is a verse found only in Luke:

> Then Jesus [having just been crucified] said, "Father, forgive them; for they do not know what they are doing." (23:34)

Brown notes that this "verse is omitted in important textual witnesses, some of them very early. Yet other major Greek codices and early versions have it. This is an instance where the weight of textual witnesses on one side almost offsets that on the other side" (975). His own conclusion, with which I agree, is, "Overall, after surveying the pros and cons, I would deem it easier to posit that the passage was written by Luke and excised for theological reasons by a later copyist than that it was added to Luke by such a copyist who took the trouble to cast it in Lucan style and thought" (980). Primary among such theological reasons was this: "they found it too favorable to the Jews" (979). Brown concludes most appropriately, "It is ironical that perhaps the most beautiful sentence in the PN [passion narrative] should be textually doubtful" (980). It is doubly ironical, and just as significant, that no Christian copyist ever excised that "blood be upon us" verse from Matthew 27:25.

If some Christians take everything in the passion as actual, factual information, they must take both Matthew 27:25 and Luke 23:34 as historical data. But, because Jesus' prayer for forgiveness in Luke happened after the people's acceptance of responsibility in Matthew, it must surely have annulled it. Unless, of course, God refused Jesus' prayer. For Christians, like myself, who think that Matthew and Luke each created those specific verses out of their own theological backgrounds, there is a slightly different conclusion. Inspired Christian texts contain both virulent bitterness and serene forgiveness. It is necessary to know the difference and judge accordingly. And the decision to delete a verse, or which verse to delete, is an ethical one. As with Jewish responsibility and Roman innocence, it is necessary finally to call things by their proper names.

In conclusion, I cannot find any detailed historical information about the crucifixion of Jesus. Every item we looked at was prophecy historicized rather than history recalled. There was one glaring exception. The one time the *narrative passion* broke away from its base in the *prophetic passion,* that is, from the single, composite trial in Psalm 2, was to assert Jewish responsibility and Roman innocence. But those motifs were neither prophecy nor history but Christian propaganda, a daring act of public relations faith in the destiny of Christianity not within Judaism but within the Roman Empire. In a way that *was* history, not past history but future history.

CHAPTER SIX

Burial

Burying the Crucified

All five versions of the passion story have Jesus buried by somebody named Joseph. But is that a case of hope or of history? I look first at Roman expectations, at what we expect to happen to the body of a crucified criminal in Roman practice, then at Jewish exceptions, at the particular situation in the Jewish homeland, and finally and most important, at those detailed Christian stories concerning the burial of Jesus.

Roman Expectations

The hierarchy of horror was loss of life, loss of possessions, loss of burial, that is, destruction of body, destruction of family, destruction of identity. For the ancient world, the final penalty was to lie unburied as food for carrion birds and beasts. After Octavius, later emperor Augustus, had defeated Julius Caesar's murderers at Philippi in October of 42 B.C.E.,

> He did not use his victory with moderation, but after sending Brutus' head to Rome, to be cast at the feet of Caesar's statue, he vented his spleen upon the most distinguished of his captives, not even sparing them insulting language. For instance, to one man who begged humbly for burial, he is said to have replied: "The [carrion] birds will soon settle that question." (Suetonius, *The Deified Augustus* 13.1–2)

As with Brutus's companions for Augustus, so with Sejanus's companions for Tiberius. Between 26 and 31 the emperor Tiberius ruled Rome from the island of Capri off Naples, and Sejanus, prefect of the praetorian or imperial bodyguard, plotted against him in Rome itself. But in October of 31 C.E. Tiberius moved swiftly against him, and many of his fellow plotters chose immediate suicide:

For these modes of dying were rendered popular by fear of the executioner and by the fact that a man legally condemned forfeited his estate and was debarred from burial; while he who passed sentence upon himself had his celerity so far rewarded that his body was interred and his will respected. (Tacitus, *Annals* 6.29)

Lack of proper burial was not just ultimate insult, it was ultimate annihilation in the ancient Roman world. There would be no place where the dead one could be mourned, visited, or remembered. Think of all those Roman graves whose epitaphs address the passerby in direct discourse: the *I* can still speak to a *you*.

It was precisely that lack of burial that consummated the three supreme penalties of being burned alive, cast to the beasts in the amphitheater, or crucified. They all involved inhuman cruelty, public dishonor, and impossible burial. In the first two cases, that is obvious: there would be hardly anything left for burial. In the case of crucifixion, it presumes that the body was left on the cross until birds and beasts of prey had destroyed it. Indeed, in Roman texts two items occur again and again in connection with crucifixion. First, the crucified one is especially a disobedient slave or anyone considered an equivalent nobody, hence its designation as the slave penalty. Second, the crucified one is left unburied on the cross as carrion. Those twin concepts come together in an imagined interchange between Horace and one of his slaves published in 20 B.C.E.

If a slave were to say to me, "I never stole nor ran away":
my reply would be, "You have your reward; you are not flogged."
[If a slave were to say to me,] "I never killed anyone":
[my reply would be,] "You'll hang on no cross to feed crows."
(*Epistles* 1.16:46–48)

Crucifieds were left, kept, or guarded on the cross even after death if there was any chance that relatives or friends might take them down for proper burial before it was absolutely too late. Such an act would be, of course, extremely dangerous unless done with bribes or permissions. Here is a satirical story whose parody underlines the normal practices of the time.

Petronius was the emperor Nero's master of decadence before he was accused of conspiracy and forced to commit suicide in 66 C.E. Around 61, when he was at the height of imperial favor, he wrote his novel *Satyricon*, wherein one Eumolpus tells "a story that had happened in his own lifetime" (!) about a widow of Ephesus who was mourning disconsolately inside the tomb of her lately buried husband by "day and night."

Now at this moment the governor of the province gave orders that some robbers should be crucified near the small structure in which the lady was lamenting her loss. So, next day, the soldier, on guard by the crosses to stop anyone from taking down a body for burial, noticed a light glimmering quite distinctly among the tombs, and heard the moans of a mourner.

The soldier deserts his post to investigate, finds the grieving widow, seduces her, and returns "the next night as well, and the night after that."

So the parents of one of the crucified men, noting how careless was the guard, took the body down one night and performed the last rites over it. In his absence from duty the soldier was thus circumvented; and next day, finding one of the crosses without its corpse, he was scared at the prospect of punishment. . . . [He contemplated suicide, but the widow said], "I'd rather see a dead man crucified than a living man dead. She thereupon bade him remove her husband's corpse from its coffin and fix it up on the empty cross . . . and the people wondered next day by what means a dead man had ascended the cross. (*Satyricon* 111–12)

The story is satire and parody, to be sure, although the subject of crucifixion is far from funny. But, even in its gallows humor, it reminds us that nonburial and carrion-eating birds or beasts were the normal concomitants of Roman crucifixion.

To catch some glimpse of the horror of crucifixion, read Martin Hengel's inventory of texts in his book *Crucifixion*. This is his summary statement at its conclusion (86–88):

Crucifixion as a penalty was remarkably widespread in antiquity. It appears in various forms among numerous peoples of the ancient world, even among the Greeks. . . . [It] was and remained a political and military punishment. While among the Persians and the Carthaginians it was imposed primarily on high officials and commanders, as on rebels, among the Romans it was inflicted above all on the lower classes, i.e., slaves, violent criminals, and the unruly elements in rebellious provinces, not least in Judaea. The chief reason for its use was its allegedly supreme efficacy as a deterrent; it was, of course, carried out publicly. . . . It was usually associated with other forms of torture, including at least flogging. . . . By the public display of a naked victim at a prominent place—at a crossroads, in the theatre, on high ground, at the place of his crime—crucifixion also represented his uttermost humiliation, which had a numinous dimension to it. With Deuteronomy 21.23 in the background, the Jew in particular was very aware of this. . . . Crucifixion was aggravated further by the fact that quite often its victims were never buried. It was a stereotyped picture that the crucified victim served as food for wild beasts and birds of prey. In this way his humiliation was made complete. What it meant for a man in antiquity to be refused burial, and the dishonour which went with it, can hardly be appreciated by modern man.

Crucifixion as death-without-burial and the body-as-carrion was the Roman understanding of that execution which was particularly reserved for slaves, bandits, rebels, or anyone designated to be dishonored to their level. Those are the Roman expectations.

Jewish Exceptions

A first step: That quotation from Hengel draws attention to Jewish law in Deuteronomy, and this is very important in determining Roman practice in the Jewish homeland:

> When someone is convicted of a crime punishable by death and is executed, and you hang him on a tree, his corpse must not remain all night upon the tree; you shall bury him that same day, for anyone hung on a tree is under God's curse. You must not defile the land that the Lord your God is giving you for possession. (Deuteronomy 21:22–23)

Two important notes: First, that text does not refer to crucifixion *before* but *after* death. It presumes that persons who have been executed, say by stoning, have their dead bodies exposed afterward as humiliation for them and warning to others. Call it dead rather than live crucifixion. Second, that exposure must end by nightfall. It is crucifixion after death and removal by sunset that is described in two cases of defeated kings in the book of Joshua, but more explicitly in the second than the first one:

> But the king of Ai was taken alive and brought to Joshua. . . . And he hanged the king of Ai on a tree until evening; and at sunset Joshua commanded, and they took his body down from the tree, threw it down at the entrance of the gate of the city, and raised over it a great heap of stones, which stands there to this day. (8:23, 29)

> The five kings of the Amorites—the king of Jerusalem, the king of Hebron, the king of Jarmuth, the king of Lachish, and the king of Eglon—[were defeated]. . . . Afterward Joshua struck them down and put them to death, and he hung them on five trees. And they hung on the trees until evening. At sunset Joshua commanded, and they took them down from the trees and threw them into the cave where they had hidden themselves; they set large stones against the mouth of the cave, which remain to this very day. (10:5, 26–27)

I read that former text in the light of the latter one so that both indicate dead crucifixion or exposure and removal, of course, by sunset. *Such removals create no problem because those so exposed were already dead.* But if, for example, they were crucified *alive* in the Roman fashion, evening removals would have interfered completely with the long, slow exhibition of that terrible death. Seneca the Younger, like Petronius a suicide by Nero's command in 65 C.E., describes crucifixion in arguing that life is not always to be desired:

> Can any man be found willing to be fastened to the accursed tree, long sickly, already deformed, swelling with ugly tumours on chest and shoulders, and draw the breath of life amid long-drawn-out agony? I think he would have many excuses for dying even before mounting the cross! (*Epistles* 101.14)

Removal by evening of one crucified *after* death is very different from removal by evening of one crucified *before* death. Could Deuteronomy 21:22–23 prevail against *live* crucifixion?

A second step: The older Jewish practice of crucifixion of the dead had given way to the Roman one of live crucifixion under the Jewish Hasmonean dynasty in the last centuries B.C.E. A document from among the Dead Sea Scrolls is important in this regard. It is a fragment found in Qumran Cave 4 (hence 4Q) applying Nahum's prophecy (hence pNahum, or *pesher,* that is, application of, Nahum) about the fall of the Assyrian capital Nineveh in the seventh century B.C.E. to events in the early first century B.C.E. The Syrian king Demetrius III Eucerus was invited by the Pharisees, the "Seekers-after-Smooth-Things," to help them by attacking their enemy, the Hasmonean king and high priest Alexander Janneus. After a battle at Shechem in 88 B.C.E., Demetrius was unable to move on Jerusalem, and the victorious Alexander Janneus, the "Lion of Wrath," took a terrible revenge on his Pharisaic enemies. The commentary or application says that the phrase "he has filled his caves with prey and his dens with torn flesh" from Nahum 2:12b actually refers to that revenge:

> The interpretation of it concerns the Lion of Wrath [who has found a crime punishable by] death in the Seekers-after-Smooth-Things, whom he hangs as live men [on the tree, as it was thus done] in Israel from of old. (4QpNahum, fragments 3–4, column i, lines 6–8; Fitzmyer 500)

In the restored gap at the manuscript's end, live crucifixion is described as having being done "from of old" in the Jewish homeland. We also know about that event from Josephus, who gives more of its awful details:

So furious was he [Alexander Janneus] that his savagery went to the length of impiety. He had eight hundred of his captives crucified in the midst of the city, and their wives and children butchered before their eyes, while he looked on, drinking, with his concubines reclining beside him. (*Jewish War* 1:97=*Jewish Antiquities* 13.380)

Once again, that is live crucifixion, and one can only wonder if Alexander Janneus worried much about Deuteronomy 21:22–23 and removal of those crucifieds by evening.

A third step: A document from among the Dead Sea Scrolls is involved in this case as well. Since 1947 the ruins and caves of Qumran on the northwest shore of the Dead Sea have furnished evidence for the separated life and extensive library of a group of Jews usually identified as Essenes who abandoned what they considered to be the polluted Temple and invalid high priesthood of the Hasmonean dynasty. Sometime toward the end of the reign of Simon or the beginning of the reign of his son John Hyrcanus, in the second half of second century B.C.E., they built their sectarian settlement in the desert and lived in ritual purity and apocalyptic expectation of the imminent coming of God. Their compound was destroyed in 68 C.E. by the Romans during the First Roman War, but they had already hidden their library—and, we hope, themselves as well—in the surrounding caves. If that last text, 4QpNahum, told us what Hasmonean king-priests did with crucifixion, this one, 11QTemple, tells us what Essene dissidents would have done in their stead.

The Temple Scroll is, at twenty-seven feet, the longest of the Dead Sea Scrolls. Its laws extend, not only to the Temple, but to the entire city of Jerusalem, a strict interpretation of the purity rules promulgated in Deuteronomy for the Tabernacle and the Israelite camp during the desert period. It is that concern with a ritually pure Jerusalem that necessitated the more precise laws concerning those hanged or crucified:

If a man informs against his people, and delivers his people up to a foreign nation, and does harm to his people, *you shall hang him on the tree, and he shall die.* On the evidence of two witnesses and on the evidence of three witnesses *he shall be put to death, and they shall hang him on the tree.* And if a man has committed a crim[e] punishable by death, and has defected into the midst of the nations, and has cursed his people [and] the children of Israel, *you shall hang him also on the tree, and he shall die.* And their body shall not remain upon the tree all night, but you shall bury them the same day, for those hanged on the tree are accursed to God and men; you shall not defile the land which I give you for an inheritance. (11QTemple, column 64, lines 6–13; Yadin 1977–83:1.373, 288–91, 420–23; vol. 3, plate 79; my italics)

I have italicized the clauses that frame the ancient dead crucifixion with the more recent live crucifixion. The purpose of that careful juxtaposition is deliberately to equate dead and live crucifixion and keep *both* under the removal-by-sunset law of Deuteronomy. The Essenes, in other words, advocate live crucifixion for at least the two crimes of treason and blasphemy, but they also insist that Deuteronomy 21:22–23 be followed even in those cases.

Those laws clearly presume that live crucifixion was permissible to the Essenes, but do they indicate that Deuteronomy 21:22–23 was or was not obeyed in Jerusalem *while they were writing them?* Other laws in the Temple Scroll forbid any sex or defecation within the city of Jerusalem because the entire urban area was, in effect, a Temple. Toilets, for example, were to be located somewhat under a mile from the city, but that was farther than was permissible to walk on the Sabbath day. Defecation was therefore impossible on the Sabbath. I consider the laws of the Temple Scroll to be ideals for what the Essenes would do if and when they controlled Jerusalem. As such they tell us more what was *not* being done than what was being done at the time of their composition. I cannot presume, therefore, that Deuteronomy 21:22–23 was followed in Roman crucifixions in the first-century Jewish homeland.

A fourth step: Josephus knows all about Deuteronomy 21:22–23 and assumes its implementation when he is talking about ideal Jewish law:

> Let him that blasphemeth God be stoned, then hung for a day, and buried ignominiously and in obscurity. (*Jewish Antiquities* 4.202)

But then there's practice. I mentioned much earlier that the peasant Zealots took over the Temple during the First Roman War and killed Ananus II and Jesus, high priests in 62 and 64 respectively. As Josephus records,

> They actually went so far in their impiety as to cast out the corpses without burial, although the Jews are so careful about funeral rites that even malefactors who have been sentenced to crucifixion are taken down and buried before sunset. (*Jewish War* 4.317)

That is the theory, again from Deuteronomy 21:22–23, and it is useful to cite it against the Zealots. But in all those thousands of Roman crucifixions around Jerusalem in the first century, from the two thousand crucified by Varus in 4 B.C.E. through the thirty-six hundred crucified by Florus in 66 C.E. and on to the five hundred a day crucified by Titus in 70 C.E., Josephus never mentions anything about removal by sunset. He also tells us this personal anecdote:

> When I . . . saw many prisoners who had been crucified, and recognized
> three of my acquaintances among them, I was cut to the heart and came
> and told Titus with tears what I had seen. He gave orders immediately that
> they should be taken down and receive the most careful treatment. Two of
> them died in the physicians' hands; the third survived. (*Life* 420–21)

Once again, there is nothing about removal by sunset when actual practice rather than ideal law is being discussed.

A fifth and final step: Even if Deuteronomy 21:22–23 was ignored in
the Jewish homeland under, say, a governor like Pilate, insensitive to Jewish religious concerns, and a high priest like Caiaphas, sensitive to Roman
political concerns, there is one possibility left. The body of a crucified
person could be released to friends or relatives as an act of mercy. We have
explicit mention of that in a text from Philo. In his attack on A. Avillius
Flaccus, governor of Egypt, Philo mentions two ways that decent governors, as distinct from Flaccus, handle crucifixions on festal occasions.
They either postpone them, as seen in a text quoted earlier in discussing
Barabbas, or they allow burial:

> I have known cases when on the eve of a holiday of this kind [imperial
> birthdays], people who have been crucified have been taken down and
> their bodies delivered to their kinsfolk, because it was thought well to give
> them burial and allow them the ordinary rites. For it was meet that the
> dead also should have the advantage of some kind treatment upon the
> birthday of the emperor and also that the sanctity of the festival should be
> maintained. But Flaccus gave no orders to take down those who had died
> on the cross. (*Against Flaccus* 83)

Burial of crucifieds by their families is certainly possible. In fact, we now
have both material as well as textual evidence for this possibility.

In June of 1968 the only crucified skeleton ever discovered in the
Jewish homeland was found at Giv'at ha-Mivtar, just north of Jerusalem,
in a tomb dating from the first century but probably prior to the First
Roman War in 66–73/74 C.E. There were four tombs in all, carved like
small rooms into the soft limestone, each with an anteroom and then a
burial chamber whose niches were deep enough to take a human body
headfirst at burial. Such tombs were used over and over again for generations, because the bones, after decomposition of their flesh within the
niches, were buried together in pits dug in the floor or, as a much more
costly alternative, gathered together into ossuaries or limestone bone
boxes. The niches were then reused for more recent burials. In this complex there were fifteen such ossuaries, mostly packed to the top and containing the bones of thirty-five different individuals, eleven males, twelve

females, and twelve children. Of those thirty-five, one woman and her infant had died together in childbirth for lack of a midwife's help; three children, one of 6–8 months, one of 3–4 years, and another of 7–8 years, had died of starvation; and five individuals had met violent deaths: a female and a male by burning, a female by a macelike blow, a child of 3–4 years by an arrow wound, and a male of 24–28 years, 5 feet 5 inches in height, by crucifixion. His name, inscribed on the ossuary, was Yehochanan, and the box also contained another incomplete adult skeleton as well as that of Yehochanan's son, a child of 3–4 years. All of that reads like a rather sad commentary on the first century in Jerusalem, even before the great war with Rome.

After appraisal and reappraisal by scholars from Israel's Department of Antiquities and Jerusalem's Hebrew University Hadassah Medical School, the manner of crucifixion became clear (Zias and Sekeles). His arms were not nailed but tied to the bar of the cross, probably with hands to elbows over and behind it. His legs were on either side of the upright beam with separate nails holding the anklebone to the wood on each side. A small olive wood plaque was set between the nail's head and the heel bone lest the condemned man manage to tear his foot free from the nail. But the nail in the right heel struck a knot in the upright, and its point became bent so that when the man was taken down the nail, olive wood, and heel bone all remained fixed together in burial and discovery. Finally, there was no evidence that the man's legs were broken to speed his death by asphyxiation.

That discovery emphasizes two points. First, however it was managed, be it through bribery, mercy, or indifference, a crucified person could receive honorable burial in the family tomb in the early or middle first-century Jewish homeland. Second, with all those thousands of people crucified around Jerusalem in the first century alone, we have so far found only a single crucified skeleton, and that, of course, preserved in an ossuary. Was burial, then, the exception rather than the rule, the extraordinary rather than the ordinary case?

Hope Is Not History

The preceding section can only establish general parameters. From Roman practice one expects the crucified body to be left on the cross for carrion birds and beasts. Crucifixion sites, such as that of Golgotha in Jerusalem or of the Campus Esquilinus in Rome, with their permanent uprights awaiting victims who carried their own crossbars to the site, were grisly focuses for predators attracted by the smell of sweat and blood, urine and feces. The very place itself, with its flies, crows, and dogs, was an enduring warning against subversion from the lower classes. If, in the Jewish homeland, the law of Deuteronomy 21:22–23 was observed, burial by sunset was a merciful replacement for deliberate Roman non-burial. But I see in Josephus no evidence that it was observed in actual practice, and the Temple Scroll indicates the opposite. Essene law, extending the rules for dead to live crucifixion, decrees what they would do if they ran Jerusalem and thereby emphasizes what was not being done at that time. But, in both Roman and Jewish practice, there was always the possibility that relatives or friends would be allowed to take the body away and give it proper burial. And is that not exactly what happened in the case of Jesus? Yes. But was it hope or history? Roman expectation and Jewish exceptions become particular and precise in reading Christian texts. But was it hope or history?

From Fear to Hope

In my reconstruction, as you will recall from the prologue section "Dependent and Independent Passion Stories" and also can see in the appendix, the gospel of Peter contains what I term the Cross Gospel, which is more original than, independent from, and probably a source for the four canonical gospels. For Brown, the gospel of Peter is a digest from memory of Matthew, Luke, and John, along with some popular passion traditions from outside those gospels. This is another good place to test those hypotheses.

There are three texts in Peter concerned with the burial of Jesus, leaving aside for now any mention of the guards or women at the tomb. First, there is the most original one, from what I call the Cross Gospel:

> Now it was midday and a darkness covered all Judaea. And they became anxious and uneasy lest the sun had already set, since he was still alive. <For> it stands written for them: the sun should not set on one that has been put to death. And one of them said, "Give him to drink gall with vinegar." And they mixed it and gave him to drink. And they fulfilled all things and completed the measure of their sins on their head. And many went about with lamps, since they supposed that it was night, <and> they stumbled. And the Lord called out and cried, "My power, O power, thou hast forsaken me!" And having said this he was taken up. And at the same hour the veil of the temple in Jerusalem was rent in two. And then they

> drew the nails from the hands of the Lord and laid him on the earth. And
> the whole earth shook and there came a great fear. Then the sun shone
> (again), and it was found to be the ninth hour. (Peter 5:15–6:22)

I begin with that text which is, for me, from the *original stratum* of Peter
(see the appendix). It presumes that those who crucified Jesus are responsible, from Deuteronomy 21:22–23, for taking his body off the cross and
burying it before sunset. That is why, as seen earlier, the crucifiers hasten
his death by a poisoned drink. Thereafter, it is *they* who take Jesus' body
down from the cross and, from that text up to that point, one presumes
that *they* will bury it as well. The Cross Gospel, the original passion-resurrection story within Peter, takes it for granted that Jesus was crucified, removed from the cross, and buried by his enemies. Why? Explicitly,
because of obedience to Deuteronomy 21:22–23, a law of which they
were aware throughout the process and because of which the darkness
unnerved them. Is it night, and have we disobeyed the law?

Next comes a second but very different text. My working hypothesis
is that the original Cross Gospel story had to accommodate itself to the
increasing ascendancy of the canonical gospels after the middle of the
second century. Those versions told, in general, about a burial of Jesus, not
by his enemies, as in the Cross Gospel, but by his friends. Here is that
new text from what I term the canonical stratum in Peter:

> And the Jews rejoiced and gave his body to Joseph that he might bury it,
> since he had seen all the good that he [=Jesus] had done. And he took the
> Lord, washed him, wrapped him in linen and brought him into his own
> sepulchre, called Joseph's Garden. (Peter 6:23–24)

That text is a combination of canonical information that swiftly but
deftly summarizes an honorable burial for Jesus. It picks up the tomb as
Joseph's "own," found only in Matthew 27:60, and in a "garden," found
only in John 19:41. But it also makes explicit what none of the canonicals
mention, that Jesus' body was first washed. That is not independent tradition but is dependent on the canonical passion stories.

Finally, there is a third text. Imagine yourself now as the author who
has those two versions of Jesus' burial available. The older one is a presumed burial of Jesus by his enemies because of Deuteronomy 21:22–23.
The newer one is a burial by Joseph, presumably a friend, because "he
had seen all the good that he [=Jesus] had done." How do you reconcile
those twin burials and make them into one story? Here is how you do it:

> Now there stood there Joseph, the friend of Pilate and of the Lord, and
> knowing that they were about to crucify him he came to Pilate and begged

the body of the Lord for burial. And Pilate sent to Herod and begged his body. And Herod said, "Brother Pilate, even if no one had begged him, we should bury him, since the Sabbath is drawing on. For it stands written in the law: the sun should not set on one that has been put to death." (Peter 2:3–5a)

In terms of present narrative sequence that unit comes first in 2:3–5a, before any mention of burial by enemies in 5:15–6:22 or by friends in 6:23–24. It had to be placed very early in the narrative before the hearers or readers find out anything about a burial by enemies. So Joseph must now ask for the body even before the abuse and crucifixion. It is what I term a redactional preparation, a way of making certain in advance that the later burial by friends will be able to override the earlier burial by enemies. Furthermore, because Pilate oversees the crucifixion in the canonical versions but Herod does so in the Cross Gospel, that first text must integrate those divergent accounts. Hence, in that text, the story is Joseph to Pilate and Pilate to Herod: Joseph goes to Pilate, because Pilate is in charge in the canonicals, and Pilate goes to Herod, because Herod is in charge in the Cross Gospel. Finally, Herod repeats the allusion to Deuteronomy 21:22–23 from 5:15 in 2:5a.

From Peter, therefore, I take only that first text from the Cross Gospel's *original stratum* and emphasize what it presumes: that those who crucified Jesus would have buried him out of obedience to Deuteronomy 21:22–23. That does not seem to be based on any knowledge of what actually happened but is rather a hope for what surely must have happened. Jesus' companions had fled after his arrest and were not there to see what happened. Their ultimate terror was that he was left unburied. So the process of negating that awful possibility began. It began, as early as we can see it, with the crucifiers' burial of Jesus by sunset, according to Deuteronomy 21:22–23. It began with hope. But hope, for all its humanity, is not history.

From Hope to Hyperbole

In the canonical versions, from Mark through John, hope becomes fact; a possible burial by Jesus' unnamed enemies becomes an actual burial by his named friends, and a hurried or inadequate burial becomes a splendid and royal entombment. And, of course, there is no more mention of Deuteronomy 21:22–23. That was necessary only to explain why enemies might have buried Jesus; it is not needed to explain why friends would have done so. Enemies did it out of obedience to the law; friends did it out of love for Jesus.

THE MARKAN DILEMMA

Mark is the crucial text in this process. All that he had from previous tradition, as in the Cross Gospel within Peter, was a presumed burial of Jesus by his enemies. Here is his transformation of that hope into fact:

> When evening had come, and since it was the day of Preparation, that is, the day before the sabbath, Joseph of Arimathea, a respected member of the council, who was also himself waiting expectantly for the kingdom of God, went *boldly* to Pilate and asked for the body of Jesus. Then Pilate wondered if he were already dead; and summoning the centurion, he asked him whether he had been dead for some time. When he learned from the centurion that he was dead, he granted the body to Joseph. Then Joseph bought a linen cloth, and taking down the body, wrapped it in the linen cloth, and laid it in a tomb that had been hewn out of the rock. He then rolled a stone against the door of the tomb. (Mark 15:42–46, my italics)

I consider Joseph of Arimathea to be a total Markan creation in name, in place, and in function. Mark's problem is clear: those with power were against Jesus; those for him had no power. No power: not power to do, not power to request, not power to beg, not even power to bribe. What is needed is an in-between character, one somehow on the side of power and somehow on the side of Jesus. What is needed, in fact, is a never-never person. So, in 15:43, Joseph is both

(1) a respected member of the council
(2) waiting expectantly for the kingdom of God

Brown notes, for example, that Mark 15:43 is "an extremely convoluted sentence" (1213). It is also an extremely convoluted creation. Joseph is clearly, from that first sentence, a member of the council, or Sanhedrin, that had just, according to Mark 14:64 *"all* condemned him [Jesus] to death." But that second sentence is deliberately and necessarily ambiguous. Is he a disciple or not? Brown says no: "there is a possibility and even likelihood that Mark is not describing Joseph as a disciple of Jesus" (1216). I prefer to underline the ambiguity. Mark is trying to come as close as possible to having Joseph a disciple without actually saying it. He is caught with an impossible creation: one with access to power but still on the side of Jesus. That is why, while only hinting at discipleship, he still says that it took courage (note my italicized *boldly* in the quotation) to ask for Jesus' body.

Brown sees Joseph as a pious Sanhedrist who buries the crucified body not as a disciple of Jesus but as an observer of Deuteronomy 21:22–23. It is certainly possible that Deuteronomy is implicitly behind Mark's account, but all that is explicitly mentioned is that the next day was the Sabbath. The problem seems to be that the body not remain on the cross during the Sabbath. But one could, in any case, argue that Joseph was acting out of general respect for the dead. He would be like Tobit, in the fourth or third century B.C.E. novel of that same name:

> I was carried away captive to Assyria and came as a captive to Nineveh [722 B.C.E.]. . . . if I saw the dead body of any of my people thrown out behind the wall of Nineveh, I would bury it. I also buried any whom King Sennacherib put to death when he came fleeing from Judea in those days of judgment that the king of heaven executed upon him because of his blasphemies [701 B.C.E.]. For in his anger he put to death many Israelites; but I would secretly remove the bodies and bury them. So when Sennacherib looked for them he could not find them.
>
> So Tobias [son of Tobit] went to look for some poor person of our people. When he had returned he said, "Father!" And I replied, "Here I am, my child." Then he went on to say, "Look, father, one of our own people has been murdered and thrown into the market place, and now he lies there strangled." Then I sprang up, left the dinner before even tasting it, and removed the body from the square and laid it in one of the rooms until sunset when I might bury it. (Tobit 1:10, 17–18; 2:3–4)

There is one objection to all of that: *Joseph buries only Jesus and not the other two crucified bodies.* If he is a pious Sanhedrist, acting in accordance with Deuteronomy 21:22–23 or even a general respect for the dead, he will bury all three bodies. That would have solved Mark's dilemma; he would not have needed even the hint of Joseph's discipleship. But, of course, it would have raised an equally disturbing problem, the possibility of the three dead bodies being buried together and so somehow confused. Mark did his best with an impossible problem: those in power were against Jesus; those for him had no power. How could you invent a person *with* power (at least, access to Pilate) but *for* Jesus? He created Joseph as both Sanhedrist and almost-a-disciple of Jesus. Brown describes the long, later life of Joseph in Christian fiction (1233–34). His life, however, began in fiction and has flourished there brilliantly ever after.

THE OTHER SOLUTIONS

I am persuaded of my Markan reading by watching what the other three evangelists, Mark's first and most formidable critics, do with his story about Joseph. They see very clearly the dilemma of an even–that–much pro-Jesus Sanhedrist and rewrite accordingly. Here is Matthew's version (note the italicized additions):

> When it was evening, there came a *rich man* from Arimathea, named Joseph, who was also *a disciple of Jesus.* He went to Pilate and asked for the body of Jesus; then Pilate ordered it to be given to him. So Joseph took the body and wrapped it in a *clean* linen cloth and laid it in his *own new* tomb, which he had hewn in the rock. He then rolled a *great* stone to the door of the tomb and went away. (Matthew 27:57–60)

He solves the Markan dilemma by having Joseph rich but not a Sanhedrist, and then he can have him explicitly a disciple. He also improved Mark's shroud as being "clean" and Mark's tomb with two added items. It is now not only "rock-hewn," as in Mark, but it is Joseph's "own new" tomb and sealed with a "great" stone. Those last items probably emphasize the identity, security, and integrity of the body and burial of Jesus.

Luke sees the Markan dilemma just as clearly as Matthew does, but he solves it in a slightly different way, indeed in the obviously opposite way:

> Now there was a good and righteous man named Joseph, who, though a member of the council, *had not agreed to their plan and action.* He came from the Jewish town of Arimathea, and he was waiting expectantly for the kingdom of God. This man went to Pilate and asked for the body of Jesus. Then he took it down, wrapped it in a linen cloth, and laid it in a rock-hewn tomb *where no one had ever been laid.* It was the day of Preparation, and the sabbath was beginning. (23:50–54, my italics)

Luke stays very close to Mark but describes Joseph the Sanhedrist as having been against the condemnation and crucifixion of Jesus. That is but a different solution to the Sanhedrist/disciple problem. The tomb is also new in Luke. Matthew, Luke, and John all agree on this point, although it is not present in Mark. The newness answers an obvious problem: What if the body of Jesus got mixed up with other bodies in the tomb? That would raise questions like, How could you tell whether one was missing or not? What if somebody had come to visit those other bodies? Such glosses answered questions Christians would have had in their own minds even before they came from opponents as objections.

As has happened so often in the passion narrative, nobody can solve a problem as totally and absolutely as can John. From the cohort on the ground at the start to the last words on the cross, Jesus has been in serene control of events throughout John's story. So also here. No agony in the garden, no dereliction on the cross, and no inadequacy in the burial. There is no hurried or improper burial, as Nicodemus from John's own gospel comes to consummate the work of Joseph from the Synoptic versions:

> After these things, Joseph of Arimathea, *who was a disciple of Jesus, though a secret one because of his fear of the Jews,* asked Pilate to let him take away the body of Jesus. Pilate gave him permission; so *he came* and removed his body.
>
> Nicodemus, who had at first come to Jesus by night, *also came,* bringing a mixture of myrrh and aloes, weighing about a hundred pounds. They took the body of Jesus and wrapped it with the spices in linen cloths, according to the burial custom of the Jews. Now there was a garden in the place where he was crucified, and in the garden there was a new tomb in which no one had ever been laid. And so, because it was the Jewish day of Preparation, and the tomb was nearby, they laid Jesus there. (John 19:38–42, my italics)

That solves the Markan dilemma but in a characteristically Johannine fashion. John sees no problem even if Joseph were a Sanhedrist because he claims that there were secret disciples of Jesus even among the authorities:

> Many, even of the authorities, believed in him. But because of the Pharisees they did not confess it, for fear that they would be put out of the synagogue; for they loved human glory more than the glory that comes from God. (12:42–43)

He is a secret because fearful disciple, but now he has found courage to be open at last. The major Johannine change, however, is the presence of Nicodemus along with Joseph. Nicodemus also started as fearful in 3:2 since he came to Jesus "by night." But this interchange took place later concerning Jesus at the feast of Tabernacles in Jerusalem:

> Then the temple police went back to the chief priests and Pharisees, who asked them, "Why did you not arrest him?" The police answered, "Never has anyone spoken like this!" Then the Pharisees replied, "Surely you have not been deceived too, have you? Has any one of the authorities or of the Pharisees believed in him? But this crowd, which does not know the law—they are accursed." Nicodemus, who had gone to Jesus before, and who was one of them [presumably, one of the authorities?], asked, "Our law does not judge people without first giving them a hearing to find out what they are doing, does it?" They replied, "Surely you are not also from Galilee, are you? Search and you will see that no prophet is to arise from Galilee." (John 7:45–52)

John probably sees both Joseph and Nicodemus among those Jewish authorities who were secret because fearful disciples of Jesus but who now at last find the courage of their convictions and bury him properly.

Like that full cohort of six hundred soldiers coming out to arrest Jesus in John 18:2, 12 and ending up flat on the ground at his feet in John 18:6, that hundred pounds of myrrh and aloes in John 19:39 is deliberately intended as appropriate exaggeration. As Brown notes, "if powdered or fragmented spices are meant, such a weight would fill a considerable space in the tomb and smother the corpse in a mound" and "the likelihood [is] that John's 'myrrh and aloes' in 19:39 is not a reference to oil or ointment but to dry spices" (1260, 1263). John's purpose is to describe not just a royal or imperial burial but a transcendental or divine one. Jesus died and was buried as the Divine King in John's gospel.

Brown comments that "there is nothing implausible in John's scenario that there was a garden in the area north of Jerusalem where Jesus was crucified, and that he was buried in a tomb in that garden" (1270). That is absolutely correct: nothing implausible. Nothing historical either.

Names for the Nameless

The objection is obvious. We have Joseph's name. We even have his place, Arimathea, although we have no idea so far where it is. How can you say that Mark *created* a named and located person and that he progressed thence into Matthew, Luke, John, and the canonical stratum of Peter and on throughout Christian history? I recall an incident told by the famous Argentine author and parabler Jorge Luis Borges concerning his story about the Aleph, a fictional or mythical sphere containing all places on earth simultaneously. In his short story "The Aleph" he had located that object in a house on Garay Street in Buenos Aires:

> Once, in Madrid, a journalist asked me whether Buenos Aires actually possessed an Aleph. I nearly yielded to temptation and said yes, but a friend broke in and pointed out that were such an object to exist it would not only be the most famous thing in the world but would renew our whole conception of time, astronomy, mathematics, and space. "Ah," said the journalist, "so the entire thing is your own invention. I thought it was true because you gave the name of the street." I did not dare tell him that the naming of streets is not much of a feat." (Jorge Luis Borges, *The Aleph and Other Stories 1933–1969,* p. 190)

The naming of streets is not much of a feat. Neither is the naming of names. Publicly known persons, such as Pilate or Caiaphas, are real people, whether the words and deeds attributed to them are or are not historical. But does the naming of names such as "Barabbas" in Mark 15:7 or "Simon of Cyrene, the father of Alexander and Rufus," in Mark 15:21 or "Joseph of Arimathea" in Mark 15:43 preclude fictional creation not only of those names but of the actions and events associated with them?

The general early Christian tradition was to name those significant characters left nameless in the passion accounts: "Pilate's wife, the centurion stationed at the Cross, the two thieves who were crucified with Jesus, and the officer in charge of the soldiers guarding the sepulchre" (Metzger 79). But that process had even started within the New Testament itself. Mark 14:47, Matthew 26:47, and Luke 22:50 do not identify either the sword wielder or the person whose ear was severed in the garden of Gethsemane. But John 18:10 identifies them as Peter and Malchus. I take that to be Johannine creativity at work.

Names, of course, can also drop out as the tradition continues. Those sons of Simon of Cyrene, Alexander and Rufus, in Mark 15:21 disappear from Matthew 27:32 and Luke 23:26. And the name of the centurion Petronius in Peter 8:31 disappears from Mark 15:39, Matthew 27:54, and Luke 23:47. But, in general, names come in rather than drop out; names are created rather than lost. If, therefore, creative fiction adds names, could it not also create them in the process of creating the event itself? It is possible, of course, that those events and names came to Mark from historical memory, or that the events so came but he himself added the names. But those events concerning Barabbas, Simon, and Joseph are all so appropriately Markan that my own working hypothesis is more limited: he himself created both names and events. Or, in other words, if you create the events, why not create names as well?

The Guards at the Tomb

Another useful test case for the differences between Brown and myself concerning passion tradition is the account of the guards at the tomb. Recall from the section "Responsibility for Innocent Blood" in chapter 5 on the Execution that Brown finds Matthew and Peter using "vivid popular tales of the passion" (1118) that appear at a less developed stage in Matthew, in the 80s–90s of the first century, but at a more developed stage in Peter, in the first half of the second century (1335, 1345). He explains the story about the guards at Jesus' tomb within that framework but qualified as follows:

A consecutive story about the guard at the sepulcher came to Matt from the same collection of popular tradition that he tapped for previous additions he made to Mark's PN [passion narrative]. . . . I shall contend that the author of *GPet* drew not only on Matt but on an independent form of the guard-at-the-sepulcher story. (1287)

The author of *GPet* may well have known Matt's account of the guard (a judgment based on his use of Matthean vocabulary), but a plausible scenario is that he also knew a consecutive form of the story and gave preference to that. (1301 note 35)

The author of *GPet* had available two forms of the guard-at-the-sepulcher story, Matt's and another. (1307)

I give, in Table 9, those twin texts about the guards in Peter 8:28–33 and Matthew 27:62–88 in parallel columns, and I italicize words or expressions that are the same in Greek even if not in English translation. Read down each column to get the logic of its story and then read across the parallel elements to see similarities and differences.

First, the vocabulary is not very helpful in proving dependence one way or the other. There are seven or eight words the same verbatim in the Greek of that "Disciples" element, but that cannot establish dependence one way or the other. It probably indicates the response of Jewish opponents who, once Jesus' followers claimed resurrection, counterclaimed tomb robbery. It is the inevitable rebuttal: *the disciples came and stole the body.* But that verbatim similarity indicates the polemical background to this story: *we* say resurrection; *you* say tomb robbery; *we* say guards who lie; *your* move! And that sudden and unexpected mention of "Pharisees" at the start of both texts (but not thereafter) probably indicates the opponents involved when the guards at the tomb story was first composed.

Next, the sequence of elements is exactly the same in each case. It is too similar to be explained by general oral tradition or even memory from a common source. But that does not prove dependence one way or another between Peter and Matthew, as distinct, say, from their dependence on a common (written?) source.

Finally, there is the content of each story, and here there is one possible argument for the dependence of Matthew on Peter rather than of Peter on Matthew. In Peter, the *authorities* know that the *people* have repented of their participation in Jesus' crucifixion: see the "Background" element. Now focus on the "Three Days" element. In Peter they want to guard the tomb "for three days." Why? I agree here with Brown: "In the

Table 9

The Guards at the Tomb Story in Peter and Matthew

Elements	Peter 8:28–33	Matthew 27:62–66
Time		The next day, that is, after the day of Preparation,
Background	But the scribes and *Pharisees* and elders, *being assembled together* and hearing that all the people were murmuring and beating their breasts, saying, "If at his death these exceeding great signs have come to pass, behold how righteous he was!"	
Request	The elders were afraid and came to Pilate, entreating him and saying,	the chief priests and the Pharisees *gathered* before Pilate and said,
Three days	"Give us soldiers that we may watch his *sepulchre* for three days,	"Sir, we remember what that impostor said while he was still alive, 'After three days I will rise again.' Therefore command the *tomb* to be made secure until the third day;
Disciples	*lest his disciples come and steal him away*	*otherwise his disciples may go and steal him away,*
People	and the *people* suppose that he is risen from the *dead,*	and tell the *people,* 'He has been raised from the *dead,*'
Result	and do us harm."	and the last deception would be worse than the first."
Response	And Pilate gave them Petronius the centurion with soldiers to watch the *sepulchre.*	Pilate said to them, "You [can] have a guard of soldiers; go, make it as secure as you can."
Jewish authorities	And with them there came elders and scribes to the sepulchre.	
Stone, seal, & guards	And all who were there, together with the centurion and the soldiers, rolled thither a great stone and laid it against the entrance to the sepulchre and put on it seven seals, pitched a tent and kept watch.	So they went with the guard and made the *tomb* secure by sealing the stone.

GPet storyline the wish to safeguard the burial place 'for three days' (8:30) need imply only that after such a period the impostor would surely be dead" (1309 note 55). Recall, for example, the Lazarus story:

> After having heard that Lazarus was ill, he stayed two days longer in the place where he was. . . . When Jesus arrived, he found that Lazarus had already been in the tomb four days. (John 11:6, 17)

The point is that by four days Lazarus is securely, definitely, and absolutely dead and not somehow still alive inside the tomb and capable of resuscitation and removal. A similar point is made by the "three days" in Peter. By that time Jesus will be securely dead. The logic of their request is very important. If they were simply afraid of grave robbery, an empty tomb, and claims *from the disciples* of resurrection, they would have needed to guard the tomb for a much longer time. Such claims could have been made at any time, not just within three days. Three days establishes that the body is really and irrevocably a corpse so that the disciples cannot resuscitate Jesus and remove him. Thereafter, the people, finding an empty tomb and already repentant because of the "exceeding great signs" at Jesus' death, might believe *all by themselves and without any apostolic prompting* that Jesus was risen from the dead. Their plan, in other words, is to prevent resuscitation by the disciples from becoming interpreted as resurrection by the people.

Matthew, however, tells a very different story. The authorities know and quote Jesus' own prophecy that he would rise on the third day. That prophecy is made *to the disciples* thrice in Mark 8:31=Matthew 16:21; Mark 9:31=Matthew 17:22–23; and Mark 10:33–34=Matthew 20:18–19. But he also foretold it to the authorities in Matthew alone:

> Then some of the scribes and Pharisees said to him, "Teacher, we wish to see a sign from you." But he answered them, "An evil and adulterous generation asks for a sign, but no sign will be given to it except the sign of the prophet Jonah. For just as Jonah was three days and three nights in the belly of the sea monster, so for three days and three nights the Son of Man will be in the heart of the earth. (Matthew 12:38–40)

The authorities do not necessarily believe Jesus' prophecy, but they fear the disciples may fake a resurrection. A guard for three days now comes from Jesus' prophecy. Thereafter, no guard is necessary because Jesus will have been proved wrong. I find Matthew a development over Peter and not the reverse in that case. That seems to me more likely than Brown's postulate that Peter, having heard or read Matthew long before, remembered the three days but forgot its connection to Jesus' prophecy. Finally, of course, all traces of the Jewish people's repentance and the Jewish authorities' fear that they may do them harm is absent in the much more anti-Jewish (authorities *and* people) version of Matthew. All in all, therefore, not from vocabulary, not from sequence, but from content, Peter 8:28–33 is an earlier and less developed version of the guards at the tomb story than is Matthew 27:62–66. But behind Peter is not history remembered or even prophecy historicized. Behind the guards at the tomb, as earlier behind Pilate's innocence and Herod's guilt, lie apologetics and polemics along the line from Peter to Matthew. *Christians:* Jesus rose from the dead. *Opponents:* he did not, you stole his body. *Christians:* no we did not; you had guards at the tomb who know the truth, but you told them to lie.

The Women at the Tomb

The title of this section is put in deliberate parallelism with that of the last one because guards at the tomb and women at the tomb represent quite separate and somewhat contradictory traditions. The former narrative goes only from the *original stratum* (Cross Gospel) in Peter into Matthew. The latter goes from Mark into everyone else, Matthew, Luke, John, and the final or *canonical* stratum of Peter.

The Women in Mark

The women at the tomb are even more important than the guards because an argument for the event's historicity is often made as follows: no Christian would have created such a story unless it were true, for what value were women witnesses in a patriarchal world? But as with Peter's denials, women's spices must be watched very carefully in Mark. Here are his three separate texts:

(1) [*After the death.*] There were also women looking on from a distance; among them were Mary Magdalene, and Mary the mother of James the younger and of Joses, and Salome. These used to follow him and provided for him when he was in Galilee; and there were many other women who had come up with him to Jerusalem. (Mark 15:40–41)

(2) [*After the burial.*] Mary Magdalene and Mary the mother of Joses saw where the body was laid. (Mark 15:47)

(3) [*After the Sabbath.*] When the sabbath was over, Mary Magdalene, and Mary the mother of James, and Salome bought spices, so that they might go and anoint him. And very early on the first day of the week, when the sun had risen, they went to the tomb. They had been saying to one another, "Who will roll away the stone for us from the entrance to the tomb?" When they looked up, they saw that the stone, which was very large, had already been rolled back. As they entered the tomb, they saw a young man, dressed in a white robe, sitting on the right side; and they were alarmed. But he said to them, "Do not be alarmed; you are looking for Jesus of Nazareth, who was crucified. He has been raised; he is not here. Look, there is the place they laid him. But go, tell his disciples and Peter that he is going ahead of you to Galilee; there you will see him, just as he told you." So they went out and fled from the tomb, for terror and amazement had seized them; and they said nothing to anyone, for they were afraid. (Mark 16:1–8)

I have given up trying to imagine why Mark names the women so differently in each case and will ignore that here to concentrate on his reason for introducing them at all.

The intention of the *three* women in Mark 16:1–8 is to anoint Jesus' body. That purpose creates problems of narrative logic, so Mark must have needed it for some reason strong enough to override the problems it created. Why did they not anoint the body at burial? How did they expect to get into the tomb? Luke saw the former difficulty and solved it by saying they did not have enough time:

> The women who had come with him from Galilee followed, and they saw the tomb and how his body was laid. Then they returned, and prepared spices and ointments. On the sabbath they rested according to the commandment. (23:55–56)

Matthew saw both difficulties and simply said that the *two* women "went to see the tomb" in 24:1. He has nothing at all about anointing the body. John 20:1 is even more laconic; *one* woman "came to the tomb" in 20:1 although "we" is used in 20:2. The women seem to be gradually disappearing, from three to two to one. So, if Mark himself created this story about the women at the tomb, he created one with obvious difficulties built into it. Why was anointing so important for Mark?

You will recall that Mark is severely and consistently critical of the three main named disciples, Peter, James, and John. That is a profoundly and peculiarly Markan theme that runs throughout his gospel: those closest to Jesus fail him most profoundly. That theme has been interpreted as Markan criticism of other Christian communities less emphatic than his about the suffering destiny of Jesus, less enthusiastic than his for the mission to the pagans, and especially more dependent than his on traditions about Peter, the Three, and the Twelve for their theological viewpoints. It has also been interpreted as Markan consolation for those in his own community who have failed Jesus in recent persecutions attendant on the First Roman War of 66–73/74 C.E. and who need to be told that, as with Peter, the Three, and the Twelve, failure is not final, flight and even denial are not hopeless. So now at the end of the passion, we have another failure, but from three named women, Mary of Magdala on the Sea of Galilee, Mary the mother of James the Younger and Joses, and Salome.

Mark has closed a series of compositional frames with the empty tomb story in 16:1–8. I give the three main ones in summary outline, in Figure 6, before discussing them in more detail.

The innermost frames are between the agony in 14:32–42 and the tomb in 16:1–8. Three named male disciples at the start of the passion story and three named female disciples at the end of the passion story fail Jesus rather strikingly. The outermost frames are between 10:32–34 and both 15:40–41 (the first mention of the women in the texts above) and 16:1–8. Recall this text, which we have seen before:

> They were on the road, going up to Jerusalem, and Jesus was *walking ahead of them;* they were *amazed,* and those who followed were *afraid.* He took the twelve aside again and began to tell them what was to happen to him, saying, "See, we are going up to Jerusalem, and the Son of Man will be handed over to the chief priests and the scribes, and they will condemn him to death; then they will hand him over to the Gentiles; they will mock

Figure 6

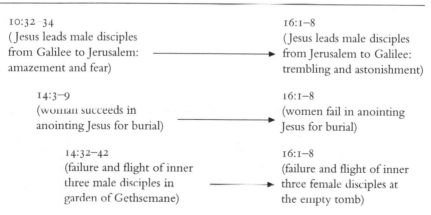

10:32–34	16:1–8
(Jesus leads male disciples from Galilee to Jerusalem: amazement and fear)	(Jesus leads male disciples from Jerusalem to Galilee: trembling and astonishment)
14:3–9	16:1–8
(woman succeeds in anointing Jesus for burial)	(women fail in anointing Jesus for burial)
14:32–42	16:1–8
(failure and flight of inner three male disciples in garden of Gethsemane)	(failure and flight of inner three female disciples at the empty tomb)

him, and spit upon him, and flog him, and kill him; and after three days he will rise again." (Mark 10:32–34, my italics)

Jesus is "leading" the male disciples up to Jerusalem, and their response is amazement and fear. What amazes and terrifies them is clear in the following verses, which give the last and most detailed of Mark's three passion predictions. But now in 14:40–41 we find (for the first time) that, just like the Twelve, there were female followers who came with Jesus from Galilee to Jerusalem, and just as Peter, James, and John are singled out among the Twelve for special roles and failures, so Mary of Magdala, Mary the mother of James and Joses, and Salome are singled out from among the women for a special role and a special failure. In the tomb they are amazed in 16:5. They are to tell "his disciples and Peter that he is *going before* you to Galilee." That is the same Greek verb from 10:32 for *walking ahead,* and it means, for Mark, that, just as Jesus led them from Galilee to Jerusalem, so now he leads them back from Jerusalem to Galilee. The result from the females in 16:8, as for the males in 10:32, is "trembling and astonishment." For Mark, then, Jesus' male and female disciples, and especially the inner three of each group, finish the passion story in flight, fear, and silence. They are afraid of Jerusalem because it is the place of suffering. They are afraid of Galilee because it is the place of pagan mission. And, says Mark, the message to leave Jerusalem (the Jewish mission) for Galilee (the pagan mission) was never delivered or received by those claiming to follow Peter and the disciples.

Male and female followers of Jesus are important for Mark, and the inner three from each group are especially important for him. But they are important as models of failure, not hopeless failure, but failure nonetheless. That explains why Mark created the empty tomb story, just as he created the sleeping disciples in Gethsemane. But what about the anointing? Why not leave it more simply as coming to visit the tomb? Why create that special problem, seen clearly by the other canonical writers who followed him on the story, but not on that purpose? These questions bring up those middle frames of 14:3–9 and 16:1–8. Here is that former text:

> While he was at Bethany in the house of Simon the leper, as he sat at the table, a woman came with an alabaster jar of very costly ointment of nard, and she broke open the jar and poured the ointment on his head. But some were there who said to one another in anger, "Why was the ointment wasted in this way? For this ointment could have been sold for more than three hundred denarii, and the money given to the poor." And they

scolded her. But Jesus said, "Let her alone; why do you trouble her? She has performed a good service for me. For you always have the poor with you, and you can show kindness to them whenever you wish; but you will not always have me. She has done what she could; she has anointed my body beforehand for its burial. Truly I tell you, wherever the good news is proclaimed in the whole world, what she has done will be told in remembrance of her." (Mark 14:3–9)

Think about women and anointings for burial. In Mark's story Jesus had told the disciples three times and very clearly that he would be executed in Jerusalem and that he would rise after three days. If one believed those prophecies, to come with ointments is certainly an act of love but hardly of faith. It is, for Mark, a failure in belief. But before he tells of that failure by named women in 16:1–8, he tells the above story of stunning faith. This unnamed woman believes Jesus and knows that, if she does not anoint him for burial now, she will never be able to do it later. That is why she gets that astonishing statement of praise, one unparalleled in the entire gospel: "wherever the good news is proclaimed in the whole world, what she has done will be told in remembrance of her." That accolade is given because, in Mark's gospel, this is the first complete and unequivocal act of faith in Jesus' suffering and rising destiny. It is the only such full act before that of the equally unnamed centurion beneath the cross in 14:39b: "Truly this man was God's Son!"

All that literary composition and theological density explain why the anointing women are so important for Mark and why his empty tomb story is so peculiarly his own. I know of no evidence of that story outside Markan dependence, not in Matthew, Luke, John, or the canonical stratum in Peter, so I conclude that it is a Markan creation, ending his gospel as he wanted it to end, in the ambiguity, for named male and female disciples, of hopeful failure. The hope is in the unnamed woman and the unnamed centurion and especially in the gospel whose author is likewise unnamed.

The Women After Mark

My working hypothesis is that the *original stratum* or Cross Gospel in Peter had only the guards at the tomb and nothing whatsoever about the women at the tomb. It was Mark himself who created the empty tomb story and its failed anointing as a fitting climax to the literary and theological motifs of his gospel. The three women are, however, as real as are the three men, and the very fact that Mark singles out *both* groups for criticism tells me of their importance in those Christian communities to which Mark's gospel offers both correction and hope. I conclude with two examples of how other writers, dependent on Mark, handled his story about the women.

From John, as usual, one expects maximum creativity. I leave for the next chapter any discussion of his empty tomb story, where, finally, we move from guards through women to apostles at the tomb. For now, I look at how he replaced that first introduction of the women in Mark 15:40–41 with this:

> Standing near the cross of Jesus were his mother, and his mother's sister, Mary the wife of Clopas, and Mary Magdalene. When Jesus saw his mother and the disciple whom he loved standing beside her, he said to his mother, "Woman, here is your son." Then he said to the disciple, "Here is your mother." And from that hour the disciple took her into his own home.
> (John 19:25b–27)

There are again three (or four?) women, but now they stand not "looking on from afar" as in Mark but "by the cross." And Mary of Magdala is now in last, not first, place. But, most important, the Beloved Disciple is also at the cross. We last saw him as "the other disciple" with Peter in John 18:16. But, as Peter failed by his denials back then, so the Beloved Disciple confesses by his presence beneath the cross now. The scene is profoundly symbolic and has nothing to do with domestic living arrangements. Even granted that Jesus is, for John, in complete control of the passion and showing not the slightest signs of suffering, a discussion of literally domestic problems seems most unlikely. Jesus consigns his community and the Beloved Disciple to one another. Brown interprets this to mean that biological family and believing community have merged: "it brings the natural family (Jesus' mother) into the relationship of discipleship by making her the mother of the beloved disciple who takes her into his realm of discipleship" (1025). Possibly. But it is the Beloved Disciple, not Peter or even James, the brother of Jesus, who is thereby declared leader of the community left by Jesus at his death. There is a polemical edge to that scene that should not be removed. Finally, Brown is unable "to resolve further the questions of the preGospel antiquity of the picture of the mother and the disciple at the cross or its antiquity" (1018). He is, as always, right in an absolute sense. But in a relative world in which one is challenged to give one's best historical construction, I find that incident a total Johannine creation.

My second and last example of creativity on a Markan theme is from the canonical stratum of Peter. Recall that, for me, there was an attempt to add to the original Cross Gospel certain traditions from the canonical versions at the last stage of that writing's history. Thus to its original guards at the tomb there was added this unit on the women at the tomb:

> Early in the morning of the Lord's day Mary Magdalene, a woman disciple of the Lord—*for fear of the Jews, since (they) were inflamed with wrath, she had not done at the sepulchre what women are wont to do for those beloved of them who die*—took with her her women friends and came to the sepulchre where he was laid. *And they feared lest the Jews should see them, and said, "Although we could not weep and lament on that day when he was crucified, yet let us now do so at his sepulchre.* But who will roll away for us the stone also that is set on the entrance of the sepulchre, that we may go in and sit beside him and *do what is due?*—For the stone was great,—and we fear lest any one see us. *And if we cannot do so, let us at least put down at the entrance what we bring for a memorial to him and let us weep and lament until we have again gone home."* So they went and found the sepulchre opened. And they came near, stooped down and saw there a young man sitting in the midst of the sepulchre, comely and clothed with a brightly shining robe, who said to them, "Wherefore are ye come? Whom seek ye? Not him that was crucified? He is risen and gone. But if ye believe not, stoop this way and see the place where he lay, for he is not here. For he is risen and is gone thither whence he was sent." Then the women fled affrighted. (Peter 11:50–14:57, my italics)

That complex combines two sources. One is the standard Markan story from 16:1–8 (given in roman print above). Note, by the way, that "young man" is as surely and stylistically Markan as any words can ever be! It is explicit evidence that Peter is here dependent on Mark. The other is the twin motifs of fear of the Jews from John 19:38 and 20:9 as well as the weeping for Jesus from 20:11, 13, 15 (given in italic print above). That combination explains why there was something left for the women to do that they had not done.

I do not see any new or independent data there. It is primarily an apologetic explanation for why those who loved Jesus were unable to render proper last rites. By this time, of course, the very presence of the women, the empty tomb, and the announcement of Jesus' resurrection in a story where Jewish and Roman authorities as well as the hearers or readers have just seen it all happen before their eyes are, to put it mildly, irrelevant and anticlimactic.

In conclusion, what is the historicity of the burial account? From Roman expectations, the body of Jesus and of any others crucified with him would have been left on the cross as carrion for the crows and the dogs. From Jewish exceptions, would not Deuteronomy 21:22–23 have been followed? Maybe, but only the barest maybe. Josephus proclaims it in theory, but the Temple Scroll indicates to me that it was not followed in Hasmonean or Herodian Jerusalem. And I doubt it was followed in Jerusalem under the happy combination of Pilate and Caiaphas. But, even if it was, the soldiers who crucified Jesus would probably have done it, speedily and indifferently, in a necessarily shallow and mounded grave rather than a rock-hewn tomb. That would mean lime, at best, and the dogs again, at worst. One's humanity and decency cries out against that solution, but decency and humanity cannot change the facts, only the results, of history. I keep thinking of all those other thousands of Jews crucified around Jerusalem in that terrible first century from among whom we have found only one skeleton and one nail. I think I know what happened to their bodies, and I have no reason to think Jesus' body did not join them. As I read the Christian texts about Jesus' burial, from the Cross Gospel in Peter, through Mark, Matthew, Luke, and on into John, I find an utterly understandable movement from hope to hyperbole, from a *hopeful* burial by his enemies obeying Deuteronomy 21:22–23 in the Cross Gospel to a *factual* burial by a named Sanhedrist and quasi-disciple in Mark, and from a hurried or inadequate burial by disciples in Matthew to a magnificent and transcendental burial by disciples in John. The burial stories are not history remembered, but neither are they prophecy historicized. What prophecies were present to be historicized? The burial stories are hope and hyperbole expanded into apologetics and polemics. But hope is not always history, and neither is hyperbole. In this case, as so often before and after, horror is history.

CHAPTER SEVEN

Resurrection

According to the Scriptures

Brown's book *The Death of the Messiah* ends at the burial of Jesus and the guarding of his tomb. It does not contain a section on the finding of the empty tomb or the apparitions of the risen Jesus. He says, when asked if he will write a commentary entitled *The Resurrection of the Messiah,* that "emphatically . . . I have no such plans. I would rather explore that area 'face to face'" (1.xii). He is, on the most important level, profoundly correct that the resurrection is a matter of Christian faith and that the Easter or Paschal mystery is not susceptible to the same historical processes as is everything else from Crime and Arrest to Execution and Burial. Still, for three reasons, I could not end my historical reconstruction without facing the *historical* challenge of the resurrection *stories.*

Persecution and Vindication

My first reason is personal and autobiographical. Since the publication of my own books, *The Historical Jesus: The Life of a Mediterranean Jewish Peasant* in late 1991 and its popularization *Jesus: A Revolutionary Biography* in late 1993, I have had rather many interviews in newspapers and magazines as well as on radio and television. In almost every single case the questions were not only historical but theological; they concerned not only the life and death but also the resurrection of Jesus. I think those questioners were correct not to end the story with a sealed stone and a standing guard.

The next reason has to do with the gospel texts themselves. No gospel ends at the closed tomb and says, in effect, the rest is indescribable mystery and community faith. The story continues, the narrative persists, and there is not the slightest overt index warning us that we are now out of the normal space-time continuum. In the gospel of Peter, Jesus' enemies see the actual resurrection itself, but in all other gospels nobody sees the resurrection, and Jesus appears only to his followers. Still, it all seems to take place in standard time and space, in Jerusalem and Galilee, in upper room or on mountaintop. That requires commentary.

Finally, there is the most important reason of all. All those historicized prophecies mentioned previously came from texts containing both persecution and vindication; there was always a dualism of suffering and triumph. Three examples will suffice, with just the key verses noted:

> [*Persecution*] Why do the nations conspire, and the peoples plot in vain? The kings of the earth set themselves, and the rulers take counsel together, against the Lord and his anointed. . . .

> [*Vindication*] I will tell of the decree of the Lord: He said to me, "You are my son; today I have begotten you. Ask of me, and I will make the nations your heritage, and the ends of the earth your possession. You shall break them with a rod of iron, and dash them in pieces like a potter's vessel." (Psalm 2:1–2, 7–8)

> [*Persecution*] My God, my God, why have you forsaken me? . . . But I am a worm, and not human; scorned by others, and despised by the people. All who see me mock at me; they make mouths at me, they shake their heads; "Commit your cause to the Lord; let him deliver—let him rescue the one in whom he delights!" . . .

> [*Vindication*] I will tell of your name to my brothers and sisters; in the midst of the congregation I will praise you: You who fear the Lord, praise him! All you offspring of Jacob, glorify him; stand in awe of him, all you offspring of Israel! For he did not despise or abhor the affliction of the afflicted; he did not hide his face from me, but heard when I cried to him. (Psalm 22:1–8, 22–24)

> [*Persecution*] Insults have broken my heart, so that I am in despair. I looked for pity, but there was none; and for comforters, but I found none. They gave me poison for food, and for my thirst they gave me vinegar to drink. . . .

> [*Vindication*] I will praise the name of God with a song; I will magnify him with thanksgiving. This will please the Lord more than an ox or a bull with horns and hoofs. Let the oppressed see it and be glad; you who seek God, let your hearts revive. For the Lord hears the needy, and does not despise his own that are in bonds. (Psalm 69:20–21, 30–33)

The *texts* in passion prophecy actually looked to both persecution *and* vindication. So did the *types* used to foreshadow Jesus. David on the Mount of Olives as model for the Arrest was not just David betrayed but

David eventually victorious. And the scapegoat for the Abuse was but one of the twin goats on the Day of Atonement, one for the departure (persecution) and the other for the return of Jesus (vindication). Passion prophecy was always a persecution-vindication dyad. That helps better to understand what Paul said about the tradition he had received:

> that Christ died for our sins in accordance with the scriptures. . . .
> and that he was raised on the third day in accordance with the scriptures.
> (1 Corinthians 15:3–4)

There is no difficulty in finding many texts referred to by that first line, but what about the second one? The usual suggestion is this:

> Come, let us return to the Lord;
> > for it is he who has torn, and he will heal us;
> > he has struck down, and he will bind us up.
> After two days he will revive us;
> > on the third day he will raise us up,
> > that we may live before him.
> (Hosea 6:1–2)

That is certainly possible but that two days/three days parallelism, like the same two times/three times parallelism for cockcrow and Petrine denial, is a Hebrew poetic device. It simply means *very soon* and is scarcely enough to balance by itself all those many prophecies of persecution. Is this the only vindication prophecy that Paul had in mind? I find it more likely that every persecution prophecy brings with it a vindication one. The texts from the prophets or the psalms used by early Christianity for Jesus' passion tend always to combine both elements. Resurrection and parousia are specifications of vindication, but innocence vindicated is the heart of passion prophecy. That, more than anything else, demands that we continue the discussion beyond persecution into vindication. We cannot stop, even from a historical viewpoint, with a closed tomb. Josephus did not stop there: he spoke of an unbroken love. Tacitus did not stop there: he spoke of a spreading contagion. Neither passion prophecy nor passion narrative stopped there: they both spoke of innocence vindicated. Actually, Brown's *The Death of the Messiah* alone stops there. I intend to continue.

A Model for Innocence Vindicated

The texts of the prophetic passion were often very explicit about the suffering and persecution to be endured but vague and general about the deliverance and vindication to follow. What model of story or what genre of narrative would serve to bring passion prophecy as persecution and vindication into a single sequence? That means, for me, how did Peter do it? How did Peter in the 40s of the first century change many discrete passion prophecies into one single tale of vindicated innocence?

In the prologue section "Dependent and Independent Passion Stories," I mentioned the Q Gospel and the Gospel of Thomas as two different documents primarily interested in the *sayings* of Jesus as Wisdom speaking here on earth. The Q Gospel dates to the 50s; the Gospel of Thomas dates between the 50s and the 70s C.E. They are quite different in many respects, but they share a common store of Jesus' sayings and a general lack of interest in Jesus' deeds. That common store of sayings and that emphasis on Jesus as Wisdom's voice must date, therefore, at least from the 40s. It is, in other words, a very early stream of Christian tradition. And an interest in Jesus' sayings but not his deeds would seem to preclude any interest in the passion (surely a "deed") at such an early moment in Christian tradition. My argument, however, is that Wisdom, from the Old Testament tradition, lies behind both sayings collections and passion narratives.

One of the best known and most widely spread texts from the ancient Near Eastern world is a folktale told about a historical character, Ahiqar, a wise councillor at the court of the Assyrian king Esarhaddon in the early seventh century B.C.E. (Lindenberger 479–84). We touched on it earlier in comparing the death of the traitor Judas with that of the traitor Nadin. The text has two parts, a story of vindicated innocence and a collection of wise sayings integrated into it in various ways in different manuscripts. That combination is artificial: the twin units may have been composed separately and independently, or the story may have been composed to introduce the sayings. They appear in the sequence first story then sayings in the oldest extant manuscript, an Aramaic document from the Jewish colony at Elephantine in Lower Egypt discovered in 1907 and dated to the late fifth century B.C.E. But, most likely, the combined text was at least a hundred years old even by then.

In the story the aging scholar-minister Ahiqar persuades Esarhaddon to accept Ahiqar's nephew and adopted son Nadin as his replacement, but the ungrateful youth later accuses his uncle of plotting against the monarch. Ahiqar is condemned to death. He is spared only because the executioner owes him a favor, kills a slave surrogate in his stead, and takes him into hiding pending a more fortunate future. The story breaks off at this point in the oldest or Aramaic text, but the later versions record how Pharaoh challenges the Assyrian monarch to send him one wise enough to perform an impossible task and how Ahiqar is produced, accomplishes the task, and is restored to power while Nadin is punished. Innocence is vindicated, but here on earth in the presence of its humiliated enemies.

The hundred-or-so *sayings* that follow that *story* in the Elephantine papyrus include many with later parallels in the Jewish wisdom literature from the Old Testament. Here is one striking example of a hymn to Wisdom herself:

> From heaven the people are favored;
> Wisdom is of the gods.
> Indeed, she is precious to the gods;
> her kingdom is *et[er]nal.*
> She has been established by Shamyn
> yea, the Holy Lord has exalted her.
> (*Ahiqar,* saying 13; Lindenberger 499)

The mention of "gods" and of the Syrian god Baal Shamyn, the Lord of Heaven, remind us that this is pagan wisdom, or, better, that it is the common stock from which both polytheistic and monotheistic wisdom proceeded. The author of the present composite text also added in some *sayings* that link more particularly and explicitly with the *story,* for example:

> My distress is my own fault,
> before whom will I be found innocent?
> My own son spied out my house,
> [wh]at shall I say of strangers?
> He was a false witness against me;
> who, then, will declare me innocent?
> (*Ahiqar,* sayings 50–52; Lindenberger 504)

But how do we get from a pagan tradition of the seventh to sixth centuries B.C.E. to the gospel of Peter in the mid first century C.E.? Recall that our oldest Ahiqar text was discovered in a Jewish colony in Egypt. Not only was the text of Ahiqar read by Jews, the person of Ahiqar was adopted into Judaism. Recall Tobit, and his care to bury his fellow Jews executed and left unburied by Sennacherib, the king who preceded Esarhaddon of Assyria:

> I also buried any whom King Sennacherib put to death. . . . Then one of the Ninevites went and informed the king about me, that I was burying them; so I hid myself. . . . But not forty days passed before two of Sennacherib's sons killed him . . . and his son Esarhaddon reigned after him. He appointed Ahikar, the son of my brother Hanael, over all the accounts of his kingdom, and he had authority over the entire administration. Ahikar interceded for me, and I returned to Nineveh. Now Ahikar was

chief cupbearer, keeper of the signet, and in charge of administrations of the accounts under King Sennacherib of Assyria; so Esarhaddon reappointed him. He was my nephew and so a close relative. (Tobit 1:18–22)

Ahiqar is now a Jew, and just as he appears here at the beginning of Tobit, so he appears as well at its conclusion:

See, my son, what Nadab [Nadin, in the Elephantine papyrus] did to Ahikar who had reared him. Was he not, while still alive, brought down into the earth? For God repaid him to his face for this shameful treatment. Ahikar came out into the light, but Nadab went into the eternal darkness, because he tried to kill Ahikar. Because he gave alms, Ahikar escaped the fatal trap that Nadab had set for him, but Nadab fell into it himself, and was destroyed. (Tobit 14:10)

Tobit's connection to Ahiqar is not history but one folktale linked to another. Still, it indicates how a Jewish and monotheistic rather than a pagan and polytheistic Ahiqar would have been available in both Jewish and Christian circles by the first century C.E. It also indicates that anyone learned enough to think of the *sayings* of Jesus against a wisdom background could just as easily think of his passion against that same background. Ahiqar shows how a *collection of wise sayings* and a *story of vindicated innocence* belong to the same tradition.

The story of Ahiqar, with its sequential elements of Situation, Accusation, Condemnation, Deliverance, and Restoration, is the generic model for a whole set of stories about pious Jews wrongly accused but eventually vindicated, especially in a Diaspora setting and a court location. Usually the royal or imperial overlords are somewhat benign or neutral, and the genre details how the wrongfully accused one is vindicated against evil accusers in the sight of those authorities.

Here are several examples of such tales:

- Joseph is saved from Potiphar's wife in Genesis 37–50, dated from 650 to 425 B.C.E.
- Shadrach, Meshach, and Abednego are saved from the fiery furnace and Daniel is saved from the lion's den in the book of Daniel 3 and 6, dated from the third to early second centuries B.C.E.
- Esther, Mordechai, and other Jews are saved from Haman's plot in the book of Esther, dated from 150 to 100 B.C.E.
- Susanna is saved from the evil judges in the book of Susanna, dated from 95 to 80 B.C.E.
- Jews are saved from profanation of the Jerusalem Temple and persecution in Egypt in *3 Maccabees,* dated from 38 to 41 C.E.

In every one of those cases, the Deliverance is not after but before death, not in heaven but on earth. The pious and/or wise protagonists are all saved either by direct or indirect, implicit or explicit divine intervention. They, like Ahiqar, do not die at all. Their Restoration is here below in front of their discomfited enemies.

The Cross That Spoke

It is not surprising that, just as some in the early Christian wisdom tradition were interested in collecting Jesus' wise sayings, others were interested in Jesus' passion-resurrection modeled on those court tales of vindicated innocence. The former gave us the Q Gospel and the Gospel of Thomas. The latter gave us the Cross Gospel, the original stratum in Peter. Both stem from the same wisdom tradition. Neither is it surprising that, just as an unknown Jew composed the book known as 3 Maccabees with its anti-Egyptian and pro-Jewish overtones in the 40s C.E., so did an unknown Christian compose the Cross Gospel (now in Peter) with its anti-Jewish-authorities and pro-Roman-authorities stance at around the same time. Behind both compositions on the same generic model lies the shock of Caligula's statue and the relief of Caligula's assassination. But, of course, as we saw earlier, Herod Agrippa I was better news for Jews in general than for Christians in particular.

The Harrowing of Hell

As in all examples of the genre of vindicated innocence we have seen so far, the Restoration of Jesus in the Cross Gospel takes place here below in front of the enemies who Condemned him. The Cross Gospel had three acts (appendix):

Act I: Trial, Abuse, and Crucifixion (1:1–2; 2:5b–6:22)
Act II: Fear, Guards, and Tomb (7:25: 8:28–9:34)
Act III: Resurrection, Confession, and Deceit (9:35–10:42; 11:45–49)

We have already seen Act I and the part concerning the posting of the guards from Act II. Return now to the sealed tomb, but remember, from 8:31–32, that the Jewish authorities stand watch there along with the Roman soldiers. Here is what happens next:

Now in the night in which the Lord's day dawned, when the soldiers, two by two in every watch, were keeping guard, there rang out a loud voice in heaven, and they saw the heavens opened and two men come down from there in a great brightness and draw nigh to the sepulchre. That stone which had been laid against the entrance to the sepulchre started of itself to roll and give way to the side, and the sepulchre was opened, and both the young men entered in. When now the soldiers saw this, *they awakened the centurion and the elders—for they also were there to assist at the watch.* And whilst they were relating what they had seen, they saw again three men come out from the sepulchre, and two of them sustaining the other and a cross following them, and the heads of the two reaching to heaven, but that of him who was led of them by the hand overpassing the heavens. And they heard a voice out of the heavens crying, "Hast thou preached to them that sleep?" and from the cross there was heard the answer, "Yea." (*Peter* 9:35–10:42, my italics)

In this version the Roman soldiers explicitly awake the Jewish authorities in time to witness the resurrection (my italics). This is a crucial point for the generic background of the Cross Gospel. Jesus' triumph must be displayed before his enemies here below on earth not just hereafter in heaven or at the parousia. But in order to have them see the resurrection, the author must describe it. He does so in two steps. First, Jesus appears as a transcendental figure greater even than the two angels who accompany him. They "sustain" him, a solemn procedure of eastern court protocol in which very high officials accompany their king with his arms resting on theirs. Naaman the Syrian mentions, in 4 Kings 5:18, how his king enters the temple of Rimmon "leaning on his arm" (thank you, Kathleen Corley). But the cross that spoke is even more interesting.

It evokes a serenely mythological but theologically profound belief from earliest Christianity often referred to as the harrowing of Hell. Jesus died and so descended into Sheol, the dark and dismal abode of the dead. But that prison house could not detain his divine being, and so he, at the head of all the righteous ones who had died before him, broke out from its confines together. That belief is barely visible in a few places in the New Testament, although it is still enshrined in the Apostles' Creed "he descended into Hell." One of its most beautiful expressions is in the Syriac *Odes of Solomon* from the late first or early second century C.E.:

Sheol saw me and was shattered
and Death ejected me and many with me. . . .

And those who had died ran toward me;
and cried out and said, "Son of God, have pity on us. . . .

And open for us the door
by which we may go forth to you,
for we perceive that our death does not approach you,

May we also be saved with you,
because you are our Savior."

Then I heard their voice,
and placed their faith in my heart,

And I placed my name upon their head,
because they are free and they are mine.
(*Odes of Solomon* 42:11–20; Charlesworth 2.771)

In the Cross Gospel, the transcendental figure of Jesus emerges from Sheol at the head of those whom death has imprisoned. They follow him in a giant crosslike procession. That, at least, is how I imagine the author's intention, not as depicting a walking, talking wooden cross. God addresses Jesus and asks: "Have you preached to them that sleep?" And the great cross-shaped procession answers God in the affirmative.

I do not think that theological vision is late but early and as religiously profound and spiritually beautiful as it is serenely mythological. (That story, by the way, had to arise among people who still wanted some/many/all dead Jews to arise with Jesus!). But it creates all sorts of problems, and I think that is why it was moved very soon to the periphery of Christian theology. Was everyone freed, or just the pious and righteous? Or were only the pious and righteous in Sheol? Did it involve pagans as well as Jews? Did they all have to become Christians first? If Jesus led them forth, then resurrection and ascension must have been immediate. But that left no time or opportunity for risen appearances or apostolic mandates. If there were such appearances, where were those risen ones during them? Those may seem like silly questions, but watch how Matthew gets himself in trouble retelling in fragmentary fashion that scene given more fully in Peter:

At that moment the curtain of the temple was torn in two, from top to bottom. The earth shook, and the rocks were split. The tombs also were opened, and many bodies of the saints who had fallen asleep were raised. After his resurrection they came out of the tombs and entered the holy city and appeared to many. (Matthew 27:51–53)

Matthew has "those that sleep" arise on Friday before Jesus, but they only appear on Sunday after Jesus. Unfortunately, rising at the head of the holy ones means that resurrection and ascension are immediate and simultaneous. There is no space or time for risen appearances or apostolic mandates. That, more than anything else, is probably what doomed the Cross Gospel.

The Report of the Guards

That magnificent resurrection scene is not the end of the story in the Cross Gospel. Because both Roman soldiers and Jewish authorities witness it together, they return to Pilate together:

> When those who were of the centurion's company saw this, they hastened by night to Pilate, abandoning the sepulchre which they were guarding, and reported everything they had seen, being full of disquietude and saying, "In truth he was the Son of God." Pilate answered and said, "I am clean from the blood of the Son of God, upon such a thing have you decided." Then all came to him, beseeching him and urgently calling upon him to command the centurion and the soldiers to tell no one what they had seen. "For it is better for us," they said, "to make ourselves guilty of the greatest sin before God than to fall into the hands of the people of the Jews and be stoned." Pilate therefore commanded the centurion and the soldiers to say nothing. (Peter 11:45–47)

The Jewish authorities now admit that Jesus is the Son of God and so does Pilate. But the former compound their crime by denying what they now know and persuade Pilate to order a cover-up. He asserts his innocence for Jesus' death but goes along with the cover-up. But, most important, those Jewish authorities admit that if they told the Jewish people the truth, the people would stone them. That phrase is absolutely determinative of the Cross Gospel's attitude toward Judaism: if only the Jewish authorities had told the Jewish people the truth!

There is nothing at all about disciples stealing the body of Jesus in that account, but it comes up again in the only canonical parallel to that story:

> While they were going, some of the guard went into the city and told the chief priests everything that had happened. After the priests had assembled with the elders, they devised a plan to give a large sum of money to the soldiers, telling them, "You must say, 'His disciples came by night and stole him away while we were asleep.' If this comes to the governor's ears, we will satisfy him and keep you out of trouble." So they took the money and did as they were directed. And this story is still told among the Jews to this day. (Matthew 28:11–15)

In the Cross Gospel the Jewish authorities are much more culpable, but their people are much less so. They have been deceived by their own leaders. But for Matthew, the Jewish authorities and the Jewish people are *equally* to blame. That explains every change in his story. He does not mind describing the authorities as culpable, but there will be no hint that the people are almost innocent. There will be no Jewish authorities present at the tomb, nor will any resurrection take place before their eyes. Hence there is nothing at all about them fearing their own people. And, because Pilate is not present to command Roman soldiers into silence, bribery and the promise of protection must suffice. Every difference in Matthew can be explained as a necessary result of not wanting to have the "people of the Jews" innocent through ignorance and deceived by their own authorities who actually know the truth.

Innocence Vindicated Hereafter

The model for the narrative genre of vindicated innocence seen earlier, from Ahiqar to 3 Maccabees, was always a restoration here below, a deliverance not *after and despite* but *before and from* death. The evil accusers had to see and accept that deliverance, and a royal or imperial setting acted somewhat like umpire in the entire process. That was the model used by the Cross Gospel in the original stratum of Peter.

Such stories were all very well in situations of social discrimination, but if more and more people were dying, they could seem like dangerous and unreal delusions. There was, therefore, a specific adaptation of the genre to situations of lethal persecution. The stories in Daniel 1–6, for example, were used as prelude to the apocalyptic revelations in Daniel 7–12 during the Jewish persecution by the Syrian monarch Antiochus IV Epiphanes between 167 and 164 B.C.E. But they were certainly not created in that lethal situation, where faithful Jewish martyrs were dying courageously rather than being miraculously saved from death like Daniel and his three companions. So, if they were to be saved, they could only be saved *after death*. Their vindication could come only in the *hereafter*. That is exactly how the generic story changes in 2 Maccabees, a book about that Syrian persecution composed between 100 and 75 B.C.E. A mother and seven sons are put to death for refusing to disobey God's law. They are not saved *before* death but repeatedly affirm that God will save them *after* death. They will be vindicated hereafter, and the king will be punished. Here are three of their dying speeches:

> You accursed wretch, you dismiss us from this present life, but the King of the universe will raise us up to an everlasting renewal of life, because we have died for his laws. . . .
>
> One cannot but choose to die at the hands of mortals and to cherish the hope God gives of being raised again by him. But for you there will be no resurrection to life! . . .

Because you have authority among mortals, though you also are mortal, you do what you please. But do not think that God has forsaken our people. Keep on, and see how his mighty power will torture you and your descendants! (2 Maccabees 7:9, 13, 16–17)

In situations of social discrimination, the *before* death model is persuasive. In situations of lethal persecution, only the *after* death model will work. It was, as far as possible, the before death or at least the here-below model that was used in the Cross Gospel. Jesus died, but that was simply to gain entrance to Sheol or Hades and release its captives. After that, he was vindicated at the mouth of the tomb before his accusers.

Mark and his community, as seen so often before, know all about lethal persecution, so that the Cross Gospel model is quite unacceptable to them. That is why Mark, although he knows the Cross Gospel narrative, resolutely avoids anything that reflects a here-below or before death deliverance for Jesus. That was not what happened to Jesus, because that was not what happened in Mark's recent community experience. It is only at the parousia or second coming of Jesus that he will be vindicated before his enemies for Mark. That is what he has Jesus tell the authorities at his Jewish trial:

"'You will see the Son of Man seated at the right hand of the Power,' and 'coming with the clouds of heaven.'" (Mark 14:62)

Mark wants nothing about risen apparitions here below and nothing about confessions of faith generated by them. Jesus is present to the Markan community only in the pain and suffering of absence, pending, of course, the imminent parousia. There can be no earthly apparitions or deliverances at the resurrection, because there were none for Mark's persecuted community. Between resurrection and parousia, there is only the suffering and dying Jesus present in the suffering and dying of his followers in the terrible situation of the First Roman War between 66 and 73/74 C.E. I give just two major examples of how Mark changes from a here-below vindication, as in the Cross Gospel, to a hereafter vindication, thereby adopting but adapting the classic model of vindicated innocence. In all of this, from Cross Gospel to Mark, we are following Jewish narrative models as, for example from above, with *3 Maccabees* for that former case but 2 Maccabees for that latter one.

The first point concerns the centurion at the cross. As you recall, the Jewish and Roman authorities both confess that Jesus is Son of God after and on account of that great risen apparition in the Cross Gospel of Peter. Not so for Mark:

> Now when the centurion, who stood facing him, saw that in this way he
> breathed his last, he said, "Truly this man was God's Son!" (Mark 15:39)

It is Jesus' death that brings the centurion to an act of Christian faith in
Mark's account. That is not, of course, history but symbol. It is the martyred death of Christians that brings their pagan executioners to faith, according to Mark. Both Matthew and Luke have difficulty with Mark's
text and change it:

> Now when the centurion and those with him, who were keeping watch
> over Jesus, saw the earthquake and what took place, they were terrified and
> said, "Truly this man was God's Son!" (Matthew 27:54)

> When the centurion saw what had taken place, he praised God and said,
> "Certainly this man was innocent." (Luke 23:47)

Matthew's centurion responds not so much to the death as the miracu-
lous events, intensified in this version, that accompany it. Luke has the
centurion respond to Jesus' death but with a declaration of Jesus' innocence rather than of Christian faith. But Mark means just what he says: it
is the martyred death that counts; it is that which brings pagans to faith.

The second point is even more important. Mark's gospel ends at 16:8
without any risen apparitions. That is true of no other gospel, and various
appropriate endings were added to Mark in the second century to rem-
edy that defect. For Mark, however, it was not defect but necessity. Jesus
had not appeared to deliver Mark's community under persecution, and
Mark believed that such interventions simply did not happen between
resurrection and parousia. Even to speak of them was dangerously misleading. So the transcendentally magnificent apparition from the Cross
Gospel was retrojected by Mark into the earlier life of Jesus and historicized as what we call the Transfiguration:

> Six days later, Jesus took with him Peter and James and John, and led them
> up a high mountain apart, by themselves. And he was transfigured before
> them, and his clothes became dazzling white, such as no one on earth
> could bleach them. And there appeared to them Elijah with Moses, who
> were talking with Jesus. Then Peter said to Jesus, "Rabbi, it is good for us
> to be here; let us make three dwellings, one for you, one for Moses, and
> one for Elijah." He did not know what to say, for they were terrified.
> Then a cloud over-shadowed them, and from the cloud there came a
> voice, "This is my Son, the Beloved; listen to him!" Suddenly when they
> looked around, they saw no one with them any more, but only Jesus.
> (Mark 9:2–8)

There are four main items from the original Cross Gospel apparition still residually evident in Mark 9:2–8, evident, that is, if one is willing to accept the basic idea that Mark transfigured his source as he relocated it. First, those "two men" whose accompaniment honors Jesus in Peter 10:39 become identified as "Elijah with Moses" in Mark. Next, the motif of height from Peter 10:40, "the heads of the two reaching to heaven, but that of him who was led of them by the hand overpassing the heavens," becomes, more simply, "and led them up to a high mountain" in Mark. Furthermore, the motif of light from Peter 9:36, the "great brightness," changes to "and his garments became glistening, intensely white, as no fuller on earth could bleach them." Finally, the "voice out of the heavens crying" in Peter 10:41 reappears as "a voice came from the cloud" in Mark. Mark, in summary, changes a risen apparition into a parousia foretaste but, more significantly, keeps it in the earthly not the risen life of Jesus. For Mark, there are and can be no risen apparitions pending the single, great, and imminent one of the parousia itself.

Apparition and Authority

In the *Cross Gospel,* the original stratum of Peter, the risen Jesus appears only to the inimical Jewish authorities and the relatively neutral Roman soldiers. That story follows the narrative model of the wise, pious, and innocent Jew attacked by evil accusers but eventually vindicated here on earth in the presence of a relatively benign imperial authority. None of that is, of course, history in the strict sense of what actually happened at one time in one place. It represents, however, in condensed dramatic presentation a Christian position that has high hopes for Roman accommodation and that blames the Jewish authorities for knowing the truth and hiding it from their own people lest they be destroyed by them for what they had done. It represents, in other words, a moment in the Christian 40s when failure had not yet turned Christians against both Jewish authorities and Jewish people (Matthew) or, more simply, against the Jews (John). But, if the risen apparition in the Cross Gospel is about *vindication* outside the Christian community, almost all the stories in the canonical gospels are about *authority* inside it.

Last of All to Me

During the winter of 53 or 54 C.E., that is, from twenty to forty years before the New Testament gospels gave us their last chapters, Paul wrote this to the Christian community at Corinth:

I handed on to you as of first importance what I in turn had received: that Christ died for our sins in accordance with the scriptures, and that he was buried, and that he was raised on the third day in accordance with the scriptures,

> and that he *appeared* to Cephas [Simon Peter],
> > then to the twelve.
> > > Then he *appeared* to more than five hundred brothers and sisters at one time, most of whom are still alive, though some have died.
> > Then he *appeared* to James,
> > > then to all the apostles.

Last of all, as to one untimely born, he *appeared* also to me. For I am the least of the apostles, unfit to be called an apostle, because I persecuted the church of God. But by the grace of God I am what I am, and his grace toward me has not been in vain. On the contrary, I worked harder than any of them—though it was not I, but the grace of God that is with me. Whether then it was I or they, so we proclaim and so you have come to believe. (1 Corinthians 15:3b–11, my italics)

What I emphasize from that text and the others to be seen in this section is their profoundly political implications. They are not primarily interested in trance, ecstasy, apparition, or revelation but in authority, power, leadership, and priority.

The thrust of that description is not just to emphasize the risen apparitions of Jesus but to insist that Paul himself is an *apostle,* that is, one specifically called and designated by God and Jesus to take a leadership role in the early church. There are three significant elements.

There is, first of all, that balance of Cephas and the Twelve as against James and the Apostles. Normally one thinks of the Twelve Apostles, with Peter mentioned always in first place. For certain Christian groups the Twelve Apostles represented in microcosm the New Testament just as the Twelve Patriarchs represented the Old Testament. But here the Twelve seem distinct from the Apostles. They have to be distinct else Paul himself cannot be an apostle. He cannot be one of the Twelve. That is why he mentions "to all the apostles" just before mentioning himself as "the least of the apostles." He cannot claim to be one of the Twelve but can and does claim to be an *apostle,* one *sent* (that is what the Greek term means) by God and Jesus. And despite the admission of belatedness at the end, as well as the insistence on divine grace, that final sentence puts it bluntly: there is *I,* and there are *they,* but we are all apostles, *I* am *their* equal.

There is a second element dependent on that first one. Paul is very interested in equating his own experience of the risen Jesus with that of all others before him. Hence he always uses that same expression, *appeared* or *was revealed to* (a literal and better translation of the Greek expression) for all instances. There can be no doubt that Paul's own experience involved trance, that altered state of consciousness well known from all the world's religions. Luke gives three accounts of Paul's initial revelatory experience, but they all agree on its ecstatic character:

> Now as he was going along and approaching Damascus, suddenly a light from heaven flashed around him. He fell to the ground and heard a voice saying to him, "Saul, Saul, why do you persecute me?" (Acts 9:3–4 = 22:6–7 = 26:13–14)

When Paul himself describes that same experience in Galatians 1:16 he simply calls it a "revelation," but it is possible that he is also referring to it in this text:

> I know a person in Christ [i.e., Paul himself] who fourteen years ago was caught up to the third heaven—whether in the body or out of the body I do not know; God knows. And I know that such a person—whether in the body or out of the body I do not know; God knows—was caught up into Paradise and heard things that are not to be told, that no mortal is permitted to repeat. (2 Corinthians 12:2–3)

Paul was a persecutor of Christianity before he was called to become its apostle to the pagans. He knew enough about this new Jewish sect to oppose it deeply, and the result of his entranced experience was not just to stop persecution, not just to become a Christian, not just to become a missionary, but to become the missionary of the pagans. I suspect that it was their opening of Judaism to paganism and their willingness to abandon any ritual tradition standing in their way that had caused his initial persecution of Christianity, and it was precisely what he had persecuted them for that he now accepted as his destiny. Paul needs, in 1 Corinthians 15:1–11, to equate his own experience with that of the preceding apostles—to equate, that is, its validity and legitimacy but not necessarily its mode or manner. Jesus *was revealed* to all of them, but Paul's own entranced revelation should not be presumed to be the model for all others. The point is, we are all alike apostles.

Finally, in Paul's account of those apparitions or revelations there are three types of recipients. There is only one general community, those five hundred brethren. There are two different leadership groups, the Twelve and the Apostles. There are three specific leaders: Peter, James, and Paul himself. I use those categories of general community, leadership group, and specific leader to understand the risen apparitions in the last chapters of the canonical gospels. Watch the movement in what follows from general community to leadership group and from leadership group to this or that specific leader.

From General Community to Leadership Group

As you recall from the prologue section "Dependent and Independent Passion Stories," what we call the Gospel of Luke and the Acts of the Apostles are but two volumes of the single integrated gospel of Luke. But there is an overlap concerning Jesus' risen apparitions at the end of the first volume and the start of the second one. There must also have been some time between their composition because they have significant differences. As I discuss those differences, watch how the emphasis shifts from general community to leadership group.

First, with regard to general community, here is what happens as two Christians leave Jerusalem on Easter Sunday. They are sad and dejected about the execution of Jesus and the failure of their hopes:

> Now on that same day two of them were going to a village called Emmaus, about seven miles from Jerusalem, and talking with each other about all these things that had happened. While they were talking and discussing, Jesus himself came near and went with them, but their eyes were kept from recognizing him. . . .
>
> Then beginning with Moses and all the prophets, he interpreted to them the things about himself in all the scriptures. As they came near the village to which they were going, he walked ahead as if he were going on. But they urged him strongly, saying, "Stay with us, because it is almost evening and the day is now nearly over." So he went in to stay with them. When he was at the table with them, he took bread, blessed and broke it, and gave it to them. Then their eyes were opened, and they recognized him; and he vanished from their sight. They said to each other, "Were not our hearts burning within us while he was talking to us on the road, while he was opening the scriptures to us?" That same hour they got up and returned to Jerusalem; and they found the eleven and their companions gathered together. . . .
>
> While they were talking about this [Emmaus experience], Jesus himself stood among them and said to them, "Peace be with you." (Luke 24:13–16, 27–33, 36)

We are dealing in that text with a *general community*. The two disciples (one male, one female?) leave Jerusalem in sadness and dejection but return there in joy and gladness. The presence and empowerment of Jesus remain in the community as it studies the scriptures *about* him and shares a meal together *with* him. This is not trance but exegesis, not ecstasy but Eucharist. Those two "missionaries" return to "the eleven and their companions." When Jesus appears again and immediately, it is therefore to this general group and not just to an inner Eleven (Judas is gone) alone. And everything else that happens in the rest of Luke 24, up to and including Jesus' ascension into heaven, happens to that *general community*. The general apostolic mandate is given to the community at large, and they all observe Jesus' ascension into heaven. Even though the Eleven are specifically mentioned, they are not exclusively singled out as the only ones to receive authority or to see that ascension.

Next, with regard to the leadership group, watch how that is all rephrased as Luke tells it a second time, but later at the start of the Acts of the Apostles:

> In the first book [Luke's gospel], Theophilus, I wrote about all that Jesus did and taught from the beginning until the day when he was taken up to heaven, after giving instructions through the Holy Spirit *to the apostles whom he had chosen*. After his suffering he presented himself alive to them by many convincing proofs, appearing to *them* during forty days and speaking about the kingdom of God. While staying with *them,* he ordered *them* not to leave Jerusalem, but to wait there for the promise of the Father. . . .
>
> "You will receive power when the Holy Spirit has come upon you; and you will be my witnesses in Jerusalem, in all Judea and Samaria, and to the ends of the earth." . . .
>
> Then *they* returned to Jerusalem from the mount called Olivet, which is near Jerusalem, a sabbath day's journey away. When *they* had entered the city, they went to the room upstairs where they were staying, Peter, and John, and James, and Andrew, Philip and Thomas, Bartholomew and Matthew, James son of Alphaeus, and Simon the Zealot, and Judas son of James. *All these* were constantly devoting themselves to prayer, *together with* certain women, including Mary the mother of Jesus, as well as his brothers. (Acts 1:1–4, 8, 12–14, my italics)

The risen Jesus now talks *only* to the Apostles. They and they alone receive apostolic authority and observe the ascension into heaven. The Eleven are clearly distinguished from all others, including the women. Finally, in Acts 1:21, the Eleven are restored to Twelve Apostles by a choice among the *males* who had been with Jesus from the beginning of his public life.

We have moved, even in Luke's twin volumes, from an emphasis on general community, even with the Eleven clearly present, to an emphasis on the Eleven or Twelve as a special leadership group. Risen apparition is not just a matter of *from* whom but *to* whom. It confers authority.

From Leadership Group to Specific Leader

In Luke 24 the general community was primarily to the forefront, even though the Eleven were also mentioned. But a specific leader, Simon Peter, was also evident at two points. This is what happens as soon as the women return to report about the empty tomb:

> But Peter got up and ran to the tomb; stooping and looking in, he saw the linen cloths by themselves; then he went home, amazed at what had happened. (Luke 24:12)

This is what happens as soon as the two return from Emmaus to report about Jesus' apparition to them:

> That same hour they got up and returned to Jerusalem; and they found the eleven and their companions gathered together. They were saying, "The Lord has risen indeed, and he has appeared to Simon!" Then they told what had happened on the road, and how he had been made known to them in the breaking of the bread. (Luke 24:33–35)

That awkward and intrusive central sentence tells about Peter before they get to tell about themselves. But suppose that you belonged to another Christian community or tradition, that you knew full well that emphasis on the leadership of Peter, but that you wished to oppose it in favor of your own specific leader. How do you do that? Here is how John does it in favor, as you would expect, of the unnamed Beloved Disciple, after Mary Magdalene reports about the empty tomb:

> Peter and the other disciple set out and went toward the tomb. The two were running together, but the other disciple outran Peter and *reached* the tomb first. He bent down to *look in* and saw the linen wrappings lying there, but he did not go in. Then Simon Peter came, following him, and *went into* the tomb. He saw the linen wrappings lying there, and the cloth that had been on Jesus' head, not lying with the linen wrappings but rolled up in a place by itself. Then the other disciple, who reached the tomb first, also went in, and he saw and *believed*. (John 20:3–8, my italics)

The race to the tomb has become a duel over authority. The Beloved Disciple gets there first and looks in first. Peter gets to go in first, because a text like Luke 24:12 demands it. But the Beloved Disciple believes. John does not say that Peter does not believe, or that he does believe, but he asserts quite explicitly that the Beloved Disciple did.

How could those who preferred Petrine leadership counteract that story? Scholars consider John 21 to have been added as an appendix to an already completed John 20. But it is also an appendix that elevates Peter over the Beloved Disciple, point counterpoint:

> When they had gone ashore, they saw a charcoal fire there, with fish on it, and bread. . . . When they had finished breakfast, Jesus said to Simon Peter, "Simon son of John, do you love me more than these?" He said to him, "Yes, Lord; you know that I love you." Jesus said to him, "Feed my lambs." A second time he said to him, "Simon son of John, do you love me?" He said to him, "Yes, Lord; you know that I love you." Jesus said to him, "Tend my sheep." He said to him the third time, "Simon son of John, do you love me?" Peter felt hurt because he said to him the third time, "Do you love me?" And he said to him, "Lord, you know everything; you know that I love you." Jesus said to him, "Feed my sheep." (John 21:9, 15–17)

Earlier, Peter had denied Jesus thrice at a "charcoal fire" in John 18:15–18, 25–27. Here, again at a "charcoal fire," he affirms him thrice. The triple affirmation is obviously artificial, as there are only two categories (lambs, sheep) to be emphasized. But Peter is clearly and explicitly exalted above the other apostles and placed in charge of both general community (lambs) and leadership group (sheep).

The Mystery of Easter

Those preceding sections are only paradigmatic examples from Luke and John, but they are quite adequate to make my point. The risen apparitions in the gospels have nothing whatsoever to do with ecstatic experiences or entranced revelations. Those are found in all the world's religions, and there may well have been many of them in earliest Christianity. But that is not what is being described in those last chapters of the gospels. It is questions of authority that are under discussion there. Is there a leadership group in the community? Is there to be someone in charge of community and group? What type of person is it to be? Who is it to be? The answers come from what the risen Jesus says and especially to whom the risen Jesus speaks.

But then, I am asked again and again, how do you explain what happened at Easter? Was it not those specific apparitions on Easter Sunday that restored their faith? Without them would not everything have ended there and then? I give you, once more and in full, those texts from Josephus and Tacitus in my prologue:

> About this time there lived Jesus, a wise man. . . . For he was one who wrought surprising feats and was a teacher of such people as accept the truth gladly. He won over many Jews and many of the Greeks. . . . When Pilate, upon hearing him accused by men of the highest standing amongst us, had condemned him to be crucified, those who had in the first place

come to love him did not give up their affection for him. . . . And the tribe of the Christians, so called after him, has still to this day not disappeared. (Josephus, *Jewish Antiquities* 18.63)

Christus, the founder of the name, had undergone the death penalty in the reign of Tiberius, by sentence of the procurator Pontius Pilatus, and the pernicious superstition was checked for the moment, only to break out once more, not merely in Judaea, the home of the disease, but in the capital itself, where all things horrible or shameful in the world collect and find a vogue. (Tacitus, *Annals* 15.44)

Three points: There was a movement. The authorities executed the founder. But the movement continued and spread. Those three points are history. I do not find anything historical in the finding of the empty tomb, which was most likely created by Mark himself—at least I cannot find it anywhere except under his influence. The risen apparitions are not historical events in the sense of trances or ecstasies, except in the case of Paul. Josephus's *unbroken love* or Tacitus's *spreading contagion* are explanations, but neither of them explains why this love holds or this contagion spreads where others did not. I see one other important historical item that needs to be added.

The Kingdom movement was an empowering rather than a dominating one. The historical Jesus did not send others out to speak about himself or bring others to him. He told them they could do just what he was doing. They could heal one another, share their food together, and thereby bring the Kingdom into their midst. The God of that Kingdom was one who empowered people, unlike Caesar, whose kingdom dominated people. The Kingdom movement, in other words, was not the Jesus movement, and to remove Jesus was not to remove the Kingdom. When he was executed, those with him lost their nerve and fled. They did not lose their faith and quit. What they found, even after his execution, was that the empowering Kingdom was still present, was still operative, was still there. Furthermore, and however one expressed it, Jesus' presence was still experienced as empowerment, not only by those who had known him before, but by others hearing about him now for the first time. Easter faith is no more or less a mystery than any other faith, but it did not start on Easter Sunday. It started among those first followers of Jesus in Lower Galilee long before his death, and precisely because it was faith as empowerment rather than faith as domination, it could survive and, in fact, negate the execution of Jesus himself. It is absolutely insulting to those first Christians to imagine either that faith started on Easter Sunday through apparition or that, having been temporarily lost, it was restored by trance and ecstasy that same Sunday. An empty tomb or a risen body susceptible to food and touch were dramatic ways of expressing that faith. Trances or ecstasies were dramatic ways of experiencing that faith. Risen appearances, as in the last chapters of the gospels, were dramatic ways of organizing and managing that faith. But Christian faith itself was the experience of Jesus' continued empowering presence, however one expressed that, however one explained that, and however one defended that in public discourse. It was the continued presence of absolutely the same Jesus in an absolutely different mode of existence.

History and Faith

Autobiographical Presuppositions

The questions or objections put to me after public lectures or on radio call-in shows are usually theological rather than historical, usually personal and autobiographical rather than methodological and theoretical, usually more about faith than about fact. This epilogue looks at a few of those basic questions so you can assess where my own presuppositions and prejudices, my own life experiences and situations may have influenced my historical reconstruction for better or for worse. By presupposition, I do not mean that I had all these ideas before I began my work. They have developed in interaction with it so that I cannot any longer tell which influenced which.

One very basic presupposition is the validity of my previous books on the historical Jesus. Here is my best and most succinct summary of those studies published between 1991 and 1994. The Kingdom of God movement was Jesus' program of empowerment for a peasantry becoming steadily more hard-pressed, in that first-century Jewish homeland, through insistent taxation, attendant indebtedness, and eventual land expropriation, all within increasing commercialization in the booming colonial economy of a Roman Empire under Augustan peace and a Lower Galilee under Herodian urbanization. Jesus *lived,* against the systemic injustice and structural evil of that situation, an alternative open to all who would accept it: a life of open healing and shared eating, of radical itinerancy and fundamental egalitarianism, of human contact without discrimination and divine contact without hierarchy. That, he said, was how God would run the world if God, not Caesar, sat on its imperial throne. That was how God's will was to be done on earth—as in heaven. But heaven was in very good shape. It was earth that was the problem. He also died for that vision and that program. I emphasize that, for Jesus, the

Kingdom *of God* meant just what it said, a religious vision and a religious program but incarnated in rather than separated from the social, political, and economic realities of everyday life. That emphasis is necessary because of a truly cheap crack in Brown's book. He describes

> the myth that Jesus was a political revolutionary, either the Che Guevara type gathering a band of armed followers, or the Gandhi type practicing and encouraging nonviolent resistance. Such an impression has been furthered on the popular level by what may be called "media hype," since the view of Jesus as an advocate of Jewish or peasant liberation can be presented with enthusiasm and does not require radio, newspaper, or TV presenters to take a stance about Jesus' religious claims that might offend viewers. (677–78)

My understanding of Jesus as a peasant revolutionary, but a radically social rather than an aggressively military one, with both vision and program for the Kingdom of God, has definitely influenced my analysis of the passion stories. Jesus could have been executed for his activities at any time in Herodian Galilee. And, on one level, his execution requires no more specific cause than his general program. But he was executed in Jerusalem through a conjunction of the highest Jewish and Roman authorities. The elimination of a dangerous peasant nuisance like Jesus need not have involved any official trials or even consultations between Temple and Roman authorities. It was, in my view, handled under general procedures for maintaining crowd control during Passover. If individuals cause serious trouble in the Temple, crucify them immediately as a warning. In historical reconstruction I opt for the minimum necessary rather than the maximum possible. But the death is inexplicable without the life, and my general view of that life has also deeply influenced my general view of the facts and details about Jesus' death and burial. After two thousand years of Christianity, it is hard for us even to imagine the brutal offhandedness with which a peasant nobody like Jesus would have been dispatched in a Jerusalem under Caiaphas and Pilate.

But is not all that peasant stuff but a projection onto Jesus of my own Irish background? Did I not grow up trained to dislike British imperialism, and am I not just passing on that dislike to ancient Roman imperialism? Are my early influences, then, permanent prejudices?

Peasants? My paternal grandparents were lower-class peasant farmers, and my maternal grandparents were middle-class urban shopkeepers. When I stayed at their respective homes in the very early forties (I was born in 1934), the former were still living well outside the nearest town,

Letterkenny in County Donegal, in a whitewashed thatch-roofed cottage (for real, not for tourist entertainment) with open fireplace for cooking, no internal plumbing whatsoever, several chickens and one goat for animals, donkey and trap for transportation, and sometime town jobs for added support. The latter lived in a market town, Ballymote in County Sligo, above and beside their shop in a house whose internal plumbing was adequate even by present standards. Does that early experience with my paternal grandparents explain why I made Jesus a peasant? Conversely, then, why did that other equally early experience with my maternal grandparents not make him a shopkeeper, running a carpentry business out of his home in Nazareth? Maybe Jesus was a peasant, and those experiences made me simply more sensitive to what that might have meant.

Empires? I grew up among the first generation of postcolonial Irish in the protected lee of the foundering British Empire. Schooling, in that situation, bred strange contradictions. High school, for example, was in Donegal, a county connected to the Republic by a narrow sliver of land and surrounded on all its non-Atlantic sides by Northern Ireland, then as now a part of Britain. It was a boarding school, not from social privilege but from geographical necessity, because Donegal's small towns required some centralized institution. Still, even with all instruction in Gaelic, the curriculum was adopted bodily from the elite private schools of England. In Irish history class, I learned what awful things Britain had done to Ireland. That should have made me dislike empire? But in courses on the Greek and Roman classics, with texts chosen by British education to prepare its youth for imperial administration, I learned, say, from Caesar's *Gallic Wars,* to admire the syntax and ignore the slaughter—even of our ancient Celtic ancestors. That should have made me admire empire? On festive occasions when the boarding students were released to visit their local relatives, I usually went to a paternal uncle-in-law who, when he was a little drunk (that is, on all festive occasions), would show me from a well-greased rag beneath his bed a Luger used not in the fight for Irish independence but in the Irish civil war that immediately succeeded its partial acceptance. From all that pedagogical confusion I hold two truths with equal and fundamental certainty: one, the British did terrible things to the Irish; two, the Irish, had they the power, would have done equally terrible things to the British. And so also for any other paired adversaries I can imagine. The difficulty, of course, is to hold on to both those truths with equal intensity and not let either one negate the other. And to know when to emphasize one without forgetting the other. Our humanity is probably lost and gained in the necessary tension between them both. I hope, by the way, that I do not sound anti-British. It is impossible not to admire a people who gave up India and held on to Northern Ireland. That shows a truly Celtic sense of humor.

After high school in Ireland I entered a Roman Catholic religious order, the Servites, which is what brought me to the United States in 1951. I was ordained a priest in 1957 but spent my entire priestly life as a graduate student or seminary professor. In 1969 I left the order and the priesthood and managed, as I hoped, to disentangle being a priest from being a scholar. So, I am often asked, is it all revenge? You intend to attack the Roman Catholic Church and/or Christianity in general and/or the Bible in particular? I cannot find anywhere in my heart a desire or need to attack on any of those fronts.

A historical reconstruction that is anti-dogmatic is even more silly than one that is pro-dogmatic. In both cases, the researcher is trapped in somebody else's agenda. I have deliberately kept my distance from the Roman Catholic *hierarchy* in the last twenty-five years lest I get trapped in such negativity, but I could never think of myself as outside the Roman Catholic or Christian *tradition.* Others, of course, can so think, but that is their problem, not mine. Attack, even in a book like this one that deliberately opposes another one, is not as important to me as understanding, education, options, and alternatives.

From that almost twenty years spent in a medieval religious order, I took one absolutely basic conviction that has already appeared at the end of this book's prologue. *Reason* and *revelation,* or history and faith, or historical reconstruction and credal articulation cannot contradict each other unless we are misreading one or both of them. I try to hold them always in tensile dialectic, for although in theory revelation is superior to reason, in practice reason is usually the final judge. Otherwise, we have no way to evaluate a Jonestown or a Waco situation before it is too late. I have no rationalist presumption that reason is always right nor that revelation is always wrong. Nor vice versa. To be human is to live in their tensile dialectic and our humanity can be equally lost when that dialectic falters too far in either direction. Reason, however, is disciplined by the physical, the social, and the human sciences. They are by no means infallible; they are just all we have on the reason side of the dialectic. Thus, for example, when we learn from the physical sciences all we can about evolution, we are correct to judge that Genesis 1 does not describe how God created the world but that God, even in creation, did not skip the Sabbath but abided by its law. The Sabbath is, as it were, bigger than creation itself.

Maybe I might have figured that out from the literary structure, theological emphasis, or postulated author of Genesis 1, but what really worked for me was that reason (evolution) could not contradict revelation (Genesis 1). Therefore, Genesis 1 could not be taken literally but must be taken metaphorically or symbolically. That conclusion is, of course, widely accepted in Christian thought today but the principle involved tends to get forgotten as we move from the start (Genesis 1) and end of the world (Apocalypse) to the start (conception) and end (resurrection) of Jesus' life. But metaphor, myth, and symbol always cluster closely around beginnings and endings because at the start they must carry our hopes and at the end they must bury our fears. I take, in other words, that dialectic of reason and revelation straight through from one end of the Bible to the other and from one end of Jesus' life to the other. Another word for that dialectic of reason and revelation is divine consistency. It does not concern what God *can* do but what God *does* do, in the first century or the twentieth century or any century.

Theological Presuppositions

All religions that I have ever known or can ever imagine are trinitarian in structure. And I use that term very deliberately, because this is how I understand the Christian Trinity. There is, first of all, that *ultimate referent* known in supreme metaphors as power, person, state, or order, as nature, goddess or god, nirvana, or way. There is, next, some *material manifestation,* some person, place, or thing, some individual or collectivity, some cave or shrine or temple, some clearing in the forest or tree in the desert where that ultimate referent is met and experienced. There is, finally, at least one *faithful believer* to begin with and eventually more to end with. But, since there are always non-believers as well, some prior affinity must exist, as it were, between believer, referent, and manifestation. The spirit of referent and manifestation must already be present to the believer else why does one accept belief and another refuse it. There is always, in other words, a trinitarian loop involved. For me, therefore, all faith and all religion, not just my own Christianity, is trinitarian in structure.

When I confess that Jesus is divine, Christ, or Lord, is Lamb of God, Word of God, Son of Man, Son of David, or Son of God, I do not mean those terms to be essential or substantial but relational and interactive. (Actually, I think that essential or substantial is the same as relational and interactive.) To say that Jesus is divine, for example, means for me that *I* see *Jesus* as the manifestation of *God*. Similarly, as a historian of Christian origins, I must be able to explain why, in that first century, some people saw Jesus and said, "Let's ignore him," others said, "Let's execute him," and others said, "Let's worship him." To media or audience questions insisting, "Yes, yes, but was he *really* divine," I answer again and again that, for the first as for the twenty-first century, Jesus was and is divine for those who experience in him *the* manifestation of God.

Focus, for a moment, on that italicized word *the*. To be human is to be absolutely particular, that is, absolutely relative or relatively absolute. In anything that is of supreme importance to us, be it spouse or family, hobby or passion, job or profession, language or country, there is an inevitable slippage from *a* to *the*. It is considered most imprudent to wake up next a beloved spouse whom you consider to be the most beautiful person in the world and say, however correctly, "If I had not met you, I probably would have met somebody else." Shown a newborn infant and asked, "Isn't that the most beautiful baby in the word?" the wisest answer is always in the affirmative. But out of the corner of our minds we recognize that *a* has become *the,* and we know that such is perfectly human and presents no problem—*unless* it is taken literally and the equally relative absolutes of others are negated. So also, or especially, with one's faith or one's religion. It must be experienced as *the* manifestation of the Holy, but we must never forget or deny that it is actually *a* manifestation for me and *for us*. To be human is to live in *a* as *the;* to be inhuman is to deny that necessary slippage.

My own background is Irish and Catholic, aspects of sensibility rather than of documentation and probably not subject to change as is that latter item. When I think about Jesus as the manifestation of God, I am not just referring to his words alone, or even his deeds alone, but to both of those as facets of a lived life and a somewhat inevitable death. I do not separate or emphasize words over deeds or death over life. It is the *whole* that counts, then, now, and always. The resurrection of Jesus means for me that the human empowerment that some people experienced in Lower Galilee at the start of the first century in and through Jesus is now available to any person in any place at any time who finds God in and through that same Jesus. Empty tomb stories and physical appearance stories are perfectly valid parables expressing that faith, akin in their own way to the Good Samaritan story. They are, for me, parables of resurrection not the resurrection itself. Resurrection as the continuing experience of God's presence in and through Jesus is the heart of Christian faith.

But that heart is a structure more than a content, and the structure is synthesized, almost atomically, in the name Jesus Christ, that is, Jesus *as* the Christ. The first word, Jesus, is a *fact* open in principle to proof and disproof (he did or did not exist). The second word, Christ (or Lord, or Wisdom, or Son of God, etc.) is an *interpretation,* not open in principle to proof or disproof (he is or is not such). Their conjunction is an act of faith that, as such, is interpretation, fundamental interpretation, not historical fact. This is why, for me, historical Jesus research is of importance for Christian faith. That importance was already established in Christianity at a very early stage. By the 50s, for example, the Q Gospel had reconstructed the mode of Jesus' *life* as vital to its faith, and Paul had reconstructed the mode of Jesus' *death* as vital for his. Each of the four gospels reconstructed a vision of the historical Jesus and argued for it as a/*the* manifestation of God for its community. For Christianity, the reconstruction could differ, and even how it manifested God could differ, but the structure held: Christianity is historical reconstruction interpreted as divine manifestation. It is not (in a postmodern world) that we find once and for all who the historical Jesus was way back then. It is that each generation and century must redo that historical work and establish its best reconstruction, a reconstruction that will be and must be in some creative interaction with its own particular needs, visions, and programs. And such historical reconstruction is open in principle to any researcher able and willing to undertake its disciplined constraints. It is that Jesus reconstructed in the dialogues, debates, controversies, and conclusions of contemporary scholarship that challenges faith to see and say how that is for now the Christ, the Lord, the Son of God. Diversity in scholarship, by the way, no more disqualifies history than diversity in Christology devalues faith or diversity in gospel invalidates the New Testament. The gospels are, for me, even more normative as process than as product. Each of them laminates together the Jesus of the 30s C.E. with their interpretations of him from the 70s, 80s, and 90s. Each of them laminates history and faith almost inextricably together. Ours is the same task, all over again, and again, and again. The gospels are our normative models for that process, and we cannot evade it by simply repeating either their history or their faith and calling it our own.

I do not accept the argument that Christian faith itself tells us what we need to know about the historical Jesus. Christian faith tells us how the historical Jesus (fact) is the manifestation of God for us here and now (interpretation). You cannot believe in a fact, only in an interpretation. And no amount of faith can turn an interpretation into a fact. Here occurs a lethal deceit that too often renders savage the heart of Christianity. We argue that we have facts not interpretations, that we have history not myth, that *we* have truth and *you* have lies. That will not work any longer, not for us and not for anyone else. We need to compare one another's myths and metaphors to see how fully human is the life they engender, but we cannot deny that *everyone* builds firmly on such inevitable foundations. Christians, like all other human beings, live from out of the depths of myth and metaphor. But there still remains, now especially, the urgent challenge to accept our own foundational myth without shame or denial and that of others without hate or disparagement.

Historical Presuppositions

Historical reconstruction in that first common-era century is delicate and sensitive because out of that common spiritual matrix came two great world religions, earliest Christianity and rabbinic Judaism. Here are three presuppositions that could be historical or theological depending on viewpoint and that will probably be resented by some people in both religions.

First, each of those religions is as legitimate a branch of that common trunk as is the other. Second, each of those religions asserted itself as the sole legitimate heir of the past and denied the validity of the other's claim. Third, because Christianity eventually obtained the political and military support of the Roman Empire, it was able to promote its claim and even persecute its opponent in a way not open to Judaism.

In more detail: The reconstructed historical Jesus must be understood within his contemporary Hellenistic Judaism, a Judaism responding with all its antiquity and tradition to Greco-Roman culture undergirded by both armed power and imperial ambition. But that contemporary Judaism was, as modern scholarship insists ever more forcibly, a richly creative, diverse, and variegated one. By the end of the second century of the common era, two hundred years after Jesus, *rabbinic* Judaism, like *catholic* Christianity, was deeply involved in retrojecting its ascendancy onto earlier history so that it would later be as difficult to discern any earlier plurality in one as in the other. By that time those two great religions had emerged as distinct products of a common matrix, as twin daughters of a common mother. Each claimed to be the only legitimate heir, and each had texts and traditions to argue that claim. Each, in fact, represented an equally legitimate, equally valid, equally surprising, and equally magnificent leap out of the past and into the future. It would, in truth, be difficult to say, had Moses woken from slumber around 200 C.E., which of the two would have surprised him the more. All that was, however, two hundred years *after* Jesus.

I use terms like *Christians* and *Christianity* in this book exactly as I would use terms such as *Essenes, Pharisees, Sadducees,* or *Zealots.* What we are watching, in the beginning, are intra-Jewish fights for the soul of Judaism and the leadership of its future. Each group can call the other very nasty names. Any one group can even imagine that it alone has the proper vision and appropriate program for the future and that all the other leadership groups are wrong or inadequate. Slowly but surely, and at different speeds in different places and times, Christians are separating and being separated from Judaism. Slowly but surely, and at different speeds in different places and times, more and more Jews are refusing the Christian and accepting the rabbinical alternative for their future. You can measure an individual's or community's sense of Christian failure, marginalization, or disenfranchisement by the bitterness of its invective against the Jewish authorities, and/or the Jewish people, and/or, most simply, the Jews. But only when pagans are speaking does "the Jews" clearly mean "the Jews" as distinct from us. When Jewish Christians are speaking, and no matter how bitterly they are attacking, it means "you other Jews who oppose us" or even "all other Jews because they oppose us." Similarly, an American individual or group can speak about or against "Americans," saying, for example, that "Americans are too violent," and be easily understood to mean "All you other Americans except me or us." But even when and if Jewish Christians stopped thinking of themselves as Jews and so used "the Jews" as pagans had always used it, the most serious line is not crossed. It is not invective that turned lethal or separation that proved fatal but power. Once the Roman Empire was Christian, all others were in danger—Jews, of course, but pagans too, and also dissident Christians.

I conclude this epilogue where the prologue began, with darkness at high noon. There are actually four successive stages in the growth of the passion tradition.

The first stage is the *historical passion,* and it would have originally contained every detail known to those who participated in it. It is what actually happened. But, because those who knew did not care and those who cared did not know, it comes to us today as little more than the barest minimum: crucified by a conjunction of Jewish and Roman authority under Pontius Pilate in Jerusalem at Passover. In other words, the best summary answer to this book's titular question *Who Killed Jesus?* (and why) is found in Josephus's conjunction of Jesus' life and death (for why) as well as "Pilate . . . hearing him accused by men of the highest standing amongst us . . . condemned him to be crucified" (for who).

The second stage is the *prophetic passion.* It is the work of learned followers of Jesus, not from the peasant but from the retainer class, not from illiterate workers but from literate scholars. They searched their Scriptures seeking understanding of what had happened both to Jesus and to themselves. Was everything within the will and plan of God? Could they find in their sacred writings certain texts, themes, and types that would explain it all, explain especially what had happened and would yet happen to Jesus? And that process continued on its own trajectory even after the next phase started.

The third stage is the *narrative passion,* which took that somewhat esoteric scholarly exegesis and turned it into popular story, with the earliest extant example in the Cross Gospel section of Peter.

The fourth stage is the *polemical passion.* This is the terribly unfortunate, ethically indefensible, and eventually lethal argument that equates the *narrative passion* with the *historical passion* and claims that its detailed fulfillment of the *prophetic passion* renders Christian belief obvious and Jewish disbelief indefensible. Now watch all that at work.

In the *historical passion,* there was no darkness at noon when Jesus was executed any more than there was when Caesar was assassinated. In the *prophetic passion* there was Amos 8:9 foretelling a world turned upside down for its social injustice by the advent of an avenging God: daytime would become nighttime. In the *narrative passion* there is darkness for three hours from noon onward as Jesus dies on the cross. Jesus, in other words, dies in fulfillment of the sacred Scriptures of his people as read by his followers. Finally, there is the *polemical passion.* One example suffices:

> Do you seek at what hour exactly the sun failed? Was it the fifth hour or the eighth or the tenth [counting from 6:00 a.m.]? Give the exact hour, O prophet, to the unheeding Jews; when did the sun set? The prophet Amos says: "On that day, says the Lord God, I will make the sun set at midday" (for there was darkness from the sixth hour) "and cover the earth with darkness in broad daylight." (Cyril of Jerusalem, *Catechesis* 13.25; McCauley and Stephenson 2.21)

Think of place and time. Cyril was bishop of Jerusalem, and he preached the sermons from which that excerpt is taken during Lent of 349, well after Constantine became the Roman Empire's first Christian ruler. Think of content and attack. I do not question Cyril's honesty or integrity, but the injustice and invalidity of such anti-Jewish polemic is the major conclusion of this book. Of course the narrative passion agreed in detail with the prophetic passion; it had been quarried from its contents. Darkness at noon, indeed.

The Gospel of Peter

Compositional Strata in the Gospel of Peter

The prologue section "Dependent and Independent Passion Stories" gives background information on this gospel of Peter. My working hypothesis is that three strata or layers are discernible in this text (Crossan 1988).

The first stratum is the *original* one (in ordinary print below). I call it the Cross Gospel and date it to the 40s of the first century. Its pro-Roman stance might indicate a location like Sepphoris. It contains these three units:

(1a) Trial, Abuse, and Crucifixion (1:1–2; 2:5b–6:22)

(1b) Fear, Guards, and Tomb (7:25; 8:28–9:34)

(1c) Resurrection, Confession, and Deceit (9:35–10:42; 11:45–49)

Trial, Abuse, and Crucifixion are, of course, conducted by Jesus' enemies, but it is also they who bury him, guard the tomb, and thereby witness the resurrection. What is most significant is the distinction drawn between the Jewish authorities and the Jewish people. They start off in agreement against Jesus but end with very different positions: the authorities must conceal the truth lest their own people stone them for what they have done.

The second stratum is the *canonical* one (in italics). It is taken from the canonical gospels and concerns a burial of Jesus not by enemies but by friends, a presence at his tomb not of enemies (the guards) but of friends (the women), and, finally, an apparition of Jesus not before his enemies but before his friends (as the mutilated manuscript breaks off in mid-account). It contains these three units:

(2a) Joseph and Burial (6:23–24)

(2b) Women and Youth (12:50–13:57)

(2c) Disciples and Apparition (14:60–)

This stratum involves a major shift from an emphasis on Jesus' enemies in control of events to Jesus' friends in at least some control of some events. These insertions take place as the Cross Gospel comes under pressure to conform to the canonical versions after the second half of the second century.

The third stratum is the *redactional* one (in underlined text). It was used to assist the combination of those two earlier strata and was created, of course, in the process of their combination. It contains these three units:

(3a) Request for Burial (2:3–5a)

(3b) Arrival of Youth (11:43–44)

(3c) Action of Disciples (7:26–27; 14:58–59)

Each unit of this stratum is inserted at some earlier stage within the original or Cross Gospel to prepare and smooth over the insertion of the later canonical stratum.

There are two separate systems used for designating the divisions of this text, as if the verses of a biblical book continued straight through the chapters and did not begin anew with each one. Thus, for example, the verse 4:14 is immediately followed by 5:15. The chapters change but the verses continue. I follow that standard hybrid method of citation.

I have made two corrections in the following standard translation (Maurer and Schneemelcher 223–26): the Greek of 6:21 has "they" rather than "the Jews" and that of 8:29 has "the elders were afraid" not "were afraid."

Translation of the Gospel of Peter

. . . [1:1] But of the Jews none washed their hands, neither Herod nor any one of his judges. And as they would not wash, Pilate arose. [1:2] And then Herod the king commanded that the Lord should be marched off, saying to them, "What I have commanded you to do to him, do ye."

[2:3] Now there stood there Joseph, the friend of Pilate and of the Lord, and knowing that they were about to crucify him he came to Pilate and begged the body of the Lord for burial. [2:4] And Pilate sent to Herod and begged his body. [2:5a] And Herod said, "Brother Pilate, even if no one had begged him, we should bury him, since the Sabbath is drawing on. For it stands written in the law: the sun should not set on one that has been put to death."

[2:5b] And he delivered him to the people on the day before the unleavened bread, their feast. [3:6] So they took the Lord and pushed him in great haste and said, "Let us hale the Son of God now that we have gotten power over him." [3:7] And they put upon him a purple robe and set him on the judgment seat and said, "Judge righteously, O King of Israel!" [3:8] And one of them brought a crown of thorns and put it on the Lord's head. [3:9] And others who stood by spat on his face, and others buffeted him on the cheeks, others nudged him with a reed, and some scourged him, saying, "With such honour let us honour the Son of God." [4:10] And they brought two malefactors and crucified the Lord in the midst between them. But he held his peace, as if he felt no pain. [4:11] And when they had set up the cross, they wrote upon it: this is the King of Israel. [4:12] And they laid down his garments before him and divided them among themselves and cast the lot upon them. [4:13] But one of the malefactors rebuked them, saying, "We have landed in suffering for the deeds of wickedness which we have committed, but this man, who has become the saviour of men, what wrong has he done you?" [4:14] And they were wroth with him and commanded that his legs should not be broken, so that he might die in torments. [5:15] Now it was midday and a darkness covered all Judaea. And they became anxious and uneasy lest the sun had already set, since he was still alive. <For> it stands written for them: the sun should not set on one that has been put to death. [5:16] And one of them said, "Give him to drink gall with vinegar." And they mixed it and gave him to drink. [5:17] And they fulfilled all things and completed the measure of their sins on their head. [5:18] And many went about with lamps, since they supposed that it was night, <and> they stumbled. [5:19] And the Lord called out and cried, "My power, O power, thou hast forsaken me!" And having said this he was taken up. [5:20] And at the same hour the veil of the temple in Jerusalem was rent in two. [6:21] And then they drew the nails from the hands of the Lord and laid him on the earth. And the whole earth shook and there came a great fear. [6:22] Then the sun shone (again), and it was found to be the ninth hour.

[6:23] *And the Jews rejoiced and gave his body to Joseph that he might bury it, since he had seen all the good that he [=Jesus] had done.* [6:24] *And he took the Lord, washed him, wrapped him in linen and brought him into his own sepulchre, called Joseph's Garden.*

[7:25] Then the Jews and the elders and the priests, perceiving what great evil they had done to themselves, began to lament and to say, "Woe on our sins, the judgment and the end of Jerusalem is drawn nigh."

[7:26] <u>But I mourned with my fellows, and being wounded in heart we hid ourselves, for we were sought after by them as evildoers and as persons who wanted to set fire to the temple.</u> [7:27] <u>Because of all these things we were fasting and sat mourning and weeping night and day until the Sabbath.</u>

[8:28] But the scribes and Pharisees and elders, being assembled together and hearing that all the people were murmuring and beating their breasts, saying, "If at his death these exceeding great signs have come to pass, behold how righteous he was!"—[8:29] the elders were afraid and came to Pilate, entreating him and saying, [8:30] "Give us soldiers that we may watch his sepulchre for three days, lest his disciples come and steal him away and the people suppose that he is risen from the dead, and do us harm." [8:31] And Pilate gave them Petronius the centurion with soldiers to watch the sepulchre. [8:32] And with them there came elders and scribes to the sepulchre. And all who were there, together with the centurion and the soldiers, rolled thither a great stone and laid it against the entrance to the sepulchre [8:33] and put on it seven seals, pitched a tent and kept watch. [9:34] Early in the morning, when the Sabbath dawned, there came a crowd from Jerusalem and the country round about to see the sepulchre that had been sealed. [9:35] Now in the night in which the Lord's day dawned, when the soldiers, two by two in every watch, were keeping guard, there rang out a loud voice in heaven, [9:36] and they saw the heavens opened and two men come down from there in a great brightness and draw nigh to the sepulchre. [9:37] That stone which had been laid against the entrance to the sepulchre started of itself to roll and give way to the side, and the sepulchre was opened, and both the young men entered in. [10:38] When now those soldiers saw this, they awakened the centurion and the elders—for they also were there to assist at the watch. [10:39] And whilst they were relating what they had seen, they saw again three men come out from the sepulchre, and two of them sustaining the other, and a cross following them, [10:40] and the heads of the two reaching to heaven, but that of him who was led of them by the hand overpassing the heavens. [10:41] And they heard a voice out of the heavens crying, "Hast thou preached to them that sleep?" [10:42] and from the cross there was heard the answer, "Yea."

[11:43] <u>Those men therefore took counsel with one another to go and report this to Pilate.</u> [11:44] <u>And whilst they were still deliberating,</u>

the heavens were again seen to open, and a man descended and entered into the sepulchre.

[11:45] When those who were of the centurion's company saw this, they hastened by night to Pilate, abandoning the sepulchre which they were guarding, and reported everything they had seen, being full of disquietude and saying, "In truth he was the Son of God." [11:46] Pilate answered and said, "I am clean from the blood of the Son of God, upon such a thing have you decided." [11:47] Then all came to him, beseeching him and urgently calling upon him to command the centurion and the soldiers to tell no one what they had seen. "For it is better for us," they said, "to make ourselves guilty of the greatest sin before God than to fall into the hands of the people of the Jews and be stoned." Pilate therefore commanded the centurion and the soldiers to say nothing.

[11:50] *Early in the morning of the Lord's day Mary Magdalene, a woman disciple of the Lord—for fear of the Jews, since (they) were inflamed with wrath, she had not done at the sepulchre of the Lord what women are wont to do for those beloved of them who die—took* [12:51] *with her her women friends and came to the sepulchre where he was laid.* [12:52] *And they feared lest the Jews should see them, and said, "Although we could not weep and lament on that day when he was crucified, yet let us now do so at his sepulchre.* [12:53] *But who will roll away for us the stone also that is set on the entrance to the sepulchre, that we may go in and sit beside him and do what is due?—*[12:54] *For the stone was great,—and we fear lest any one see us. And if we cannot do so, let us at least put down at the entrance what we bring for a memorial of him and let us weep and lament until we have again gone home."* [13:55] *So they went and found the sepulchre opened. And they came near, stooped down and saw there a young man sitting in the midst of the sepulchre, comely and clothed with a brightly shining robe, who said to them,* [13:56] *"Wherefore are ye come? Whom seek ye? Not him that was crucified? He is risen and gone. But if we believe not, stoop this way and see the place where he lay, for he is not here. For he is risen and is gone thither whence he was sent."* [14:57] *Then the women fled affrighted.*

[14:58] Now it was the last day of unleavened bread and many went away and repaired to their homes, since the feast was at an end. [14:59] But we, the twelve disciples of the Lord, wept and mourned, and each one, very grieved for what had come to pass, went to his own home.

[14:60] *But I, Simon Peter, and my brother Andrew took our nets and went to the sea. And there was with us Levi, the son of Alphaeus, whom the Lord . . .*

S O U R C E S

For more complete references, see the bibliography in Crossan, *The Cross That Spoke,* pp. 414–25.

Basore, J. W.; R. M. Gummere; T. H. Corcoran; and F. J. Miller, trans. 1917–72. *Seneca.* 10 vols. Loeb Classical Library. Cambridge, MA: Harvard Univ. Press.

Brown, Raymond E. 1987. "The *Gospel of Peter* and Canonical Gospel Priority." *New Testament Studies* 33: 321–43.

———. 1994. *The Death of the Messiah: From Gethsemane to the Grave. A Commentary on the Passion Narratives in the Four Gospels.* 2 vols. with continuous pagination. Anchor Bible Reference Library. New York: Doubleday.

Charlesworth, James H. 1983–85. "Odes of Solomon." In *The Old Testament Pseudepigrapha,* edited by James H. Charlesworth, vol. 2, pp. 725–71. Garden City, NY: Doubleday.

Collins, John J. 1983–85. "Sibylline Oracles." In *The Old Testament Pseudepigrapha,* edited by James H. Charlesworth, vol. 1, pp. 317–472. Garden City, NY: Doubleday.

Colson, F. H.; G. H. Whitaker; J. E. Earp; and R. Marcus. 1929–62. *Philo.* 12 vols. Loeb Classical Library. Cambridge: Harvard Univ. Press.

Crossan, John Dominic. 1985. *Four Other Gospels: Shadows on the Contours of Canon.* Minneapolis: Winston/Seabury. Reprint, Sonoma, CA: Polebridge Press, 1992.

———. 1988. *The Cross That Spoke: The Origins of the Passion Narrative.* San Francisco: Harper & Row, 1988.

———. 1991. *The Historical Jesus: The Life of a Mediterranean Jewish Peasant.* San Francisco: HarperSanFrancisco. Paperback ed., 1993.

———. 1994. *The Essential Jesus: Original Sayings and Earliest Images.* San Francisco: HarperSanFrancisco.

———. 1994. *Jesus: A Revolutionary Biography.* San Francisco: HarperSanFrancisco.

Danby, H. 1967. *The Mishnah.* London: Oxford Univ. Press.

Donahue, John R. 1973. *Are You the Christ? The Trial Narrative in the Gospel of Mark.* Society of Biblical Literature Dissertation Series, no. 10. Cambridge, MA: SBL.

Edwards, James R. 1989. "Markan Sandwiches: The Significance of Interpolations in Markan Narratives." *Novum Testamentum* 31: 193–216.

Fairclough, Henry Rushton. 1926. *Horace: Satires, Epistles, Ars Poetica.* Loeb Classical Library. Cambridge, MA: Harvard Univ. Press.

Fitzmyer, Joseph A. 1978. "Crucifixion in Ancient Palestine, Qumran Literature, and the New Testament." *Catholic Biblical Quarterly* 40: 493–513.

Harris, J. Rendel; Agnes Smith Lewis; and F. C. Conybeare. 1913. "The Story of Aḥiḳar." In *The Apocrypha and Pseudepigrapha of the Old Testament,* edited by R. H. Charles, vol. 2, pp. 715–84. Oxford: Clarendon Press.

Hengel, Martin. 1977. *Crucifixion in the Ancient World and the Folly of the Message of the Cross.* Philadelphia: Fortress Press.

Hutton, M.; R. M. Ogilvie; E. H. Warmington; W. Peterson; M. Winterbottom; C. H. Moore; and John Jackson. 1914–70. *Tacitus.* 5 vols. Loeb Classical Library. Cambridge, MA: Harvard Univ. Press.

Koester, Helmut. 1980. "Apocryphal and Canonical Gospels." *Harvard Theological Review* 73: 105–30.

———. 1990. *Ancient Christian Gospels: Their History and Development.* London: SCM Press; Philadelphia: Trinity Press International.

Lindenberger, James M. 1983–85. "Ahiqar." In *The Old Testament Pseudepigrapha,* edited by James H. Charlesworth, vol. 2, pp. 479–507. Garden City, NY: Doubleday.

Lindsay, Jack. 1960. *The Satyricon and Poems of Gaius Petronius.* London: Elek Books.

MacDonald, Dennis Ronald. 1990. *The Acts of Andrew and the Acts of Andrew and Matthias in the City of the Cannibals.* Christian Apocrypha, no. 1, in Texts and Translations, no. 33. Atlanta: Scholars Press.

Marique, Joseph M.-F. 1962. "The Fragments of Papias." In *The Apostolic Fathers,* translated by Francis X. Glimm, Joseph M.-F. Marique, and Gerald G. Walsh, pp. 373–89. Vol. 1 of *The Fathers of the Church.* Washington, DC: Catholic Univ. of America, 1947–.

Maurer, Christian, and Wilhelm Schneemelcher. 1991. "The Gospel of Peter." In *New Testament Apocrypha,* rev. ed., edited by Wilhelm Schneemelcher and R. McL. Wilson, vol. 1, pp. 216–27. Louisville, KY: Westminster/John Knox Press.

McCauley, Leo P., and Anthony A. Stephenson. 1968–70. *The Works of Saint Cyril of Jerusalem.* 2 vols. Vols. 61 and 64 of *The Fathers of the Church: A New Translation.* Washington, DC: Catholic Univ. of America Press.

Metzger, Bruce M. 1970. "Names for the Nameless in the New Testament: A Study in the Growth of Christian Tradition." In *Kyriakon,* Festschrift Johannes Quasten, edited by Patrick Granfield and Josef A. Jungmann, vol. 1, pp. 79–99. Münster: Aschendorf. Reprinted in his *New Testament Studies: Philological, Versional, and Patristic,* pp. 23–43. New Testament Tools and Studies, no. 10. Leiden: Brill, 1980.

Nickelsburg, George W. E. 1980. "The Genre and Function of the Markan Passion Narrative." *Harvard Theological Review* 73: 153–84.

Roberts, Alexander; James Donaldson; and A. Cleveland Coxe. 1926. *The Ante-Nicene Fathers*. American reprint of the Edinburgh ed. New York: Scribner's.

Rolfe, John C. 1979. *Suetonius*. 2 vols. Loeb Classical Library 31, 38. Cambridge: Harvard Univ. Press [1913, 1951].

Schäferdiek, Knut. 1991. "The Acts of John." In *New Testament Apocrypha*, rev. ed., edited by Wilhelm Schneemelcher and R. McL. Wilson, vol. 1, pp. 152–209. Louisville, KY: Westminster/John Knox Press.

Thackeray, H. St. J.; R. Marcus; A. Eikgren; and L. H. Feldman. 1926–65. *Josephus*. 10 vols. Loeb Classical Library. Cambridge: Harvard Univ. Press.

Theissen, Gerd. 1991. *The Gospels in Context: Social and Political History in the Synoptic Tradition*. Minneapolis: Fortress Press.

———. 1992. *Social Reality and the Early Christians: Theology, Ethics, and the World of the New Testament*. Translated by Margaret Kohl. Minneapolis: Fortress Press.

Yadin, Yigael. 1977–83. *The Temple Scroll*. 3 vols. Jerusalem: Israel Exploration Society.

———. 1984. "The Temple Scroll: The Longest and Most Recently Discovered Dead Sea Scroll." *Biblical Archaeology Review* 10 (5/Sept–Oct): 32–49.

———. 1985. *The Temple Scroll: The Hidden Law of the Dead Sea Sect*. New York: Random House.

Zias, Joseph, and Eliezer Sekeles. 1985. "The Crucified Man from Giv'at ha-Mivtar: A Reappraisal." *Israel Exploration Journal* 35: 22–27.

DATE DUE